GRASP CHINA

By Christine Ching

Translated by Christine Ching• Frank Wang• Phoebe Lam

DEDICATION

To my Dad and my Mom, who love me unconditionally.
To my husband Frank, who always loves me and gives me full support in the making of Grasp China.
To my daughter Caylen, who gave me the inspiration to write this book.
To Phoebe, who helped me with the translation.
To Tina, who helped me with the amazing book cover design.
To all my friends who have contributed their stories to this book.

FOREWORD

If a multinational company does not have a clear "China growth story", Wall Street will likely to have doubts about the company's future. Today almost every business school has a class on "Conducting Business in China." Understanding China has become an important part of many people's job. I got the idea of writing a book about China when I worked on my first consulting project in China 16 years ago. I made a lot of mistakes. I also spent a lot of time learning about China in China. At that time, I wished there was a "bible" that taught me everything I need to know about working and surviving in this country. It should be easy and fun to read, yet very practical. I searched around but I still couldn't find exactly what I wanted. So I thought maybe I could write one! Unfortunately I did not know China enough at that time to do it. After living and working in China for over a decade, I learned a lot about "China wisdom," and I felt like it was time to share what I have learned. Like what the title suggests, this book is intended to help you to get a grasp of China in a short period of time. It is particularly written for those of you who are coming to China on a business trip or relocating to China for work or study for the first time. Since I love to listening to and telling stories instead of just stating the rules, this book consists of many personal stories or from my close friends. It will give you a realistic picture of what it is like living in China, yet is interesting to read.

Grasp China is meant to be an easy to read, comprehensive guidebook on working, living, and understanding social live in China. After reading this book, you should be able to enjoy your first trip to this country!

Table of Contents

Top 10 Watch Outs in China

1. Lack of personal space

Chinese mega and Tier 1 cities have on average 8 million inhabitants, which makes them incredibly crowded no matter where you are. Chapter 1.2 talks about city tier classification and Chapter 1.4 gives you an idea of how crowded these mega cities have become. Because of the population density, western style politeness won't get you anywhere, literally speaking, and sometimes you will have to push and shove like the rest in order get to your destination or just get things done. For instance, when you find yourself in a subway train during rush hours, many people are completely oblivious to how crowded the trains are and would continue to push their way in. Another place to witness relentless pushing and shoving is elevator during rush hours. If you don't act like the rest of your local colleagues, you could be waiting outside of the elevator door for 20 minutes during rush hour. Since everyone is used to pushing their way into a confined space, there is very little sense of personal space in the Chinese mindset. In fact, one could argue that how efficiently the Chinese people pack themselves into a small space is a feat in itself. If you are to travel to crowded places in China, it is advised that you do not wear very nice shoes, nor open-toe.

2. No Queues

Chinese people are not very accustomed to lining up mainly because of the deeply rooted need for competition for resources. While you may not find people cutting the line in department stores or shopping malls, be prepared to fight for a spot with the crowd if you are buying things from smaller stores, getting permits from government offices, or buying tickets at the train station. The younger generation is more willing to form queues nowadays, but the older generations often find it unnecessary. Chapter 4.6 will show you how chaotic it could be at the train station and how you could maneuver the situation.

3. Regional stereotypes

People from different parts of China behave quite differently according to local Chinese views. Sometimes there are quite strong stereotypes for certain regions. For instance, some employers refuse to hire people from Henan province because they believe there are many swindlers; while some employers prefer hiring people from Hunan. Some said that it is very hard to read what is in a Beijingnese mind. Even an okay from him does not mean he agrees. There are also interesting rivalries between Beijingnese and Shanghainese. To understand more about the stereotypes of people from different parts of China, go to Chapter 2.1.

4. Dinner Invitation

Do not take business dinner invitation lightly, unless you fully understand the motives behind. Attending lunch signals a different level of commitment than attending dinner. If you are the one organizing a business dinner, you will need to pay attention to seating arrangement, menu etc. Chapter 3.4 goes deeper into the significance of dining in China.

5. Dig In

It is a hygienic practice in western group dining to have communal utensils for sharing. However, this practice is seldom practiced in China, since most Chinese believe that sharing food from the same dishes bring people closer together, like a family. Therefore, you may want to get vaccinations for diseases that are easily transmitted through saliva, such as hepatitis, before traveling to China.

6. Drinking Rules

Drinking is a big part of business culture in China. There are many drinking rules one should observe. For instance, when you clink your glass with your peer or your guest, you should hold your glass with both hands and position it lower than the other party's glass to show respect. There are also specific orders in giving toasts and sequence in how drinks are served at business dinner. Chapter 3.5 summarizes the top ten rules at the drinking table.

7. Fake Alcohol

Well, not all alcohol sold in the market is fake, but given the lucrative profit margin, many small shops or restaurants tend stock cheap knockoffs rather than the real thing. Sometimes the owners can't even tell the difference. Therefore, it is not advisable to purchase alcohol from small stores, where authentic bottles are recycled and filled with fake liquor. This is especially true for western red and white wine. Consuming fake alcohol not only could give you a very bad hangover, but also could damage your liver and eyes!

8. Giving Face

Face is a very important concept in China. It means maintaining the most basic mutual respect that forms the fabrics of the society. For example, when you meet with a group in a business setting, you should understand the seniority of each person and greet the most senior person in the group first and work your way down. Respect ranking is an important element of giving face. There is no such thing as 'leapfrog' in China. If you skip a rank because you want to get things done faster, you are not giving face to your peer. Chapter 3.3 talks about how to give face to others and the importance of ranking.

9. Receiving and Giving Gifts

If someone work-related sends you a gift, think twice before you accept. There is a heavy emphasis in Chinese culture on reciprocation. When you receive and accept a gift, you must return the favor. After all, there is no free lunch in the world. So what kind of gift can you accept? And what kind of gift can you give? The gifting section in Chapter 3.3 tells you more about the art of gifting.

10. Budget Extra Time and Expenditure

When living in China, you often find yourself visiting a government agency or institution multiple times in order to get one simple task done. As the economy is growing rapidly, everyone in the country is in a hurry. Existing rules and procedures are not updated quickly enough to catch up with the changes, particularly when the matter is related to foreign passport holders. No one can offer you the full picture, or you will be faced with contradicting rules. Therefore, buffer extra time and budget if you are planning to start a business in China. Go to Chapter 3.6 to learn more about the problems my friend Fred ran into when he started his business in China.

CHAPTER 1

China is NOT one China

Before your very first China business trip, internship, or summer school program, you should be equipped with a basic level of understanding of the Chinese market to make the visit meaningful. But where and how do you start? There is so much to learn about "China." Where should you place your focus on? Is it geography, ancient Chinese history, contemporary culture, or current social norms? This first section will highlight the regional differences within China, with a focus on city tier classification and income disparity to illustrate the key notion 'China is NOT one China', as it has important implication on how companies conduct business.

1 . 1

Orientation

Basic Geography

"China is not a single contiguous entity. Each of the 34 provinces in China can be considered a country of its own, similar to the European Union member countries." This insight came up most frequently when I interviewed either locals or expats for this book. China is a big and diverse country economically and geographically. As such, you should not over simplify the country as a single entity. You must have a basic understanding of China's geography and understand the cultural differences among the provinces, particularly since each province in China is actually quite big. For instance, the population of Shanxi province is already bigger than that of Canada, and population of Shanghai is at similar level as Australia! Only when you understand China's geography will you then understand how people's living conditions and behaviors vary in different parts of China. A simple example is that in Anhui province, gifts are always given in multiples of two as a symbol of luck while odd number is considered bad luck. As a consumer brand, if you were to introduce a gift pack in Anhui, you should have twin-pack in order to observe local customs. If you understand the characteristics of different parts of China, you will be able to quickly blend into the local community and at the same time drive your business growth efficiently!

Illustration 1.1: Map of Mainland China with Provincial Capitals (Various islands in the South China Sea are omitted)

We will dedicate a fair amount of effort on Chinese geography at the beginning of this book. As we discuss the different provinces in detail, there will be many interesting facts and customs unique to that province to make it more vivid and memorable. First, let us start with the basic facts, which could be a bit dry for those who are already initiated.

China is the world's fourth largest country, with an area of 9.6 million square kilometer, and ranks in size behind Russia, Canada, and the US. In terms of political administration, China has 34 administrative regions that can be categorized into four types:

- 23 provinces (including the province of Taiwan according to the Chinese government) which is similar to the 50 states in the US;

- 5 autonomous regions which are heavily populated by ethnic minorities like the Tibetans and are conceptually similar to the US independent areas like the Guam;

- 4 municipalities that directly report to the central government, such as Beijing and Shanghai and are similar to the concept of Washington DC;

- 2 special administrative regions - Hong Kong and Macau which retained different political systems from mainland China due to the British and Portuguese colonial histories.

But more often, Chinese like to classify themselves as either southerners or northerners, which is very similar to the American concept of being from the east coast, west coast, the south or the mid-west. Typically the demarcation between northern and southern

China is the Yangtze River (aka "Chang Jiang 长江 ") and Huaihe River (淮河).

Given the scope of its diverse geography and economy, it is impractical for any business organization to manage its presence in China as one uniform region. Typically organizations break down China geographically into four sales regions: North, East, South and West. Each sales region is assigned a Head of Sales and its own sales force team. For some companies, they may even carve out the Central region as the fifth sales region as the economy in that area is large enough to justify a separate team. The following categorization by region is based on the Chinese government's official classification. As you will see, doing business in China is unavoidably intertwined with dealing with various government approvals. As a consequence, aligning your teams accordingly will avoid a lot of unnecessary headaches down the road.

East Region – Shanghai & Jiangsu & Zhejiang, Anhui, Henan

The East region constitutes of the centrally-governed municipality of Shanghai and four surrounding provinces. Since the East region is the wealthiest among the four, many MNCs (Multi-National Companies) choose to penetrate the East region first as their go-to-market strategy before going deeper into other regions. Also the high population density in the region and its long history of exposure to western companies means that it has a deeper pool of local professional talents compared to the other regions from recruiting standpoint.

East China Region

Illustration 1.2: East China Region

When local Chinese mentions the East region, Shanghai is likely the first city that comes to mind. Shanghai (上 海), also known as "Hu (沪)," is the largest city in the region. It is one of the four centrally governed municipalities, which means it does not belong to any provinces but reports directly to the central government. The system is designed so that the central government can influence the policies, make investments, and receive tax revenues directly without interference from the provincial government. Shanghai is one of the first few cities (others being Shenzhen and Guangzhou, located in southern China) to open up its economy to the west. Given Shanghai's rich history of being one of the most prosperous cities in Asia prior to the Communist rule, its physical infrastructure and culture are closest in resemblance to the west. Therefore many MNCs are attracted to set up their China headquarters there, especially companies that are consumer-oriented such as Starbucks, McDonald's, Kimberly-Clark, CocaCola, Gap, Disney, General Motor, LVMH, Uniqlo, just to name a few. Shanghai is now an international metropolis, with the highest number of MNCs establishing their China headquarters including a large number of foreigners living in Shanghai. You can see a western face at almost every street corner! If you are interested in relocating to China, Shanghai is unquestionably the most "foreigner friendly" city and has the most job opportunities for expatriates.

Shanghai borders two of the wealthiest provinces in China: Jiangsu （ 江 苏) and Zhejiang (浙 江). Many people including some locals often confuse their locations. Here is an easy trick to remember them. Since the letter "J" comes before "Z," Jiangsu province is located on top (i.e. north) of Shanghai, while Zhejiang is located just below (southwest) of Shanghai. The provincial capital of Jiangsu is Nanjing （ 南 京), which is also one of the four ancient capitals of China (the other three are Beijing (北 京), Xi'an (西 安), and Luoyang (洛 阳)). Suzhou (苏 州), another important city located in Jiangsu, is a beautiful city famous for its ancient style Chinese gardens and silk products. In fact, Suzhou is wealthier than Nanjing due to its tourism and other high tech industries. Other than its beautiful gardens, Jiangsu produces a national delicacy called hairy crab, which is highly popular with the locals during the fall season. (More on hairy crab in Chapter 2.2)

Hangzhou (杭 州), the provincial capital city of Zhejiang, is the most well-known city in the province. Hangzhou is best known for its West Lake (aka "Xihu 西 湖 "), a large scenic lake located in the middle of the city, giving it a poetic feel. Lately, Hangzhou has gained a lot of media coverage as it is where Alibaba is head quartered (and also where the first G20 Summit in China was held). Among its other natural assets are a number of grand temples and the famous Dragon Well tea. Hangzhou is the vacation destination for people all over China and the world. Chairman Mao used to stay in the National Guest House which is a resort located at the west side of the lake. Even though it is guarded by military and police, the National Guest House is opened to the public. Other famous and rich cities in Zhejiang province include Ningbo (宁 波), Wenzhou (温 州), and Yiwu (义 乌) – where the world's largest small consumer products trade market is located. Because of all these export and tourism driven industries, Zhejiang is a very wealthy province. Even a small county in Zhejiang produces higher GDP than a large city from the West region in China.

If you continue toward inland from Shanghai, you will reach Anhui province (安徽), which is located west of Jiangsu and Zhejiang provinces. Hefei is the provincial capital of Anhui. Anhui is famous for its women – specifically for domestic help or maids. In China, maids are called "Ayi (阿姨)", which is a literal translation of "aunt." Since there are many wealthy and working families in Shanghai, Jiangsu and Zhejiang, there is a high demand for household maids. A lot of women from Anhui choose to take on the profession of Ayi so that they do not have to go very far from hometown. Anhui Ayi are actually quite reputable in China for their hard working ethics.

Going further inland from Anhui we will reach Henan province (河南). "He (河)" in Chinese translates into the word river, and "Nan (南)" means south, so one can guess literally that Henan is located south of a river. The river here refers to the Yellow River (黄 河), where ancient Chinese agricultural civilization originated. The capital city of Henan province is Zhengzhou (郑州). You may not have heard of Zhengzhou, but if you are a fan of Chinese martial arts, then you should have heard of the Shaolin Temple. Shaolin Temple is located on the outskirts of Zhengzhou. In fact, many fans from all over the world flock to the Shaolin Temple to learn Chinese martial arts. In ancient China, this area is considered to be the center of the country and the most prosperous.

North Region – Beijing & Tianjin, "Huabei" Sub-Region, Northeast Sub-Region, Inner Mongolia

The North region covers two centrally governed municipalities, six provinces, and one autonomous region. It can also be divided into four sub-regions: Beijing & Tianjin; "Huabei (华 北)" sub-region; Northeast three provinces; and Inner Mongolia.

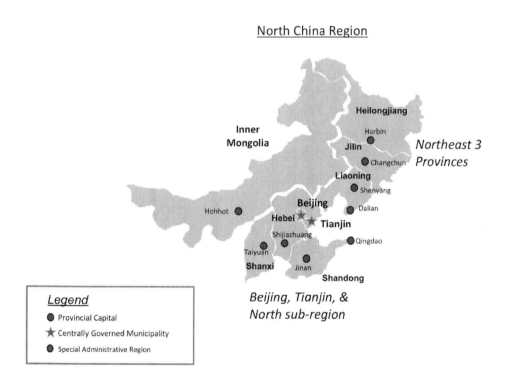

Illustration 1.3: North China Region

In terms of its standing and significance, Beijing (北 京) is definitely the most significant city for North China or even the entire China, while Shanghai is the most important city in East China. Beijing is the capital of China, as well as one of the four centrally governed municipalities. It is famous for numerous historical attractions which this book will not cover, as you can easily find online. On the other hand Beijingnese have their unique characteristics which are not only interesting to outsiders but also very consequential to conducting business in the area. We will delve into more details about people from various regions' personalities and attitudes in Chapter 2.1. From a geographical standpoint, Beijing is an inland city surrounded by Hebei province. Unlike Guangzhou and Shanghai, which are located next to waterbodies of rivers, lakes and the ocean, Beijing's landscape and climate is quite dry. The government even initiated a project costing over $85 billion to build a canal to transport water from the south to the north of the country, opposite to normal flow direction, just to support residential needs. There are also rumors about the central government considering moving the capital city out of Beijing to another city, because the underground water in Beijing will be completely depleted in the next 50 years. Whether this is true or not, we will have to stay tuned and let time reveals the truth.

Within one hour's drive or 30 minutes by high speed rail, one can reach another centrally governed municipality, Tianjin (天 津). If we use the analogy saying Beijing is the emperor's favorite son, then Tianjin is his adopted child. Tianjin has been trying very hard to become a major metropolis, but most people prefer to invest and live in Beijing where the central government and all the state-owned enterprises are located. Luckily Tianjin has a deep harbor which serves as a major port and logistics center for the Northern provinces.

"Huabei (华 北)" or North sub-region consists of Hebei province (河 北), Shandong province (山 东) and Shanxi province (山 西). Hebei's provincial capital is Shijiazhuang. Hebei surrounds Beijing and Tianjin entirely. Rental prices in Beijing have increased dramatically and became out of reach for many people over the past few years. Many migrant workers no longer could afford to live in Beijing. Some had to move to Hebei province spending hours a day commuting on the crowded light rail. When we meet friends who live in the suburban area of Beijing, we often make fun of them by saying they actually live in Hebei province instead of Beijing! Heavy industries like steel and iron manufacturing are key industries supporting Hebei's economy. As Hebei is located relatively inland, lack of wind from the ocean plus all the pollutants from the heavy industries have made Hebei the most polluted province in China. In the top 10 cities with worst air quality list published by The Ministry of Environmental Protection in China in 2014, Hebei accounted for 7 [1]. Poor air quality in Beijing and Tianjin is partly due to their proximity to Hebei province. Make sure you bring a N95 grade mask to block the air pollutants if you have to visit Hebei, particularly during winter times when residents burn coal for heat.

Shandong province is located southeast of Hebei province (and north of Jiangsu province). As one of the coastal provinces, Shandong is also a wealthy province best known for its education (as it is the home to Confucius). When it comes to Shandong, the city of Qingdao probably has the highest profile thanks to Qingdao beer (Tsingtao Brewery) and its German root. But the provincial capital is actually Jinan (济 南). Yantai (烟 台), another major city in Shandong, is closest to South Korea. You can actually see South Korea across the strait from Yantai when the weather is clear.

West of Hebei province is Shanxi province; its provincial capital is Taiyuan (太原). Shanxi is best known for coal mine owners. There were many privately owned and unregulated coal mines in Shanxi before. Rapid infrastructure developments in China over the last twenty years have caused energy prices to rise out of control. As a result, many coal mine owners quickly turned into billionaires. While many billionaires are quite frugal, these recent riches are quite willing to spend, oftentimes just to show off. They are definitely a key consumer segment for luxury brands from Europe and the US. I have heard stories of a coal mine owner spent hundreds of thousands of dollars on Range Rovers and Hummers just to haul coal from mining pits, because he finds these military grade vehicles to have sufficient horsepower and torque, and the size fits in the coal mine perfectly! You can only imagine the other luxuries they own at home. If you get to visit Taiyuan next time, make sure to spot luxury cars next to the luxury stores like LV, Gucci and Hermes. Even though a few Shanxi coal mine owners are super rich, in general Shanxi is still a relatively poor province because of weak industrial developments. Hence wealth is concentrated and income disparity is large within Shanxi.

Located in the northeast corner of China are three provinces, Liaoning (辽 宁), Jilin (吉 林), and Haerbin province (哈 尔 滨) or known to the west, Harbin. People often group the three provinces as one cluster and address them as the Northeast three provinces, as they share a similar culture. Liaoning province, with its provincial capital of Shenyang (沈阳), is located at the southernmost part of the three. Within Liaoning, if Shenyang is considered the top city, Dalian (大 连) is a powerful runner up. Just like many other provinces, the so called number two city is usually better developed economically than the provincial capital, which serves mostly as a political center. When Suzhou and Hangzhou are known for beautiful women, Liaoning is known for being the cradle of fashion models. When you walk on the streets in Liaoning, you can easily spot women who are over 6-feet tall!

Go further north and you will reach Jilin province, with provincial capital of Changchun (长　春). Jilin is known for wild ginseng, an ancient Chinese traditional medicine that is famous for improving health and increasing longevity. Changchun is an old industrial city where the communist party built up its heavy machinery and military manufacturing base half a century ago partially benefiting from its proximity to Russia. Today the state-owned enterprises no longer have the competitive edge in the market, while the city is also showing its age and wear and tear. It is considered the rust belt of China.

As we move further north, there is the northernmost Chinese province of Heilongjiang, with its provincial capital city of Harbin. In Harbin, it is most famous for "ice and snow." If you happen to be in the region in the winter, don't miss the annual International Ice Sculpture

Festival, if you can stand the outdoor temperature of -30C (-22F). A large number of tourists all over the nation attend the festival every year in the middle of the winter. I was once visiting the ice lighting show at night, and I had to wear four layers of pants, four layers of clothes, plus a down jacket just to keep warm! Imagine the amount of time just to get ready to go out. Nonetheless, it is an incredible experience to see grand ice sculpture of large architectures and statues with neon lights shining from inside the ice. Perhaps the Vodka in glasses made of ice can warm you up, just like James Bond in the Ice Palace in the movie Die Another Day. Kids can also enjoy various ice sports and activities in the -30C temperature.

Gallery 1.1: Snow Festival in Harbin

Last but not least in Northern China is the Inner Mongolia Autonomous Region (内 蒙 古), with provincial capital of Hohhot (呼和浩特). Located in the northern frontier, Inner Mongolia shares borders with Mongolia and Russia. Technically an Autonomous Region is governed similarly to a province, with the governor being a representative from the minority group. Inner Mongolia has been known for its vast grasslands and the nomads. But these days, it is better known for this particular natural resource which every country sought after – rare earth. Many people, including myself, thought that Inner Mongolia is located far, far away. But in fact, it only takes 10 hours of driving from Beijing to reach Inner Mongolia on modern paved highway. It is becoming a new holiday destination for Beijing residents to spend a long weekend. Next time when you travel to Beijing, if time permits, give it a try in Inner Mongolia and experience the nomadic life!

Southern Region – Two "Hu's, Two" Guang's", Fujian & Jiangxi, Hainan Island

The Southern region covers seven provinces, which can be divided into four sub-regions: Hubei (湖 北) & Hunan (湖 南); Guangdong (广东) & Guangxi (广西); Fujian (福建) & Jiangxi (江西); Hainan Island (海南岛).

The two "Hu's" refer to Hubei province and Hunan province. "Hu (湖)" in Chinese means lake. The lake that separates these two provinces is the famous Dongting Lake (洞庭湖).

South China Region

Two "Hu's"

Hubei
Wuhan

*Fujian &
Jiangxi*

Changsha
Nanchang

Hunan   **Jiangxi**

Fujian   Fuzhou

○ Xiamen

Guangxi   **Guangdong**
Guangzhou

Shenzhen   Hong Kong
Nanning

Macau

Hainan   Haikou   *Guangdong,
Guangxi*
○
Sanya

Legend

● Provincial Capital

★ Centrally Governed Municipality

● Special Administrative Region

Illustration 1.4: South China Region

Hubei province is located to the north of Dongting Lake. Wuhan (武 汉) is the provincial capital city of Hubei province. It is also the geographical center point in China today. Wuhan is the key transit point for the high speed railway connecting north-south bound (Beijing to Hong Kong) and east-west bound (Shanghai to Chengdu). Many fast moving consumer goods (FMCG) companies purposely conduct market research in Wuhan to represent consumers from Central China.

Hunan province is located to the south of Dongting Lake. Changsha (长沙) is the capital city of Hunan province. Mao Zedong (毛 泽 东), one of the most influential and controversial leaders of China, was from Hunan. If you love spicy food, Hunan is definitely the place for you.

Besides breaking down China into North, East, South and West regions, some companies may establish an additional central regional office that consists of Henan, Hubei, and Hunan provinces as these three neighboring provinces are quite sizable in terms of population and are of similar economic development level.

HUNAN? HUBEI? HENAN? HEBEI?

Confused by the various permutations of the Hu and He, Nan and Bei? You are not alone. Many, including myself, have trouble memorizing the location of these provinces. Here is one way to remember them. First you need to remember what the words mean in Chinese: "Hu 湖 " is lake, "He 河 " is river, "Nan 南 " is south and "Bei 北 " is north. Water flows from the He (river) in the north to the Hu (lake) in the south. The order from north to south is then: Hebei, Henan, Hubei and Hunan. If that is still difficult, then just remember He comes before Hu alphabetically; Bei also comes before Nan.

When it comes to the South region, Guangdong (广东) probably receives the most media coverage since it was one of the first provinces in China that was opened up for foreign investment. Guangdong province is also the only province in China with over 100 million in population (based on resident population, which will be explained in a later section). Because of its large population base, it also has very strong consumption power. Guangdong has two famous cities: Guangzhou (广州), the capital city of Guangdong, which is also where P&G China is headquartered; and Shenzhen (深圳), the first special economic zone in China bordering Hong Kong, now also house the headquarter of the China internet giant Tencent. Guangdong in general is most well-known for low cost electronic goods and garment manufacturing. For instance, Foxconn's largest facility in China is located in Guangdong province where iPhone and iPad are manufactured. Today, the Huaqiangbei (华强北) area in Shenzhen houses some of the world's most efficient electronic hardware manufacture supply chain companies for handhelds, USB drives and bluetooth speakers, etc. If you are in the electronics business, or planning a startup in smart network appliances, you don't want to miss this place.

West of Guangdong province is Guangxi province (广西). Even though they are neighboring provinces, Guangxi is far behind in terms of economic development compared to Guangdong due to its mountainous regions. Most of its original residents are ethnic minorities.

To the northeast of Guangdong is Fujian province (福建). Fujian province is also one of the wealthiest coastal provinces in China. It is located across the strait from Taiwan. In fact, it is so close to Taiwan that one can see military guards on the other side on a sunny and clear day with just a pair of regular binoculars. The capital city of Fujian province is Fuzhou (福州). Within Fujian province, Xiamen (厦门) is probably the best known as it is one of the top tourist destinations in China. Fujian is the manufacturing base for most sports shoes and apparels in China. What else are Fujian people famous for? Billionaire father-in-law! Recently, there were reports in the news about billionaires from Fujian giving their daughter multi-million dollars wedding and billions of dollars as dowry! So if you are single and available, consider finding yourself a girlfriend from Fujian! You may become a billionaire overnight!

If you go inland (west) from Fujian province, you will reach Jiangxi province (江西). During the Chinese civil war, the communist army hid in Jiangxi and fought back to take over the country. It is commonly referred to as the "Old Revolutionary Base" by local Chinese. Similar to Guangxi province, economic development in Jiangxi is relatively poor.

Hainan Province, located at the southern tip of China, is an island. The most famous cities in Hainan province are Haikou (海 口), the provincial capital city, and Sanya (三 亚), a beautiful tropical beach front city where Miss World Beauty Pageant have been hosted for a few years. Hainan has become the most popular tourist destination among the local population in recent years since it is the only natural tropical beach destination in China. As a result, real estate construction and prices have grown rapidly over the last few years in Hainan.

Western Region – Southwest 1+3 Region, Northwest 3 Provinces, 3 Autonomous Regions

Why do we, or most multinationals for that matter, leave the West region to the last when discussing China? Compared to the rest of the country, West region's economic development has been the slowest. The West region accounts for 70% of China's total land mass, yet it only accounts for 30% of the country's population. Most of the area is filled with rugged mountains, resulting in very high logistics costs and lower levels of productive economic activities. Many MNCs usually delay their go-to-market investments in the West region as the last priority. The West region also accounts for the largest number of provinces. There are nine provinces/ autonomous regions and one centrally governed municipality. To help you remember, the West region also can be divided into three large sub-regions: Southwest 1 +3, Northwest 3 provinces, and 3 Autonomous regions situated on the plateau.

Southwest 1+3 consists of Chongqing city (重 庆), Sichuan province (四 川), Yunnan province (云 南), and Guizhou province (贵 州). Chongqing, the last city to be established among the four centrally governed municipalities, was separated from Sichuan province in June 1997 (one month before the Hong Kong handover to China). Although Chongqing is defined as a city, its land area is

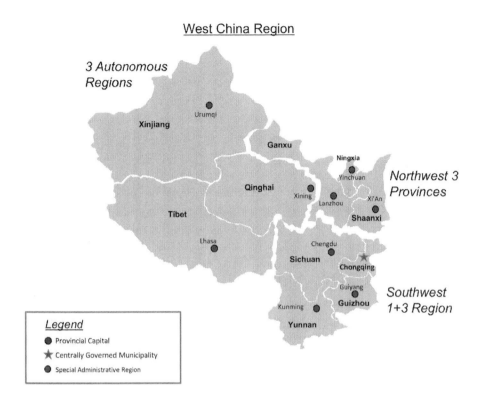

Illustration 1.5: West China Region

almost as large as a small province. Climate-wise, Chongqing is often considered one of China's three furnaces (referring to its extreme heat during the summer). The other two furnaces are Nanjing in the East region, and Wuhan in the South region. If you plan to visit these three cities during the summer, be sure to pack extra change of clothes. Many locals also describe Chongqing as a tiring city as the whole city is built on mountains, and traveling between destinations becomes a workout. Landscape-wise it is very similar to San Francisco, but not as scenic, as the city is built on industrial companies which have slowly polluted the air and water over the past few decades.

To the west of Chongqing is the province of Sichuan, with Chengdu (成都) as its capital. Sichuan is the home to the giant panda, which is China's national treasure. Since Sichuan province is situated inside a basin, it is quite humid all year round. Locals add spice to their daily diet, especially in winter, to keep warm and to get rid of the "humidity" inside the body (according to traditional Chinese medicine practices, "humidity" trapped inside the body is bad to health). As mentioned before, a lot of FMCG companies conduct market research in Wuhan to represent consumers from central China. By the same token, they conduct research in Chengdu as representative of the West region. One of the key reasons is that Chengdu is the wealthiest city in the region, representing a large portion of the local consumption power.

Continuing counterclockwise to the south of Sichuan, there is Yunnan province, with its provincial capital of Kunming (昆 明). Yunnan province guards the southwest border of China. It is neighbor to Myanmar, Laos, and Vietnam. The state-owned tobacco industry in Yunnan is one of the largest pillar industries in the province, accounting for almost 50% of the local government's revenue! Other than tobacco, tourism is another major industry in Yunnan. Thanks to its diverse topography creating beautiful scenery like snowy mountains and lakes, Yunnan is one of the top tourist destinations for mainland Chinese. Due to its proximity to Tibet, there are strong Tibetan influence in northern Yunnan, particularly in the Shangri-la area. If you are not able to visit Tibet or unable to obtain a separate travel pass in addition to your China visa, visiting Yunnan is your best alternative to get a flavor of the Tibetan culture.

Gallery 1.2: Overlooking Meili Snow Mountain from a Monstery, Shangri-La, Yunnan

Finishing the southwest loop is Guizhou province (贵州). Guizhou still has a predominantly rural population, so its development is relatively backward. One of the largest industries is the manufacturing of Chinese white liquor called "Moutai (茅台)," which is the de facto national liquor often drank by military officers, government officials, and businessmen at banquets. The base flagship model, a "106 proof white liquor," or 53% alcohol, used to sell for around US$300 a bottle (500ml). After the government cracks down on corruption in recent years, the market price dropped by half now. We will talk more about "Moutai" in the wine and dine part in Chapter 3.

While the Southwest sub-region is not wealthy overall, the Northwest sub-region is even poorer due to the lack of rain fall and rugged mountain and desert terrains. Northwest sub-region consists of three provinces where the ancient Silk Road passed through towards the West in which trade across continents took place centuries ago. Shaanxi province (陕 西) marks the starting point of the Silk Road. Shaanxi's provincial capital is Xi'an (西安), where the famous terracotta warriors guarding the first Chinese emperor Qin's tomb are located. Also, be careful not to mix up Shaanxi province with Shanxi province as the Chinese pronunciation is very similar except for the tone.

Head west along the Silk Road is the Ningxia Autonomous Region (宁夏) where a large number of Chinese Muslims live. Ningxia is also the wine region of China, where a lot of local vineyards are located. Some of the more famous local wine brands are Great Wall, Imperial Horse. Continue further west and you will reach the last stop of the Silk Road within China's border – Gansu province (甘 肃). Gansu's provincial capital is Lanzhou (兰 州), which is famous for Lanzhou ramen noodles! After all, ramen is not just Japan's specialty. Lanzhou is an industrial city where large petro-chemical plants were built in the 1950's as a strategic location away from the Soviet Union and the coast lines where western countries could have easily attacked. Thus they picked a spot in the desert area with little access, similar to Las Vegas without the glamour.

Finally we have reached the last three provinces/ autonomous regions situated far away on the plateau. West of Gansu province is Qinghai province (青　海). Qinghai is where the Yangtze River and Yellow River begin, therefore it is also known as "the source of rivers." Qinghai has a low population density. It was known for its hard labor camps for criminals, political dissidents and others who needed to be reformed in the old days, similar to Siberia of the old Soviet Union.

China's northwestern corner is home to the Xinjiang Autonomous Region (新　疆), with provincial capital of Urumqi (乌 鲁 木 齐). Xinjiang is the largest in land area among all provinces/ autonomous regions in China. There have been a number of ethnic violence incidents in the region since the communist army occupied the region and converted its occupying army personnel into civilians and took residence alongside the local Uyghurs.

Tibet Autonomous Region (西　藏) guards the southwest border of China and is directly south of Xinjiang. Tibet's provincial capital is Lhasa (拉萨). Those of you who have visited Lhasa should notice that even KFC has opened a store in Lhasa! I wonder if the taste of fried chicken would be different when cooked in a low pressure environment! Due to the independence movements and protests by some of the monks and locals, it is very difficult for foreigners from the US and Europe to gain access to the region for tours, even though one may get a visa for China easily. In airports, flights to Lhasa need to go through special security checks. If you plan to visit the beautiful and exotic Tibet, you may want to consult a travel agent about the pass before you purchase any tickets.

Taiwan Province, Hong Kong, Macau

A well-informed reader would immediately point out that Tibet is not the last province in China. In fact, it should be the last one in mainland China. To a lot of Chinese that support the unification of one China, there is the province of Taiwan. For some Taiwanese readers this could be sensitive and even offensive. This book is not meant to take a position on the issue, so please continue to read before you draw any conclusion where the author stands. When I was in strategy consulting industry, I was staffed on a China project, guiding a junior consultant on a PowerPoint slide that contained a map of China. The junior consultant forgot to include Taiwan in the map. Later the project manager discovered the issue and criticized the junior consultant. The project manager said that if the Chinese client saw this slide, they could react strongly by firing the team as this is a clear sign of not knowing China well! And if a government official saw this, our firm could get into serious trouble with consequences ranging from unable to consult for the government, SOEs to unable to conduct business in China. Anecdotally a few years ago, IKEA printed its catalog including a map indicating its store locations, which unfortunately left out Taiwan. As a result, the catalog did not clear censorship by the government as a publication and must be reprinted. In China, all publicly distributed materials such as magazines and catalogs need to go through approval by the local government propaganda agency. As you can see, this is a simple mistake with serious consequences. As a kind reminder, the Chinese government has recently updated its boundary with the Spratly Islands in the South China Sea included on the map in all Chinese passports. So sure to use the official map when your company needs to create a map of China to avoid unnecessary headaches.

As for the two Special Administrative Regions of Hong Kong and Macau, they are not part of the scope for this book. In fact, most MNCs manage Hong Kong, Macau, and Taiwan businesses separately from the mainland China operations. This is because consumer behaviors and needs, as well as the retail channel landscape are very different. This book will focus only on mainland China.

Coastal Region

Besides dividing China up into North, East, South and West regions, China's coastal area is often publicly cited by the central government and foreign media as an important region. Coastal region consists of Shanghai plus the five coastal provinces, namely Guangdong, Fujian, Zhejiang, Jiangsu and Shandong province. Accounting for only 30% of China's population, this region contributes to over 50% of China's GDP. Many MNCs' China market entry strategy typically focuses on penetrating the relatively affluent coastal region first as consumers residing in this part of China are wealthier and more receptive to foreign brands than consumers living further away from the coast.

Pearl River Delta, Yangtze River Delta

If you are a regular reader of the Wall Street Journal, Bloomberg or Financial Times, you would probably recognize the terms Pearl River Delta and Yangtze River Delta, which lead the development of the country. These deltas are cluster of cities where the government issued favorable land, tax and labor policies to attract investments to promote growth of their industries. Pearl River Delta and the Yangtze River Delta are definitely the two wealthiest and most developed city clusters in China. Because of their relatively advanced economy and infrastructure compared to the rest of the country, these two regions are positioned to take advantage of international capital and internationalize its economy ahead of the rest of the country. Here is a simple list of the cities that is included in each delta:

Pearl River Delta consists of nine cities within the Guangdong province, namely Guangzhou, Shenzhen, Zhuhai, Foshan, Huizhou, Zhaoqing, Dongguan, Zhongshan and Jiangmen.

Yangtze River Delta consists of fourteen cities that span across Shanghai, Jiangsu, and Zhejiang province. It includes six cities from Zhejiang province, namely Hangzhou, Ningbo, Huzhou, Jiaxing, Shaoxing, Zhoushan, and eight cities from Jiangsu province, namely Nanjing, Zhenjiang, Yangzhou, Taizhou, Changzhou, Wuxi, Suzhou and Nantong.

What is City Tier?

Within mainland China, there are 31 provinces, autonomous regions and centrally governed municipalities. According to statistics published by the Chinese government, there were over 3000 cities and counties in China. With such a large number of cities and counties, how does a business distinguish the importance of one city versus another? How do you know the economic development level in Jiangmen City, and whether a company should use a distributor or employ direct sales to tackle the market? What about comparing Jiangmen and Lufeng, which city is wealthier? Which city should deserve more of your time and effort? To make it easier to identify a particular city's development level and importance, many MNCs categorize 3000+ Chinese cities into five tiers. The categorization is the same as the PRC government's administrative region definition. [2] Nielsen China (one of the largest market research companies in China) also follows the same city tier classification in its China retail database, which is the largest and also most commonly used retail database that tracks market size and market share data in China.

First level consists of the most well developed cities, the Big Four Cities or Key Cities which includes Beijing, Shanghai, Guangzhou, and Shenzhen. The four cities are generally referred to as "Bei-Shang-

Guang-Shen (北 上 广 深)" by locals, which is the first Chinese character from each of the four cities. These four cities are very close in terms of the level of their economic development, with GDP per capita around US$17,000-24,000 (RMB100,000-150,000) in 2015. Note that only Beijing and Shanghai are centrally governed municipalities, while Guangzhou and Shenzhen are under the jurisdiction of Guangdong province.

Gallery 1.3: Residential District in Xi'An (Tier 1 City), Shannxi Province. Photo taken by Mr. Zhang, Yi Zhe

The next level is Tier 1 cities. There is a total of 32 Tier 1 cities, which includes all of the provincial capital cities; the two centrally governed municipalities Tianjin and Chongqing; plus Dalian, Qingdao, Ningbo, and Xiamen. [2] These are the top tier cities in which they receive majority of a provincial government's resources. Tier 1 cities also get priority in major infrastructure investments over lower tier cities within the province, such as airport, highways, subways etc.

Gallery 1.4: Office District in Nanjing (Tier 1 City), Jiangsu Province. Photo taken by Mr. Zhang, Yi Zhe

Next level down is Tier 2 cities. There are a total of 288 Tier 2 cities. [2] These are classified as the prefecture level cities according to the government's administrative classification. The level of economic development within Tier 2 cities is actually quite diverse. Some Tier 2 cities are quite wealthy. Dongguan（东莞）in Guangdong, Suzhou（苏州）in Jiangsu, and Wenzhou（温州）in Zhejiang are all located within the coastal area with close proximity to the Big Four and Tier 1 cities. On the other hand, some Tier 2 cities are relatively poor, such as Zunyi（遵义）from Guizhou and Dingxi（定西）from Gansu, which are more likely to be located in the inner western region of China. Since the five coastal provinces are relatively affluent, they account for a disproportionately higher percentage of Tier 2 cities of 25%.

Gallery 1.5: Commercial District in Yangzhou (Tier 2 City), Jiangsu Province. Photo taken by Mr. Zhang, Yi Zhe.

Next is Tier 3 cities. There is a total of 361 Tier 3 cities. [2] In the government's administrative classification, these are county-level cities. Tier 3 cities are typically small counties located on the outskirts of Tier 1 and 2 cities. In general, most people refer to China as having around 600 cities. This number is based on adding up the Big Four, Tier 1, Tier 2 and Tier 3 cities. For most companies, it is not easy to penetrate into Tier 3 cities as they are smaller in size and located further away from the Tier 1 cities.

Gallery 1.6 Small shop in Gemuer (Tier 3 City), Qinghai Province. Photo taken by Mr. Zhang, Yi Zhe

Gallery 1.7 Modern shopping center in Kunshan (Tier 3 City), Jiangsu Province

The lowest tier is Tier 4 cities. Even though they are called cities, they are actually small counties or large towns. In the government's administrative definition, these are counties with a government representative office. There are over 1,500 Tier 4 cities. With presence in over 1000+ cities in China, KFC is probably the only F&B retail chain that is able to penetrate into Tier 4 cities. [3]

Going further down the hierarchy are townships, which is often referred to as the rural areas. Township is the most basic level of administrative institution, including small towns and villages. There are over 20,000 towns, over 12,000 townships, plus other minor categories such as district offices in China. They add up to 40,000+ township-level entities. Of course there are also numerous small villages and towns scattered around the rural areas that have not been included in the official statistics.

Gallery 1.8 Local household in rural village. Taken at Chenxiaoyuan village, Huchang Town, Hubei province. Photo taken by Mr. François Trézin

Gallery 1.9 Construction site in rural village. Taken at Chenxiaoyuan village, Huchang Town, Hubei province. Photo taken by Mr. François Trézin

To better illustrate the city tier classification, here is an example of different city tiers within Guangdong province:

Key City: Guangzhou, Shenzhen

Tier 1 City: none

Tier 2 City: Dongguan, Zhuhai, Qingyuan, etc.

Tier 3 City: Zengcheng, Yingde, etc.

Tier 4 City: Qinxing county, Fogang county, etc.

Township: Longtang town, Henghe town, etc.

China City Tier Classification 2014

City Classification	Government Definitions [2]	No. of Cities	Note
Key Cities	Beijing, Shanghai, Guangzhou, Shenzhen	4	685 cities in total
Tier 1 Cities	21 Provincial Capital: Harbin, Changchun, Shenyang, Shijiazhuang, Xi'an, Zhengzhou, Jinan, Taiyuan, Hefei, Wuhan, Changsha, Nanjing, Ningbo, Guiyang, Kunming, Hangzhou, Nanchang, Fuzhou, Chengdu, Lanzhou, Haikou 5 Autonomous Region Capital: Hothot, Lhasa, Nanning, Wulumuqi, Yinchuan 2 Centrally Governed Municipality: Tianjin, Chongqing 4 Individually Planned Economic Cities: Qingdao, Dalian, Ningbo, Xiamen	32	
Tier 2 Cities	Prefecture-level cities (i.e. Wuxi, Tangshan, Suzhou, Dongguan)	256	
Tier 3 Cities	County-level cities (i.e. Yiwu, Yixing, Benxi)	361	
Tier 4 Cities	Counties / Location of county government	1,500+	
Township (rural areas)	Towns and Villages	40,000+	

[2] Source: China Statistical Yearbook 2015, Figure 25-1

Illustration 1.6: China City Tier Classification 2014

Income Disparity

Household Income Level by City Tier

To a certain extent, city tier classification reflects the levels of economic development of a city and income of its residents. Illustration 1.7 is a comparison of monthly household income by city tier in China. It is calculated by multiplying the [Per Capita Disposable Income] by [Average Household Size of 3], divided by [12 months]. All future reference of income in this book will be based on average monthly household disposable income. In Illustration 1.7, household income of a city from each region within each city tier is shown. As you can see, income level drops as we go down each tier. Moreover, income disparity is quite large even within the same city tier. Income levels in the East and South regions are generally higher than those in the North and West regions. There is a common saying in China of "East rich, West poor" to reflect the regional income disparity.

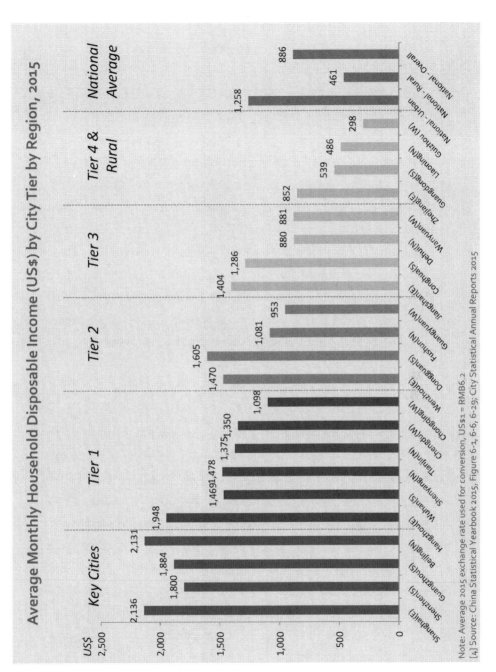

Average Monthly Household Disposable Income (US$) by City Tier by Region, 2015

Key Cities	Shanghai (E)	2,136
	Shenzhen (S)	1,800
	Guangzhou (S)	1,884
	Beijing (N)	2,131
	Hangzhou (E)	1,948
Tier 1	Wuhan (S)	1,478
	Shenyang (N)	1,469
	Tianjin (N)	1,375
	Chengdu (W)	1,350
	Chongqing (W)	1,098
Tier 2	Wenzhou (E)	1,470
	Dongguan (S)	1,605
	Fushun (N)	1,081
	Guangyuan (W)	953
Tier 3	Jiangshan (E)	1,404
	Conghua (S)	1,286
	Dehui (N)	880
	Wanyuan (W)	881
	Zhejiang (E)	852
Tier 4 & Rural	Guangdong (S)	539
	Liaoning (N)	486
	Guizhou (W)	298
National Average	National - Urban	1,258
	National - Rural	461
	National - Overall	886

US$: 2,500 · 2,000 · 1,500 · 1,000 · 500 · 0

Note: Average 2015 exchange rate used for conversion, US$1 = RMB6.2
[4] Source: China Statistical Yearbook 2015; Figure 6-1, 6-6, 6-29; City Statistical Annual Reports 2015

Illustration 1.7 Average Monthly Household Disposable Income (US$) by City Tier by Region, 2015

There are several interesting findings when perusing the figures:

When I wrote the first version of this book back in 2012, Shenzhen was earning the highest disposable income among the Big Four as it was China's first special economic zone. But within the last few years Shanghai's economy grew rapidly and overtook the top place, at around US$2,136 (RMB13,241). Even though residents in Shanghai are already earning the highest income in China, the household income level in Shanghai is still quite low compared to other international metropolis. For instance, average household income in Hong Kong, London, and New York is around US$3,200-3,400 in 2015. Shanghai is only at 60% of the international metropolis level. However, as you will learn from later chapters, living costs in Shanghai are not necessarily lower than those metropolis, especially when it comes to real estate.

As the capital city of China, Beijing surprisingly does not earn the highest household income among the Big Four. This may be due to the presence of a disproportionately high number of civil servants and employees of State Owned Enterprises (SOE) in which the "stated" salary is generally lower than those in the commercial sector, which lowered the overall average in Beijing. But is it true that household income in Beijing is lower than that in Shanghai? It is hard to say if you include all the benefits and "additional unreported incomes". But of course, no one can get to that level of transparency. In fact, a friend of mine who runs an online cake shop once told me that she found the consumption pattern very different between Shanghai and Beijing. Shanghai has a large middle income class which generates large consumption power for aspirational luxury consumer goods. Whereas in Beijing, the middle income class segment is actually not that big. Income distribution in Beijing is like an hour glass, with a large group of very high income families who are senior SOE and government officials, and a large base of lower income segment. Consumer needs are diverse and thus, making it hard for her to come up with the product portfolio that could appeal to both ends of the spectrum.

Average Monthly Household Disposable Income by City Tier (2015)

CITY TIER (NO. OF CITIES IN EACH CATEGORY)	RANGE OF MONTHLY HOUSEHOLD DISPOSABLE INCOME (US$)	AVERAGE MONTHLY HOUSEHOLD DISPOSABLE INCOME (US$)
Key City (4)	$1,800-2,140	$2,000
Tier 1 City (32)	$1,000-1,950	$1,350
Tier 2 City (256)	$280-1,600	~$800
Tier 3 City (361)	$220-1,400	~$550
Tier 4 City (1500+)	$220-600	~$480
Township (4000+)	Below $500	~$450

Note: US$ = 6.2 RMB

Illustration 1.8 Average Monthly Household Disposable Income by City Tier (2015)

Unlike the Big Four cities where the income range is relatively similar, income range among the Tier 1 cities is quite wide. Hangzhou, the highest earning Tier 1 city, at US$1,948 (RMB 12,079), almost doubled the income of the lowest earning Tier 1 city, Xining, capital of the western inland province of Qinghai, at RMB US$1,017 (RMB 6,308). In fact, Hangzhou's income level is even higher than that of Guangzhou and Shenzhen. Even though Hangzhou and Xining are both provincial capitals and Tier 1 cities, the income disparity is quite alarming. It is not uncommon to see some of the small counties and towns in the well-developed East region to surpass some of the less developed provincial capitals in the West region. This is a further proof of the "East rich, West poor" phenomenon.

Things become more dynamic among Tier 2 cities. Dongguan in Guangdong province earns the highest income among Tier 2 cities. Its average monthly household income in 2015 has reached US$1605 (RMB 9,948). How can a Tier 2 city with close proximity to Hong Kong achieve such a high household income? This is attributed to the export industry boom where many smart business people from Hong Kong, Taiwan, and other foreign countries invested in manufacturing plants in Dongguan since the early 1980s, which in turn attracted many other businesses and employment opportunities to the city, therefore greatly enhancing the income of Dongguan's labor force. During this time, Dongguan created Taiwan's richest man, Terry Gou, owner of Foxconn, whose company is one of the largest employers in Dongguan that assembles iPhones and laptops for the world. Having said that, the wealth distribution is quite uneven in China. The average of haves and have nots produced the artificial average figure, but in reality there are the ultra-rich and the everyday poor living within the same city. A news article by Financial Times published in early 2016 cited a study by Peking University, one of the top higher education institutions in the country, that 25% of the country's wealth was owned by 1% of the households, resulting in a Gini Coefficient of 0.49, which is considered by the World Bank to have severe income inequality. [5] Therefore, driving up the income level of the citizens and building a middle income class have become a top priority of the Chinese government.

Gallery 1.10 Restaurant Hiring Advertisement in Shanghai (Hiring for waiter, bartender, cleaning lady).

Note: Monthly salary starting at RMB 3,600 (US$ 580)

If we compare the highest income Tier 2 city to the lowest income Tier 2 city, the highest income city has almost 6 times as much income as the other. The lesson here is never to assume that every Tier 2 city is rich, since it all depends on which region the city is located in. In general, the average household income in Tier 2 cities is around US$800, which is considered quite decent in China's living standard.

The level of household income in Tier 3 cities has a dramatic fall from their Tier 2 counterparts. In Tier 3 cities, average household income is only at around US$550 (RMB 3,400). When it comes to Tier 4 cities, income level in small counties and rural villages is even lower. In most cases, the total household income is only at US$220-$600 (RMB 1,400-3,700).

Although national statistics have shown that monthly household income is at US$890 (RMB 5,500), the reality could be quite different. Just a year or two ago, I remembered having a hard time recruiting families in Tier 1 and Tier 2 cities with monthly income over US$700 (RMB 4,000) to participate in a market research. In the end, we had to lower the minimum income level to US$500-$700 (RMB 3,000-4,000) to recruit enough households for the research. This implies that when pricing your product, it is dangerous to assume that your target wealthy customers in big cities who seem to have insatiable appetite for European luxury goods, would have the same unlimited consumption power. In recent years, because of high housing prices which are comparable or even exceeding their US counterparts, many young families' disposable income after mortgage payment is not that high. Error! Hyperlink reference not valid. will discuss more about housing prices. In the past decade, nominal salary increase has not kept up with the real estate market. As a result, China's consumer market is mainly led by low price tier local brands.

Fresh Graduates Monthly Pay

Besides looking at the official per capita income figures as an indicator of the country's overall income level, another important measure is the university graduates' starting salaries. In 2015, Chinese college graduates' starting salary ranges between US$ 350 to US$ 530 (RMB 2200 - 3300), an average of US$450 (RMB 2750), all figures are before tax. MNCs pay the highest amount at US$450 (RMB 2,741); followed by state-owned enterprises and government jobs paying US$ 365 (RMB 2,238) and US$ 345 (RMB 2,112) respectively. Compared to developed countries, you can immediately find the amount too meager to make a living, especially when an Ayi (domestic helper) working in Beijing or Shanghai easily make US$850 in cash. In recent years, there are reportedly female graduates who prefer to work as live-in maid rather than getting a normal job, which is not too shocking after seeing the salary discrepancies. A maid's wage is decent, cash payment without tax liabilities, simple labor work, no pressure from real life work, and free room and board... But it is discouraging to see the college education wasted.

Although national average income for fresh graduates is only around US$450, but in Beijing and Shanghai, a fresh graduate can earn up to US$890 (RMB5500) if including allowances and subsidies for working for a large company. In Guangzhou and Shenzhen, it is about US$650 (RMB4000) a month. Eventually businesses have to pay a minimum salary to keep the supply of talents stable. This brings to another topic of the supply of new graduates. Every year China produces 6-7 million college graduates compared to 2 million just ten years ago in 2003 attributed to the reforms in higher education institutions since year 2000. The tiered university system means graduates from less prestigious universities tend to have a hard time competing for a job that makes a living.

CHINA NATIONAL CIVIL SERVANTS EXAMINATION

Although the base salaries of civil servants are not high, they have good fringe benefits and job security. There have been an increasing number of college graduates who apply to become civil servants in China. In the national civil servants examinations that took place in 2015, there were nearly 1.3 million applicants entered the exam. In the end, only 22,000 people were hired. The admission ratio is at 58:1, which is even lower than the undergraduate admissions rate at Harvard or Stanford! [6] This level of intense competition is exemplary of the Chinese education system.

Illustration 1.9 compares the salaries of fresh graduates in major regions/ countries around the world. It indicates that fresh graduate salary in Tier 1 cities in China is approaching the level of Taiwan, however, it is still far below the level in other developed countries.

The lower income level in Greater China area forces a lot of new grads to live with their parents or share apartments immediately after graduation. Luckily, the cost of attending college in China is also much lower than that in the US or UK. On average, four-years of college education in China cost around US$ 4,000-8,000. In the US, it is around US$ 20,000-40,000, which is 5 times more than that in China!

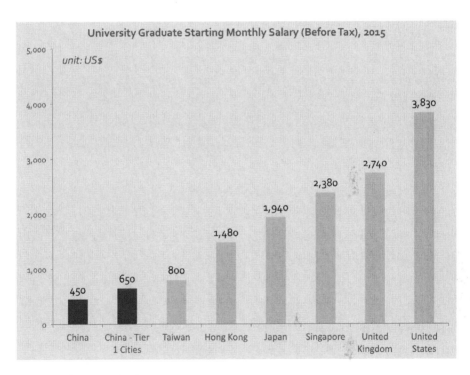

Illustration 1.9 University Graduate Starting Monthly Salary (Before Tax), 2015

1 . 4

Penetrating Different City Tiers

Even elementary students are well aware of the vast population in China: nearly 1.4 billion by 2016, which is also the highest in the world. One out of every five people in the world comes from China, which does not include the overseas ethnic Chinese population. Because of the attractive demographics, many market reports point to China as a large market with strong consumption power right behind some of the top developed countries such as the US and Europe. Many MNCs even place China as first priority market in their global expansion plan. For instance, China is already Starbucks second largest market after the US home market. But within the China market, does everyone spend similar amounts? Does everyone buy the same brand/ product? In this section, we will go into details breaking down the population by city tiers and the associated consumption. We will also talk about the implication of city tier definition to the consumer products market in terms of product offering and sales and distribution.

Before we dive into the population distribution details, we need to understand this concept that is unique to China – the "Household Registry" system "Hu Kou (户口)". The "Household Registry" system has a direct impact on how population is calculated in China.

Household Registry System "Hu Kou 户口 "

In most western countries like the UK or the US, your residential address determines to which district you belong. You receive your social benefits such as public school education, healthcare, and social insurance from your current residence district. It is not uncommon to see families moving around the country because of work or education. Residential district changes as one moves. In China, this is not the case. Because of resource scarcity, relatively better public resources such as schools, hospitals and social welfares are offered in larger cities compared to regions populated by agricultural labors. To avoid the outpouring of labor from rural areas into the cities, the Chinese government established a Household Registry system "Hu Kou," a domestic passport system, to artificially restrict the free flow of resources, especially labor. This means a person's household registry is based on where one's parents' and grandparents' Hu Kou accounts are located, not based on where the person is currently residing. For example, if Ms. Wu's Hu Kou account is in a village, even if she moves to Shanghai, she is not entitled to any social benefits provided by Shanghai city government. And if she gives birth to her child in Shanghai, her child's registry still belongs to her village (not to mention that Ms. Wu will need to pay 100% of the hospital bill in order to give birth at a local hospital in Shanghai, and which is almost free for locals with the Shanghai Hu Kou). Later on when Ms. Wu's child reaches school age, her child will not be able to attend any public schools in Shanghai, and not able to attend college entrance exam offered in Shanghai. Let me use another real life example. My last live-in maid in Shanghai discovered a small tumor in her nose.

Originally she planned to have surgery in a Shanghai hospital. But after discovering the cost of the surgery in Shanghai would be USD $3,000, given her household registry is located in a small village in Anhui province, she had to ask for sick leave to travel to her registered Hu Kou village to have the same minor operation for a mere USD $200 co-payment. The difference justifies for the week-long medical trip, but was certainly not economically efficient from the society's overall wellbeing perspective. When living in China, we always hear about news reporting patients with serious disease who could not get the proper treatment in rural areas, and need to borrow large sums of money to come to large cities for proper treatment. With the Household Registry system in place, the country is effectively divided into smaller sections where true labor mobility is not possible. And this system is unlikely to be abolished in the near future for political and economic reasons.

Population and Consumption by City Tier

The way population in China is calculated is quite complicated. Population data can be divided into two categories, the Household Registry "Hu Kou" population and resident population. Registry population is calculated based on household registry data, regardless of current residence. Based on Registry population, only 35% of China's population is considered urban population while the other 65% is considered as rural population. This also implies that a majority of China's population is still unable to enjoy the better social benefits like healthcare, education, and pension provided by the cities. As mentioned before, cities provide much better social benefits than

MIGRANT WORKERS & CHILDREN LEFT-BEHIND

Migrant workers are a byproduct of the Household Registry system. As we see from earlier sections, earnings from large cities are much higher than those in smaller counties and villages, not to mention more abundant job opportunities, causing a young migrating labor flow seeking a better life. As many of these migrant workers have little education and job training, they were only suitable for low level labor work, such as construction, factories and service industries. When traveling in large cities in China, you will notice most restaurant service staff is not local. According to the China Statistics Bureau there were 274 million migrant workers in China in 2014. Even though these migrant workers spend the majority of the time living in the city, they are not entitled to any social benefits offered by the city. It would be economically devastating if they get seriously sick or hurt. But thanks to the young demographics, such incidents have been rare. But what if these migrant workers get married and have kids? Since these children are not entitled to attend local public schools, parents will have no choice but to send them back to their hometown and have the grandparents take care of them. The term "left-behind child" refers to this social phenomenon where children were raised by the older generation while parents supports the family by working in other cities.

rural areas. As a result, many people from small cities or rural area will try to move their "Hu Kou" to the large cities through college education and work program established by each receiving city, much like the US green card process.

Population statistics by the other category, resident population, is calculated based on the location one resides for over six months in a given year. It is very common in today's China for a person's hometown different from resident location. For instance, my live-in maid's Hu Kou is in a small village in Anhui province. But when it comes to calculating resident population, she is counted as Shanghai's. Whenever a migrant worker moves to a new city, he or she will need to report to the local police station to obtain a temporary residence permit, similar to a domestic visa. Without the temporary residence permit, he or she will not be able to secure a job in the city. In fact, foreigners (including visitors from Hong Kong, Macao and Taiwan) also need to register with local police station within twenty-four hours of arrival. Don't worry if you are staying at a hotel, the system automatically reports to the police station when your passport pages are scanned at the front desk.

In 2011, the China Bureau of Statistics announced that urban population in China has finally exceeded the tipping point to 51.3%. The latest figure in 2014 indicated that urban population has risen to 54.8%, implying rural population fell to 45.2%. The government cited that this is a key milestone to China's effort in urbanization. You can probably guess already that this figure was based on resident population, instead of Registry population which is more reflective of how resources are being distributed in the country. The gap of

270 million between resident and Registry population is what we often hear in the news about migrant workers working in the cities. Not only is income higher in the cities, but there are also more job opportunities, which are key driving forces for the 270 million migrant workers to leave their hometown and families and move to the city in order to improve their quality of life. Shenzhen is a classic example of an "Immigrants City" where its resident population far exceeds its Registry population. According to the China Bureau of Statistics, Shenzhen only has 3.3 million Registry populations, whereas its actual resident population is over 10 million, driving its real estate prices to be one of the highest in mainland China! As you can see, the gap in terms of the two population figures is actually quite significant!

Illustration 1.10 compares resident population distribution by city tier to consumption distribution. Population distribution is based on resident population instead of household registry population, which is more reflective of consumer spending in a given city tier. This single graph took me the longest time to collect various statistics and analyze among all other graphs in this book. Not to mention that there are many statistics data in China that is contradicting each other! As we can see from the graph, China is gradually moving towards building mega cities. The Big Four have already accounted for more than 5% of China's population. Guangzhou and Shenzhen on its own have over ten million in resident population, while Beijing and Shanghai has over 20 million. Big Four and Tier 1 cities together (36 cities in total) account for one-fifth of China's total resident population, meaning each city on average has nearly 8 million people living and working. Big cities in China are becoming even more crowded. No wonder why real estate prices in Tier 1 cities are skyrocket high.

Household income level shown in the previous section has already indicated that there exists a large income disparity between large and small cities. Consumption level is another indicator reflecting people's living standards. Unfortunately there is no simple answer, but you can generally guess that the majority of consumption in China still comes from a small number of large cities, given that is where most of the wealth is accumulated. As Illustration 1.10 indicates, the Big Four, Tier 1, and Tier 2 cities account for 36% of total resident population, but they account for more than 60% of the country's total consumer consumption. This is why most MNCs' China entry strategy always starts with Big Four, Tier 1 and Tier 2 cities first. Conversely, the remaining 64% of the population, which is often referred to as the "Bottom of the Pyramid" in media, only account for less than 40% of total consumption. For businesses that require scale of economy to drive revenue and profit, unlocking the Bottom of the Pyramid has become the key growth opportunity.

Illustration 1.10 not only shows wealth disparity in China, but also reminds you that China is not one single entity. Different city tiers, different regions represent different levels of income and consumption, driving different consumer behaviors and needs.

Price differentiation in China's consumer product market

Having multiple city tiers is one of China's unique characteristics, with each city tier representing a different income level. Due to the large income disparity in China, the Chinese consumer market is

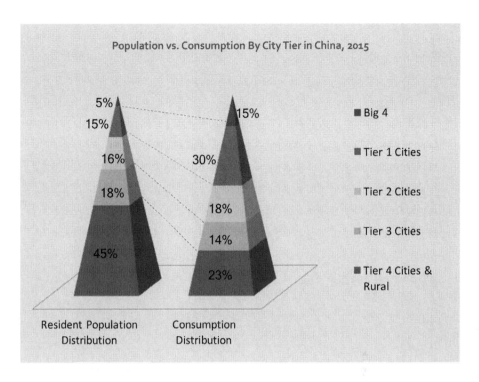

Illustration 1.10 Population vs. Consumption By City Tier in China, 2015

made up of many price segments. In developed western countries like the US and the UK, the income gap among the majority of the population is relatively narrow, so most consumer products consist of only two to three price levels: high-, mid-, low-tier price segment. In China, almost every product has three or more price segments due to the country's large income disparity. Each segment is also quite substantial in size, with low and mid-tier products still account for the majority of the market in volume terms. Let's use baby diapers as an example. In China, the diaper market can be divided into five big price segments. Each segment represents the purchasing power of a consumer group.

Most MNCs in China concentrate their product offerings in the high and mid-price range. There are a few reasons to that: (1) MNCs have a much higher cost structure than local companies when doing business in China, such as following local regulations by the word, paying all taxes as instructed by the Big Four accounting firms, strict quality control, global R&D, expatriates costs. As a result, international brands need to be priced higher than domestic brands to be profitable. (2) If a MNC wants to sell its product into China's smaller cities, the MNC will need to invest significantly on production capacity, brand building, sales and distribution. After all China has over 600 cities, 1,600 counties, 40,000 towns, and countless small villages. The headquarters of the MNCs do not necessarily view it worthwhile to invest too much into a single market. (3) Global product portfolio does not have low tier products so they will need to invest more in R&D to serve these markets. Therefore, most MNCs have made a strategic choice to position their products in the high price tier segment targeting only the high end consumer group. Going down to lower tier segments would cost the MNCs a lot of resource, and may not even justify the ROI. An alternative is to buy a local low-end player to jumpstart the penetration, but the merger synergy has been proven to be difficult.

In China, there are only a handful of MNCs like Procter & Gamble, Coca-Cola, and Wrigley launching low price tier products,

China Diaper Market Segmentation (2016)

Price Tier	Per Piece Price (Size M)	Market Importance (By Volume)	Example Brands
Do Not Use	50% of newborns and toddlers do not wear disposable diaper. They either wear cloth diaper or wear nothing!		
Low Tier	<US$0.1/pc	~23%	PetPet
Value Tier	US$0.1-0.17/pc	~11%	Pampers Red, Chius, Daddypoko
Mid Tier	US$0.17-0.23/pc	~45%	Huggies Silver, Pampers Green, Mamypoko, Anerle, Fitti
Premium Tier	US$0.23- 0.28/pc	~13%	Huggies Gold, Pampers Platinum
Super Premium Tier	> US$0.28/pc	~8%	Huggies Platinum, Kao, Koon

Illustration 1.11 China Diaper Market Segmentation (2016)

truly targeting the bottom of the pyramid. Yet, mid to low price tier segments are still occupied by domestic brands. Among the domestic brands, Large Local Enterprises (LLEs) and State Owned Enterprises (SOEs) are undoubtedly the important players. But one should not underestimate the hundreds of thousands of small local brands and copycat brands by Small and Medium Enterprises (SMEs). These small brands sell at price level that is even lower than that of LLEs. When you are surprised by how cheap a local brand can be, you can always find cheaper local alternatives in the market!

Let's take female sanitary napkins as an example. International brands generally sell for US$ 0.11 (RMB 65 cents) or more per piece. Domestic brands manufactured by LLEs would sell for US$ 0.06-0.10 (RMB 40-60 cents) per piece. When you look at the really small local brands or copycat brands, they sell for US$ 0.05 (RMB 30 cents) or less. Mathematically, a pack of twenty sanitary napkins would sell for less than US$ 1! But you may start to wonder how can these small brands operate at such low cost level? The answer is that these companies only pay attention to sales growth and cost control. They would rather spend money on advertising than on quality control like ensuring the safety of raw materials used, product performance, environmental protection, or employee's safety. No wonder there have been endless environmental pollution reports, food safety disasters and product safety problems in China over the last decade.

Penetrating Different City Tiers

Precisely because of the higher-price positioning, many international brands simply are unable to penetrate into Tier 3 and 4 cities, not to mention towns and villages. It would be quite remarkable if a MNC can distribute its products in the top 300 cities out of the 600 Tier 1, 2, and 3 cities in China.

When it comes to expanding sales and distribution network, MNCs generally follow the city tier hierarchy: the key cities first, then Tier 1 cities, followed by Tier 2 cities, followed by Tier 3 cities, etc. Going by city tiers translates directly to following the gradient of the level of wealth and purchasing power. MNCs with product offerings in high price tier typically follow this method, as the affordability diminishes toward the lower tier cities.

When it comes to sales and distribution, Large Local Enterprises or LLEs, including Taiwanese Enterprises, tend to do a much better job than MNCs. One key factor is that the LLEs' product offerings focus on low price tiers, which can attract low income consumers from Tier 3 and 4 cities and rural areas. In fact the consumer demand pull for these affordable products helps to drive sales down to small cities and villages. Some of the domestic brands from LLEs that are best in class in terms of distribution include: Wahaha bottled water, Diaopai laundry detergent and Hengan "Mind Act Upon Mind" toilet paper. Taiwanese brands like Master Kong instant noodles and Uni-President instant noodles are also known to have the widest distribution in China.

Compared to LLEs and Taiwanese enterprises, MNCs are not as strong in sales and distribution. PepsiCo even handed over the distribution of its beverage business to Taiwanese enterprise Master Kong in 2012 to leverage on Master Kong's wide distribution network while focusing only on brand building. Starbucks also gave the distribution rights of its bottled Frappuccino in China to Master Kong in 2015. Nonetheless, there are several MNCs who are role models in sales and distribution in China. KFC is one shining example. Within the China expat circle, there is a popular saying of "if you want to expand your distribution in China, follow the footsteps of KFC." KFC is the classic example of a MNC who expanded distribution in China using the city tier approach, starting from top tier cities and gradually move down to lower tier cities. KFC opened its first store in Beijing in 1987, then spent nine years to open the first 100 restaurants covering the top dozen cities in China, then spent another eight years to cover 200 cities with 1,000 restaurants. As of 2015, KFC is in 1000+ cities and towns in China with around 5,000 restaurants. [3] KFC is undoubtedly the largest fast food restaurant chain in China with its own logistics supply chain. Not surprisingly KFC China has been managed by a group of Taiwanese professionals with an increasing number of local Chinese managers, who recently negotiated a spin-off from its listed parent company.

Among fast moving consumer goods (FMCG) companies, Coca-Cola, Wrigley, Procter & Gamble's Crest toothpaste and Safeguard soap are among the top brands with the most extensive distribution in China. Nielsen China's retail sales database covers over 3.3 million retail outlets. The aforementioned brands all have reached over 2 million outlets. They have also reached 65% in numerical distribution, not to mention that their weighted distribution is at 99-100% level. Given the huge land mass in China, not many brands can achieve 20% of distribution. So how did these MNC brands achieve such incredible results? My friend from Wrigley told me that the company used the "foot soldier tactics": its distributors would hire an army of sales representatives to ride bikes or drive a minivan with goods along all the highways in China. The sales rep would get out at every exit of the highway to check whether there are retail stores. They sell products to both modern large stores and small traditional mom-and-pop stores. That's how Wrigley built its distribution in China one brick at a time, and eventually covering over 2 million outlets in the country.

Gallery 1.11 You can find Coca Cola even in small mom and pop stores in rural area of Lhasa. Photo taken by Mr. Zhang, Yi Zhe

One of the most classic approaches of sales and distribution in China used by small local brands is called "Villages Encircling the Cities," a term coined by Chairman Mao when he led the Communist Party army to win China over 60 years ago. This is common among small local brands that do not have the resources to compete with large domestic brands or international brands in big cities. Since the cost of doing business in big cities, such as store listing fees, advertising costs, and retail rent is very high, these small local brands choose to start in towns and villages where there is little competition or knowledge of the product category. While they price products low to attract local consumers, they do avoid the higher cost of doing business in big cities. As a MNC, one should not underestimate these small local brands: they can be quite profitable and entrenched in their local markets. Once these small brands make their first pot of gold from towns and villages, they can use the proceeds to enter into Tier 4 cities, then Tier 3, Tier 2, Tier 1 and so on. Finally some of the successful ones can penetrate into the key cities! The most classic example is Wahaha bottled water. It started from Tier 3 and 4 cities, and then progressed into Tier 1 and 2 cities. It used to be the number one bottled water brand in China, only later surpassed by Master Kong's bottled water. Another example is Liby laundry detergent, which used to be a small local brand in Guangdong and finally grew to become one of the top five detergent brands in China. Beingmate baby rice cereal brand also started from small cities many years ago, and subsequently became successful and entered the larger cities. Beingmate is now a listed company in China. The lesson is that China is a vast market with numerous consumer tiers, and there are many different ways to win the market other than the Harvard Business School cases.

The Emerging Middle Class

While some companies target the bottom of the pyramid for scale and volume, many are looking to serve the emerging Chinese middle class, which is transforming from "pyramid-shaped" society to "olive-shaped." Achieving the middle-class status was a hot topic across China, which was regularly discussed on television programs and media. How to define the middle class has always been a tricky question. Even the ex-Financial Secretary of Hong Kong, Mr John Tsang, once mentioned in his blog that drinking coffee and watching French movies are some of the characteristics of the middle class. In addition, he described himself as middle class even though he was making HKD 370,000 (US$47,000) a month! Many people may not agree with Mr Tsang's definition, but it did open up plenty of room for discussion. "The Times" from Great Britain once ran an article that read "How the Chinese middle class really live." It described the typical Chinese middle class family as having a kitchen equipped with IKEA products, driving a Hyundai Tucson SUV, consuming organic foods, planning to send their children to a British international school, wanting to purchase property abroad, etc. The general public reaction to the article was that the criteria given by the Times were too lofty and unachievable.

Personally, I prefer the definition given by Mr. Zong Qinghou, chairman and CEO of Hangzhou Wahaha Group, one time the richest Chinese ranked by the media. He described a middle-class family as one with its own property and an annual income of US$32,000 (RMB 200,000), likely to be after tax. However, an essential criteria in Mr. Zong's statement is that the family should own property; otherwise, the family cannot be considered middle class. [7] With that in mind, a family should have at least US$2,700 (RMB 17,000) in monthly income to satisfy that requirement. If we compare that figure to the 2015 statistics for the monthly disposable income of city-dwelling citizens of US$1,258 (RMB 7,800), we can see that the majority do not meet the middle-class standard yet.

Nevertheless, with the continuing growth of the Chinese economy, many foreign companies and investors believe that there will be more and more middle class families in China as disposable income continues to increase. Even the Chinese government has set a target to double per capita income by 2020 from 2010, implying monthly household income to reach around US$1,000, resulting in the middle-class in China approaching 600 million, almost twice the size of the entire US population today. The purchasing power potential from consumption upgrade is enormous. Many companies eagerly await the rapid growth of the Chinese middle class, which translates to rapid growth for their businesses.

Regardless of the shape of the Chinese society, given the large population base and the associated consumption power, there are ample opportunities in every segment. There are international companies like P&G, Wrigley who are successful in targeting the low income segment by penetrating into the bottom of the pyramid. Mainstream and aspirational luxury brands like Zara, Gap, Starbucks, IKEA, Disney English are growing rapidly by addressing the needs of the booming middle class families. High end luxury brands are also gaining shares from Chinese consumers, particularly from e-commerce channels and Chinese tourists traveling abroad. Chinese consumers is already the world's biggest buyers of luxury goods now, according to a news article from "The Guardian." [8]

Opportunities are not only with large multi-national companies, but also small and medium companies. I have met many foreigners who run very successful businesses spanning across various industries in China, such as restaurants, insurance, trading, design, energy, consumer research, etc. If you want to start your business in China, now would be a good time since the start-ups ecosystem is maturing. Venture capitals are flourishing, investing every promising opportunity. Some local governments have introduced favorable policies such as tax exemption and grants to small businesses to promote entrepreneurship.

Both large and small companies need to understand the local consumers' needs to be successful. The most successful multi-national companies in China are the ones who develop products that are relevant to the Chinese customers' unique tastes. The cookie cutter approach of bringing in products or services from the home market may work, but likely to limit your market potential. Both companies I worked for before in China have developed products specifically tailored to Chinese consumers' needs and preferences. That is one of the reasons why they are both successful companies in China. One thing is for sure, the old saying of "I will be rich if I can make one dollar from each Chinese consumer" is no longer valid. In fact, if you did hear that, you should question the business judgment of the person. Focusing on a specific consumer segment, closely understanding their needs and knowing where to find them, will give you a higher chance to succeed in China.

CHAPTER 2

Daily Life in China

This was what happened on my first business trip to China: my local colleagues were kind enough to take me out to dinner. As everyone was socializing at the table, I couldn't really participate in my Chinese colleagues' conversations as I was not familiar with any of the topics. I feel left out and had to sit and wonder what they were talking about, particularly when I am actually quite a talkative person! To help you avoid this kind of social awkwardness and gain a better understanding of the lives of the Chinese people, the following section will highlight some of their more popular topics of interest today. Not only can you engage in conversations with the locals, but also understand the daily lives of local Chinese.

2 . 1

Pride and Prejudice from Different Provinces

More than once my local Chinese friends mentioned their opinions of people from different regions of China. People are obviously proud of their home provinces and tend to stereotype people from rival provinces. Let me first put out a disclaimer: what is written below came from conversations with friends or observations from the media. There is nothing personal, and it is also not meant to belittle anyone from any particular provinces.

North vs. South

The biggest stereotype in China is about people from the North versus people from the South. As mentioned in Chapter 1.1, the Yangtze River and Huaihe River split China into the Northern and Southern regions. This geographical divide also gives rise to different life styles. Here are two examples to illustrate the differences:

Diet: People who reside in the North base their diet on wheat-based food. Their daily diet usually consists of noodles, buns and dumplings as staple foods. Whereas people in the South eat rice-based food, including steamed rice and rice noodles.

Heating: Central heating is mandatory in most of the office and apartment buildings in the North, with residential heating bills subsidized by the government. While the winter is more severe in the North, it is actually warm and cozy inside, but quite dry. This is similar to living on the New England region of the United States in the wintertime. But in the South, buildings are not equipped with central heating. Some families have HVAC (Heating, Ventilation and Air Conditioning) units for use in both summer and winter times. In the northern parts of the South Region like Shanghai and the Yangtze River Delta, most modern office buildings are equipped with heating systems, so it would be warm in the office during winter when the temperatures drop into single digits Celsius (high 30's in Fahrenheit). The only but key difference is that the lobbies of most office buildings do not have heating. One winter in Shanghai, I waited for a colleague at the office lobby to have lunch. My colleague was late, so I had to wait in the lobby that was freezing cold for 20 minutes. What was worst was that I did not dress warmly that day. When I complained to my colleague about his tardiness, he blamed me for not dressing appropriately for the Shanghai winter. In fact, he was right. Other than office building lobbies, many small restaurants and shops and locals' apartments do not have heating, therefore you may feel more of the winter in Shanghai than in Beijing. If you need to go to the East regions for a business trip from December to March, make sure to dress in layers.

The differences between the North and the South are not only limited to daily life, but also reflected through attitudes and behaviors. So how do Northerners and Southerner view each other? Northerners are usually seen as tough, direct, and are not bothered with trivial matters. On the other hand, that also means they seem to be somewhat careless and are always concerned about saving face. For Southerners, they are seen as detailed-oriented, pragmatic, but calculative at the same time. One can easily draw the obvious conclusion that service industry is likely to be more developed in the Southern region.

Stereotypes of People from Different Provinces

Other than the differences in lifestyles between Northerners and Southerners, people from different provinces also have different "nicknames." If you know these nicknames, you can better understand the culture differences and at the same time impress your friends and colleagues!

Hubei-nese, or people from Hubei, are always seen as very clever and capable, yet cunning and hard to deal with. There is an old Chinese saying "nine-headed birds rule the sky, Hubei men rule on earth" as a metaphor to show how capable and strong-minded Hubei men are. So don't even think about trying to take advantage of Hubei-nese, they are not easy to deal with!

Hunan "Luózi 骡子" (Donkey): We know that donkeys are hard-working, tough, and able to survive in harsh conditions. Yet, they are also seen as being stubborn, emotional, and have bad temper. That's why some employers like to hire Hunanese given their hard working nature, so long as they can cope with the Hunanese' temperament.

NORTHERNERS' CONCERN ABOUT SAVING FACE

What does it mean by Northerners worrying about saving face? Here's one example cited by my Northerner friend. When a Northerner goes to a restaurant, he will usually order at least 2-3 dishes, even if he is only eating by himself. This is because he feels embarrassed and worries that the restaurant staff will look down on him if he orders too little. If he has company at dinner, then he definitely feels the urge to order as many dishes as possible to fill up the dining table. Otherwise, he will lose face in front of his friends. I remember once I saw an interview of a famous Chinese actor on TV, the TV host asked the actor if there is one advice he wants to give to the public, what would it be? He actually said that he wishes Chinese people would not over-order food in order to save face, since that leads to a lot of food wastage. You can see how prevalent it is in China for people to over-order food in order to look good in front of others!

Jiangxi "Laobiao 老表" (Cousin): Jiangxinese like to address people from the same province as 'Laobiao', which means cousin. Note that you need to sound genuine and nice if you are going to address Jiangxinese as Laobiao, otherwise they may think you are making fun of them as being old-fashioned as Laobiao can also mean old-fashioned or not trendy in Chinese.

Sichuan "Chuan Hàozi 川 耗 子 " (Mouse): in Sichuanese dialect, Hàozi means mouse. Chuan Hàozi refers to the Sichuanese as being smart and agile, yet timid, like mice. If anything happens, they are the first one to run away. There is also another saying about Sichuanese and mice: Wherever there are Chinese people, you will find Sichuanese and mice. They are literally everywhere in China! On the contrary, I never find my Sichuanese friends to be like mice. In fact, I think the Sichuanese are good at enjoying life. They like to play poker and Mahjong with friends and drink tea all day. Everyone chills at tea house; no matter you are rich or poor. No one will care about ranking or etiquette in a tea house. At night, they go to restaurants for dinner with friends and family. Next time if you travel to Sichuan, make sure to pay a visit to the local tea house. You will surely be affected by the laid-back culture of Sichuan.

Shanxi "Lao Xi'er 老 西 儿 ": There are two origins of this saying. The first one is that Shanxi province is located to the west of Tai Hang Mountain, so Shanxinese are considered as people from the west, which is literally Xi'er in Chinese. The other saying is related to the habit of Shanxinese of consuming vinegar, and "Xi" is pronounced similar to vinegar in ancient Chinese. Shanxi is well known for its production of black vinegar, similar to the Italian Balsamic, except made from five different locally harvested grains. Besides being well known of consuming vinegar in their daily diet, Shanxinese are also known to being quite stingy. In fact, many successful merchants in ancient China came from Shanxi. There is even an old Chinese saying that Shanxinese would rather lose their lives but not their money! So if you have to do business with Shanxinese, be prepared for a difficult negotiation.

The following paragraph is very controversial, particularly among Henan-ese! On more than a few occasions I have been told to beware of Henanese as they are swindlers. If I go to Henan for business trip, all my friends will tell me to be aware of any strangers approaching. Some employers in China even refuse to hire Henanese! Why do Henanese have such a bad reputation in China? That goes back to 20-30 years ago when Henan was the most populated province in China, yet it was a very poor province with limited resources. As a result, a lot of Henanese had no choice but to work in other provinces in order to earn a living. Some Henanese resorted to cheating in order to make money. Over time, people came to remember Henanese as swindlers. But all these were yesterday's story, or just anecdotal stories resulting from similar statistics multiplied by a large population base in Henan. It is no longer fair to stereotype Henanese as swindlers today. But next time when your colleagues or business partners refer to Henanese as swindlers, you should at least know where it all started.

Wenzhou is a small, yet very rich, Tier 2 city located in Zhejiang province. Wenzhounese are not particularly famous in Chinese history. They only became famous starting about twenty years ago because of their venturing personality. Wenzhounese made their first bucket of gold through export manufacturing and trading (or sometimes smuggling) with the outside countries in the 1980s. Then they re-invested the money in real estate and stock markets. Later on, they started to invest in anything that can turn into a quick profit: coal, cotton, oil, electricity, and even garlic! Wenzhounese often form a group when investing, which gives them scale in whatever they invest in and thus able to move the market and create buzz. As a result, whatever Wenzhounese speculate on, they will be able to drive up price and make a profit. After all these years of speculation, Wenzhounese have accumulated huge amount of wealth. You will be surprised by the number of billionaires in Wenzhou.

People from the Northeast provinces are usually referred to as "Dongbei Yin", in which Dongbei means Northeast and Yin in local dialect means people. Dongbei Yin are seen as bold and straightforward, which are stereotypically characteristics of Northerners. In fact, some of the best warriors in ancient China were from Dongbei. Besides being brave warriors, Dongbei Yin are also very good at bragging and exaggerating. Small things through their word-of-mouth spreading can become something huge! In Dongbei dialect, they even have their own term called "Hu You (忽 悠)" to describe exaggeration at a level close to lying. It also refers to people who unconditionally promises without ever delivering results. "Hu You" has now become a very popular term in China. Next time if you realize your local colleague is trying to fool you or brag about things, you can tell him not to "Hu You." Even though people usually see Dongbei Yin as very good at "Hu You" and thus unreliable, there is also the valiant side of Dongbei Yin. Dongbei Yin, particularly Dongbei man, is known to be very macho and loyal to friends. If you are a single girl and looking for this type, consider finding a Dongbei Yin boyfriend.

Tianjinese, nickname "Wei Zuizi 卫 嘴 子 ": "Wei" is the abbreviation for Tianjin; "Zuizi" is mouth, referring to Tianjinese being amazingly eloquent. In fact, some of the best comedians in China are Tianjinese. Why are Tianjinese so articulate? That is related

Beijing
Proud "Jing Youzi"

Shanghai
Good Husband

Henan
Swindlers "Pianzi"

Hunan
Hardworking "Donkey"

Tianjin
Articulate

Hubei
Successful

Sichuan
Laid Back

Northeast
Bamboozle "Hu You"

Shandong
Macho "Hanzi"

Wenzhou
Speculative

Gallery 2.1 Stereotypes of People from Different Parts of China to the city's background. Tianjin used to be one of the most important harbors in northern China. Back in the old days, merchants from all over China would come to Tianjin to trade. To get business done, Tianjinese needed to negotiate all the times with others. As times went by, Tianjinese were trained to be articulate and good at negotiations.

Now that we have covered the most common nicknames in China, you may wonder about Beijingnese and Shanghainese? Of course we are saving the best for last. Beijing and Shanghai are the two of the most developed and well-known cities in China. As a result, you will notice that Shanghainese and Beijingnese tend to view each other as friendly rivals. It is very similar to the rivalry sentiment between Hong Kong and Singapore, and New York and Los Angeles. If you have a chance to have dinner with Shanghainese and Beijingnese together, you should start with this question and see how heated the conversation becomes. But on a more serious note, many MNCs spend a lot of time deciding where to setup their office and where to locate their staff. The culture aspect becomes an important consideration.

Beijingnese "Jing Youzi (京油子)"

Recently there has been a slogan posted in many locations in Beijing sponsored by local government titled "Beijingnese Spirits: Honest, Sincere, Proud, Saving Face". I find this slogan insightful and highly summarized the city's residents. Let's discuss each characteristic in turn:

Honest and Sincere: Beijingnese tend to treat others wholeheartedly.

They do not like to play games and do everything by the book. They are willing to help others, no matter if you are Beijingnese or not. If a Beijingnese sees someone in trouble, he will definitely offer help.

Open-minded: Beijingnese are quite open-minded to new things. There is a saying that Beijingnese "buy from the whole of China and sell to the whole of China" to show that Beijingnese are willing to accept brands from all parts of China, which is quite different from Shanghainese who only favors local or western brands.

Proud: Even though Beijingnese are honest, open-minded people, they are very proud underneath the surface. Beijing has been the capital city for many dynasties, and is still the capital city of the People's Republic of China. As a citizen of the capital city, living at the feet of the Emperor, Beijingnese believe that they are superior to everyone else. They see themselves as the most civilized and educated group in China, while they see people from other parts of the country not as cultured in history and literature. If you visit Beijing during the summer, swing by the Hou Hai area and you will find quite a few old timer Beijingnese men gathered around and talk about Beijing history. I recalled one time I went to a Tier 1 city for business trip with my Beijingnese colleague. After he saw the headlines of the local newspaper about a robbery case, he said, in discontent, that this type of newspaper was only for the uncivilized people. Beijing newspapers were much more sophisticated that they would never have this type of low-value news in the headline. Instead the Beijing newspapers only report issues of national importance. I was quite amused but left speechless. As you can see, Beijingnese really have a lot of pride and attitudes.

If you recall Tianjinese are referred to as "Wei Zuizi," Beijingnese also have a matching nickname "Jing Youzi." "Jing Youzi" means Beijingnese are sweet talkers, very slick and smooth when dealing with people. At the same time, it is hard to figure out what the Beijingnese are really thinking. They may not mean what they say. Once an old Beijingnese told me, foreigners probably find Beijingnese the most difficult to deal with. One of the main reasons is that Beijingnese love saving face. It is uncivilized to give feedback directly to others' face. Even if they are unhappy with someone or something, they will not directly complain. Instead, they will try to use metaphor or figurative speech to express their dissatisfaction. If you don't carefully read between the lines, you may miss the true intention. In case your Beijingnese colleague gives you a compliment, don't feel happy so soon, there may be double meanings to his words! Maybe he is actually mocking you. Beijingnese are masters of the art of talking. They can scold someone without using any bad words. It is not easy to truly understand the real meaning behind a Beijingnese's words. This is the only exception to the "honest and sincere" principal when you are on their bad side.

Another important characteristic of the Beijingnese is that everyone loves talking about politics. Beijing, as the capital of China where the central government and many SOEs are based, its citizens are much more in touch with government officials, politicians and military personnel in their daily lives. They hear about government gossips and rumors all the time, especially the taxi drivers. As time goes on, everyone becomes a pseudo-politician. This is also why Beijingnese are sweet talkers "Jing Youzi." You never know who you are dealing with, it can be a senior government official, so it is better to play safe and be polite. If you are truly interested in politics, it would be a good conversation starter with Beijingnese. Just remember when your viewpoints are different from your Beijingnese friends, do not criticize, form your disagreement in a question, or just listen and nod. Any open disagreement will be considered as not giving face.

Shanghainese "Shanghai Ning (上海人)"

Shanghainese usually say "A La Shanghai Ning" when introducing themselves, which is "I am Shanghainese" in the local dialect. Similar to Beijingnese, Shanghainese are very proud of themselves. The older generation Shanghainese may even consider people from other provinces as uncultured villagers. Interestingly, while there are nicknames assigned to people from many parts of China due to historical reasons, there is no nickname given to the Shanghainese. It is likely because of the fact that Shanghai as a city has a pretty short history when compared to other Chinese cities, like Beijing or Xi'an.

Not only are Shanghainese proud of their identity, but they are also very proud of their local brands as well. They believe that local Shanghainese brands are better than brands from the rest of the country, even better than some national brands. For example, Shanghainese prefer Guang Ming (Bright Group) milk, White Cat laundry detergent, Mei Jia Jing toothpaste, which are all produced locally. This is quite a contrast to the Beijingnese. Even though Shanghainese do not prefer Chinese brands other than local

Shanghainese brands, they are open to western cultures and embrace western brands. After China opened up in the 1980s, many MNCs have set up their China headquarters in Shanghai, turning Shanghai into an international metropolitan. This makes the inhabitants even prouder of being Shanghainese. However, people from other parts of China sometimes see Shanghainese revere to everything foreign and thus not patriotic.

How do others see Shanghainese, other than being xenophiles? Usually calculative and stingy. If you say that to your Shanghainese friends though, they will vehemently disagree. Instead, they will describe themselves as pragmatic and realistic. You can see how pragmatic (or stingy) Shanghainese are from this blind date example shared by my Beijingnese friend: when you go on a blind date, you would usually meet the person for lunch or dinner. But for Shanghainese, they prefer to meet for coffee in the afternoon because that is more economical. If they have lunch or dinner, that will cost at least RMB 100-200 (US$16-$32). The cost for a meal is too high if the date doesn't turn out well. On the other hand, meeting for coffee costs only RMB 40-50 (US$6-$8). If it doesn't work out, then the "loss" is minimized. If it works out, then they can continue with dinner after coffee! In the Northerners' eyes, these behaviors by the Shanghainese are viewed as very stingy!

Yes, Shanghainese can be calculative. But they are also detailed-oriented and cautious in everything they do. They will think and plan very carefully before they make a decision (and sometimes it does take them a long time to think). To the Northerners, they may find the Shanghainese to be wishy-washy or not bold enough. There is also a common Shanghainese saying "you better shut up if you are going to speak nonsense," which is the exact opposite of "Hu You." As you can see, the Shanghainese culture is indeed very different from the Northerner's culture.

If you think Shanghainese are not into saving face because they are the pragmatic type, you are wrong again. While Northerners feel that they need to save face no matter where they are, the Shanghainese tend to feel the need to save face in front of their friends and family. My Shanghainese friend told me that when the Shanghainese have dinner with friends or family at a restaurant, they will fight for the bill. They will also not dare to check the bill, because that will give others an impression that they are stingy.

Since we are on the topic of Shanghainese, how can one not talk about Shanghainese men? Shanghainese men have a very good reputation and are the ideal husband to all women in China! After coming back from a day of work, Shanghainese men would still cook and take care of their child when they are at home. They never complain (and dare not) to their wife even if they have to do all the household chores. People even joke about Shanghainese men being a type of national treasure, putting them on the same rank as the panda! So what about Shanghainese women? People usually use the word "Zuǒ" to describe them. It means Shanghainese women are controlling and chatter a lot. This is why Shanghainese women are able to control their husbands and train them to be obedient!

NORTH VS. EAST VS. SOUTH

I was once talking to an experienced venture capitalist regarding how he sees entrepreneurs from different parts of China, he shared an interesting example which I found to be quite reflective of reality: let's assume there are three entrepreneurs coming up with a similar restaurant business idea. A Northern entrepreneur would start by saying he wants to open a high-end restaurant, and he will turn it into a restaurant chain. He will also say that he wants to take the restaurant business to IPO in 2-3 years. However, when it comes to actual execution, the Northerner may not have the restaurant opened until a year later. The restaurant may look quite different from what he originally promised.

On the other hand, when the entrepreneur from the South approaches the venture capitalist for funding, he probably has opened quite a number of restaurants already. It is likely that he has already tried quite a few business models and overall cash flow is already positive. He is more a "doer" than a talker and does not plan as thoroughly when he first started a business. He learns from mistakes. The last restaurant he opens would probably have improved a lot when compared to the first one.

For an Easterner, he will spend a long time planning before opening the first restaurant. He will have everything from central kitchen, logistics, all the way to the first 10-20 store locations well planned out first. It may take him one year before he opens his first restaurant, but at the same time, he will have the central kitchen supporting all 20 restaurants ready as well. The Easterner is obviously the most risk-averse among the three. As you can see, people from different parts of China do possess very distinctive personalities.

Below is a jingle that is popular on the internet about stereotypes in China, test it with your local colleagues and see what they think! (I added explanations at the end to make it easier to understand).

- Beijingnese see everyone else as grassroots; (As Beijing is the capital of China, Beijingnese see themselves as more superior than others)

- Shanghainese see everyone else as villagers; (Shanghai as an international metropolitan city, so everywhere else is like rural areas compared to Shanghai)

- Guangdong people see everyone as Northerners; (Guangdong people have no sense of north and south. Basically everyone is from the north if you are not from Guangdong)

- Henanese sees everyone as idiots; (to a swindler, everyone else is a potential target)

- Shandong people see everyone as cowards; (A lot of hero characters in Chinese folktales are from Shandong)

- Jiangsu people see everyone being poor; Zhejiang people see everywhere as being undeveloped; (Jiangsu and Zhejiang are both wealthy and well developed provinces in China)

- Shannxi people see everyone as not civilized; (Xi'an, provincial capital of Shannxi, had been the capital city of ancient China for many years)

- Xinjiang people see everywhere being congested;

- Tibet people see everyone as an atheist.

A Taste of China

Flavor Segmentation

If the first thing coming to your mind when someone mentions spicy food for dinner is Thai, Indian or Mexican, then you probably haven't been exposed to the really spicy part of Chinese cuisine. There is actually a popular saying "it is red all over China" to describe the population's love for spice. Of course Chinese cuisine is more than just spicy food. In fact, every province and region has its own unique flavors. Even instant noodles in China offer different flavors in different provinces to meet the needs of local consumers. The pioneer of instant noodle flavor segmentation in China is Master Kong. Instead of segmenting the Chinese consumers by demographics or income level, Master Kong segments the China market by flavor. [9] As a result of their innovative segmentation, Master Kong has been the market leader in instant noodles, a US$10 billion business. Here we will borrow Master Kong's instant noodle segmentation to illustrate the different flavor types by region. Overall, China can be divided into eight flavor segments. As a first cut, Master Kong divides China into two big regions: spicy regions and non-spicy regions. Spicy regions are concentrated in the west and central parts of China:

1. Numbing & Spicy Region (Mid-Western Region): "Ma La (麻辣)" is a signature taste of the cuisines of the Sichuan and Chongqing regions, meaning the food tastes both numbing and spicy. Because of the local peppercorn used in its cooking, this region's cuisine creates a numbing sensation in your mouth in addition to the spiciness of the red chili peppers. Nowadays, numbingly spicy dishes are highly popular all over China. Classic Ma La dishes include the numbing spicy hot pot "Ma La Huo Guo (麻辣火锅)," water boiled beef (水煮牛肉), water boiled fish (水煮鱼). And don't be fooled by the word "water boiled" thinking it is not spicy. Water actually refers to chili oil!

2. Sour & Spicy Region (Southwest Region): Dishes from Sichuan, Yunnan and Guizhou tend to be sour and spicy. Classic southwestern dishes include sour and spicy fish (酸辣鱼片) and sour and spicy noodles (酸辣粉).

3. Oily & Spicy Region (Northwestern Region): This region is famous for making oil preserved chilies. Locals add the chilies-in-oil to every dish that they cook. A sample dish is the spicy noodle "La Zi Mian (辣子面)" from Shaanxi province.

4. Fragrant & Spicy Region (Central Region): In my opinion, I think Hunan cuisine from Central region is the spiciest among all Chinese cuisines. One of the main characteristics of dishes from the central region is that it uses large amounts of chopped red chilies, particularly the spiciest type, for cooking. Classic dishes from the region include fish heads with chopped red peppers (剁椒鱼头) and carp fish in spicy black bean sauce (豉椒划水).

Gallery 2.2 Pig Knuckle (Top); Numbing Spicy Hot Pot "Ma La Huo Guo (麻辣火锅)"(Bottom)

The other four regions are the non-spicy regions:

5. Seafood & Cantonese Soup Region (South Region): The Cantonese soup culture originating in the Guangdong region is quite unique. There is a vast variety of Cantonese soup, with different types of Chinese herbs as ingredients to improve health similar to Traditional Chinese Medicine. To the Cantonese, a meal without soup is not a proper meal. They believe that soup has the ability to enhance the inner working and well-being of the body. Next time if your local colleagues offer you Cantonese soup, make sure you ask about the ingredients before drinking if you are not the adventurous type. Cantonese are very creative in the use of ingredients when making soups. For instance, chicken feet, pig lungs, and even duck kidneys are common in the making of Cantonese soups! Besides soups, Guangdong and Fujian areas are also well-known for their costal seafood production. Just beware of the budget as some rare catches from the deep sea can be quite pricey!

6. Sweet Jiangnan Region (Eastern Region): The sweetest of all Chinese cuisines probably comes from Shanghai, Jiangsu, and Zhejiang areas. I guess people having a sweet life also prefer sweet flavors! Many dishes from the East region is cooked using sweet soy sauce, so each dish looks dark red and covered in thick sauce. Some of the famous dishes from the eastern region are Hangzhou Sweet Braised Pork "Dong Po Rou (东坡肉)," Shanghai Pork Rib in Sweet Soy Sauce "Hong Xiao Pai Gu (红烧排骨)," and WuXi Sweet Pork Buns "Tian Rou Xiao Long Bao (甜肉小笼包子)."

7. Savory Sauce Region (Northern Region): Similar to the east region where dishes tend to be heavy on the sauce, people from the north prefers savory sauce. Classic dishes from the region, Savory Sauce Pork Noodle "Zha Jiang Mian (炸酱面)," Beijing Style Pork in Savory Sauce "Jing Jiang Rou Si (京酱肉丝)," are quite oily and salty. In fact, if you have high cholesterol, high blood pressure, or high blood glucose, you should be aware not to over consume dishes from the north.

8. Savory & Sour Region (Northeastern Region): When it comes to dishes from the northeast, first thing people would think of is its stew. The way people from the northeast make stew is to put all the ingredients into a clay pot and keep cooking until they are tender. Stew is usually served in hotpot style (on cooking alcohol lamp) to ensure that the dish remains hot throughout dinner. Since the northeast is one of the coldest regions in China, people love to eat stew as it quickly warms the bodies. Classic stew dishes from the northeast include pork and dough stew (猪 肉 炖 粉 条), potato and beef stew (土豆炖牛肉), chicken and mushroom stew (小鸡炖蘑菇), Dongbei sauerkraut (fermented vegetables) stew (东北炖酸菜), and Dongbei mix stew (东北乱炖).

What was described above is only a simple categorization of flavors in China. Its main purpose is to give you an idea of different local flavor as you travel. For instance, when you visit central or west region, you should immediately know that most dishes are going to be spicy. If you cannot take spice, make sure you tell your host or colleague ahead of time. Today each city offers a wide variety of choices to satisfy all taste buds and preferences. Every province, every region in China has its own unique cuisine and flavor. If you want to learn more about different cuisines in China, check out a Chinese food documentary called "A Bite of China." It was extremely popular even among Chinese. If you are a gourmet eater, then I encourage you to try the local dishes when you travel to different areas in China. May be you can create your own version of "A Bite of China." There is a Chinese term "Chi Huo（吃货）" referring to aspiring and adventurous epicureans who can consume a large amount of food. If you fit the description, make sure to introduce yourself to locals as "Chi Huo." Your local friends will surely take you to excellent local joints.

Gallery 2.3 Chinese cuisine flavor segmentation by region

Local Specialty

Just like when you travel to Chicago, you will try the Chicago style deep dish pizza. There are also local specialty foods you should try when you visit different cities in China.

Dates "Zao (枣)" from Beijing – besides Peking roast duck, you may also want to try dates. Dates are one of the most popular daily snacks for the Beijingnese, and they are also used in the making of desserts like date cakes or other local dishes.

Numbing & Spicy Skew "Ma La Tang (麻辣烫)" from Chongqing and Chengdu – if you have a spicy taste bud and a strong stomach, then you should give Ma La Tang a try. A very common street food, Ma La Tang is cooked by dumping meat and vegetables on stick into boiling spicy oil soup base. Not only is Ma La Tang a favorite among people from Chongqing and Chengdu, it has also become a national favorite over the past few years! You can almost find small stalls selling Ma La Tang at every street corner in city center or convenient store.

Waxberry "Yang Mei (杨梅)" from Shanghai – if you are a berry fan, then you have to try this local berry call Yang Mei. It is only available for about a month's time starting around late May. Besides eating Yang Mei as a fruit, locals also preserve Yang Mei by storing it in Chinese white liquor. According to the locals, preserved Yang Mei has the miraculous effect of curing stomachache and diarrhea! I also have a jar of preserved Yang Mei at home made by my mother-in-law, and it is proven to be highly effective in curing stomachache!

Gallery 2.4 Numbing & Spicy Skew "Ma La Tang (麻辣烫)"

Gallery 2.5 Stinky Tofu "Chou Dou Fu (臭豆腐)"

Stinky Tofu "Chou Dou Fu (臭豆腐)" – as one can read from the name, Stinky Tofu emits a repulsive smell, although people who love it think it smells great! It is actually deep fried fermented tofu. Its stinky smell comes from the fermentation, much like some varieties of cheese. So not only it is stinky, but also quite oily after the deep fry wok. Locals will eat stinky tofu with different types of sauce like hot sauce or sweet bean sauce. This is definitely one of the most challenging street food you can find in China. If you are a fan of stinky cheese, you may like this local delicacy!

Duck Blood Jelly with Vermicelli from Nanjing – duck is a specialty of Nanjing. To make the best out of ducks, local Nanjingnese even turn duck blood into jelly form and serve with vermicelli in soup. For the adventurous eater and duck fan, this is a must try when you visit Nanjing! But make sure you go to a reputable restaurant to avoid fake one.

Hairy Crab "Da Zha Xie (大闸蟹)" – it is a medium-sized crab that is named for its furry claws and legs. Hairy crab first became popular in Hong Kong and Taiwan. Only within the last 20 years has hairy crab became widely popular in mainland China. Hairy crab season usually starts around mid-autumn festival and last until end of the calendar year. Some people eat hairy crab for its crab roe, not for its meat. In fact, hairy crab has so little meat that the eating part is not easy and quite time consuming. Some high end restaurants in China offer to dismantle the crabs and extract the meat and crab roes for its customers. The price of the crab varies depending on its size and its origin, ranging from as low as US$5-10 (RMB 30-60) per crab, to as high as US$100+ each! The most famous breed is the ones from Yangcheng Lake (阳澄湖) near Shanghai.

Lychee (荔　枝) from Guangzhou – Lychee is a fruit originating from southern China. It is also known as the "King of Fruits" among the southern Chinese. Lychee is only available during summer time, and although it is a sweet and juicy fruit, do not eat too much at one time. Besides being called the "King of Fruits," lychee is also known as "Three Fires" by locals because it is a fruit that will increase the "internal heat" of your body. Eating too much lychee may cause sore throat or you may even lose your voice!

Gallery 2.6 Hairy Crab "Da Zha Xie (大闸蟹)"

Local Festivals and Rituals

Local festivals in China are usually associated with a story, special type of food, and rituals. Here we will talk about special food associated with the key festivals in China.

Mooncake "Yue Bing (月饼)" for Mid-Autumn Festival:

Mid-Autumn Festival is one of the most important holidays in China, similar to Thanksgiving in the US. It falls on 15th of the 8th month of the lunar calendar year. Chinese typically eat mooncakes together with their family members as a way to celebrate. Mooncake is a round shape Chinese pastry made of different types of filling, like lotus seed paste, red bean paste, nuts, goose egg yolk etc. The selling of mooncake or mooncake coupons is a very big business prior to Mid-Autumn Festival. Not only will people buy mooncakes for self-consumption, but also for gifting to clients, employees and government officials. (More on gifting will be explained in Chapter 3) This is a huge market for a country of 1.3 billion people, and with very high profit margin – an average box of 4 cakes sells for US$20-30 (RMB 120-180). Many food retail stores and restaurants sell mooncakes or prepaid mooncake coupons in order to tap into this big market. Even Starbucks and Haggen Daz sell mooncake during Mid-Autumn Festival. Every year I received at least 5-10 boxes of mooncakes from friends, family, and suppliers as gifts before the Mid-Autumn Festival.

Rice Dumplings "Zong Zi (粽子)" for Dragon Boat Festival:

It is local tradition to eat rice dumplings to celebrate Dragon Boat Festival, which falls on the 5th day of the 5th month of the lunar calendar year. Traditional rice dumpling is made of glutinous rice stuffed with different fillings like pork, egg yolk, green beans etc., then wrapped in bamboo leaves. Due to large festival gifting market created by mooncake, merchants are turning Dragon Boat Festival into another gifting occasion by introducing high end luxury rice dumplings into the market. They would add expensive ingredients like abalone, dried scallops, sea cucumber into the rice dumplings to increase the unit price.

Rice Cake "Nian Gao (年糕)" for Chinese New Year:

Since Chinese New Year is viewed as THE most important holiday of the year, every family will eat a lot of holiday food to symbolize prosperity. To name one food that represents the Chinese New Year spirit, it is probably the Rice Cake. Rice cake is made with rice and sticky rice, which has a very chewy texture. In the south people like to make it sweet, while in the north people like to cook rice cake with meat and vegetables. Locals eat rice cake during Chinese New Year for its good meaning: the pronunciation of rice cake in Chinese sound the same as "progressing every year."

2 . 3

Explosive Internet Growth

Explosive Growth in China Internet Market

One cannot talk about the lives of Chinese people without mentioning the internet. Over the past decade, the prevalence of internet use has increased exponentially. Below are some statistics from the China Internet Network Information Center (as of Dec 2016) to illustrate that growth [10]:

China Internet Penetration, 2016

As of Dec 2016, Chinese internet usage has reached 731 million users, which is the highest in the world;	v.s.	The sum of internet users in Europe is roughly 500 million
In rural areas, there are roughly 201 million internet users;	v.s.	That is more than all the internet users in Japan and South Korea combined
The nationwide internet prevalence rate is at 53.2% (which is high for developing countries);	v.s.	The prevalence rates for Hong Kong is 69%, Taiwan is 70%, and the USA is 78%
Within the 731 million internet users in China, 95.1% of those use mobile phones to go online, which is equivalent to 695 million people;	v.s.	Desktop, laptop, and tablet users at 60.1% (439 million), 36.8% (269 million), and 31.5% (230 million) respectively

[10] Source: [China Statistical Report on Internet Development, Jan 2017], China Internet Network Information Center

Illustration 2.1 China Internet Penetration, 2016

As astonishing as it may seem, over 95% of internet users access via mobile phones. The lack of landline infrastructure enabled China to leapfrog to the wireless age, leading the frontier of mobile apps, from banking to messaging to e-commerce. It is not an over-statement to say that China is one of the most, if not the most, advanced in mobile applications development and usage in the world driven by end-user demand. It has significantly changed the lifestyle of Chinese today.

So how does the China internet landscape look like? Anyone who is interested in Chinese literature must have heard of the story "Three Kingdoms": the backdrop of the story happened during AD 180-300, where China was ruled by three powerful kingdoms "Wei (魏)," "Shu (蜀)," and "Wu (吴)." The story was about the wars among these three kingdoms. Today's internet world in China resonates with the story of "Three Kingdoms" where it is also dominated by three powerful players Baidu, Alibaba, and Tencent; typically referred to as BAT in the media. BAT has been instrumental in leading the Chinese internet world, and changing the way people live in China.

If there is one mobile app you should download on your smart phone before your first trip to China, I would recommend WeChat from Tencent. Let me tell you why.

WeChat Mega Platform

The latest superstar in the Chinese internet world is WeChat, which is a platform combing the functionalities of social networking, instant messaging, payment, eCommerce, and even financial services.

According to CNNIC report, 80% of China's internet users used WeChat in 2016, highest among all mobile application. Tencent, a powerful instant messaging and gaming company in Shenzhen, launched WeChat primarily as an instant messaging mobile app following WhatsApp in 2011. It gained popularity rapidly as people ditched the traditional SMS system and use it for both personal communications as well as work. For personal communications, WeChat offers features like "People Nearby" and "Shake the Phone" to connect strangers nearby – a very handy tool for guys who want to meet girls. As a result, WeChat gained its initial popularity in night clubs and bars. Another added benefit of WeChat is anonymity and control by not giving out personal mobile numbers. For work communications, companies use WeChat for internal team communication and for sales force management, such as deployment of tasks, sales performance daily reporting. When I was at Starbucks, if we need to send a message to all our store managers for an urgent matter, the head of operation would communicate via WeChat in addition to the traditional mean of email, where all store managers would be notified instantly. WeChat has since become the most popular form of informal communications tool at work. But the drawback is that work and deep thought streams are constantly disrupted by incoming messages, whether it is work-related or not. The overwhelming conversations gets crowded on the tiny screen and important messages are often buried and missed. I have a foreigner friend who was annoyed by all the conversations that were posted on his work WeChat group, as most of his colleagues wrote in Chinese which he couldn't understand. In the end, he had to turn chat notification off for the work group. Fortunately WeChat has since incorporated a translation feature for those who are still curious.

Social Networking - WeChat Moments

After accumulated a large user base, WeChat introduced social networking a year later which further enhanced its stickiness. Unlike Twitter which is an open social network where anyone can follow everyone, WeChat's is similar to Facebook where your request must be accepted before you can follow someone's feed. WeChat is now the largest social networking and instant messaging platform in China as access to Facebook and Twitter are blocked by the Great China Firewall. As a result, WeChat manages to own both your work and personal life to the extent of troublesome addiction where people spent hours a day staring and typing in WeChat. I once interviewed a young college girl on WeChat, where she expressed intense anxiety of expecting a constant flow of message, or else she felt the world has forgotten her. Consequently she was compelled to send someone a message every five minutes just to get the response and attention.

WeChat Red Pocket

Another key feature that significantly increased its usage is its red pocket feature from its mobile payment WeChat Pay Wallet. It is a cultural tradition to give red pockets during Chinese New Year, from parents to kids, between friends and from boss to employees. The red pocket feature allows sending money to a group of individual accounts by creating "virtual red pockets": first designate a total amount of money to be paid out from your WeChat Wallet which is connected your bank account, and the number of red pockets. Next you select a group of friends on WeChat. Everyone in the group will receive a red pocket notification, but as the number of red pockets is limited, people need to quickly click on the red pocket to literally "grab" money from the air. Not only the chance is limited, the amount people receive can be random as well, like a lottery machine. Everyone's amount received is listed so as to compare luck, a brilliant social networking tool that fully understand the psychology.

Gallery 2.7 WeChat Red Pocket

The red pocket feature went viral when it was first introduced to the market as people see it as a fun game and perfectly matched Chinese New Year's tradition. Most importantly, anyone can participate. You can give out as little as a few cents in a red pocket, and up to a maximum of RMB 200 (US$32) per recipient. During 2016 Chinese New Year, there were 516 million people used WeChat red pocket, sending out a total of 32 billion red pockets! The amount of money that was transferred from the traditional bank accounts to the WeChat Wallet balance is quite significant.

The success of the WeChat red pocket not only helped WeChat to recruit many new users to its already large user base, but also drive the awareness of the WeChat Pay. With WeChat Pay, one can easily transfer money to others within the same app. WeChat Pay made peer-to-peer money transfer very easy and free. When I go out to have dinner with friends, I don't even need to bring my wallet. I can pay my friends simply with a few clicks on my phone. Besides peer-to-peer transfer, there are also an increasing number of retailers in large cities accepting WeChat Pay because the transaction processing time is much faster than credit card, and the subsidized processing fee is lower. So how do you set up a WeChat Pay? To get WeChat Pay function, you have to download the WeChat app from the China Apple store. In order to send and receive money, you need to link it up with a local bank account. If that sounds too complicated to you, you can also ask your friends to load up your wallet in WeChat Pay and pay them back in cash. Note that WeChat Pay does not support foreign credit cards yet.

In addition to instant messaging, WeChat offers online shopping and even financial products on its platform which is competitive to traditional bank savings products. But like any other financial products offer in China, they are only available to mainland Chinese citizens.

As of Q1 2016, WeChat has over 700 million users worldwide. WeChat is certainly the most popular instant messaging tool among Chinese all over the world. If you want to blend into your local colleagues' or friends' social circle, the first thing you need to do is to open a WeChat account and get connected with your local friends.

Taobao: More Than eBay and Amazon

While the uprise of WeChat is a recent phenomenon, Taobao has been changing the way Chinese shop over the past decade. Taobao was founded in 2003 by entrepreneur Jack Ma, started as a C2C (consumer to consumer) sites similar to eBay in the US. With China's vast landscape and the largest population in the world, coupled with ever improving logistic systems, Taobao became the most prominent online shopping website in China with over 90% of market share, and the largest by transaction volume in the world. There is practically nothing you cannot buy on Taobao, from daily necessities, home furnishing, IT equipment, to even heavy machineries or real estate. I have a few foreigner friends who pretty much bought everything for the household from Taobao. There are a few things you need to pay attention to though if you want to try out Taobao. First, you need to be able to read Chinese as there is no English or foreign language site available. Second, you need to have either a local credit card or an Alipay account (PayPal equivalent in China, also owned by Taobao) to pay for the transaction. Last, be wary of the counterfeit, unsafe and inferior quality products. If you find something on Taobao that is a lot cheaper than regular store prices, be very cautious and read people's reviews first.

As Taobao became successful, so did it make many of its early merchants millionaires. There was a time where many young people would quit their job and sell on Taobao because of lack of rigid corporate structure and most importantly, they believed it is a shortcut to get rich. Don't we all? But as more merchants get on the platform, so is competition and margin. Today, a merchant on Taobao is struggling to breaking even with all the listing and marketing expenses. The latest trend for a quick buck is to drive for Uber/Didi and profit from the VC subsidized windfall.

TMall

Besides the small merchants you find on Taobao, you will also find many large companies set up their official store on Taobao under the TMall brand. TMall was set up specifically for brand owners or its official distributors, targeting B2C (business to consumer) sales, and distinguish themselves from the individual sellers. Many international companies chose to set up their e-commerce site directly with TMall rather than their own. For instance, Starbacks, Uniqlo, etc. chose to work with TMall to set up their first online flagship stores in China. If you are buying from the TMall official brand site, then you do not need to worry about buying counterfeit products as the products are directly supplied by the brand, plus TMall enforces customer service level. Today you can find Apple, Burberry, UGG, Ray-Ban, Gap, Clinique, Estee Lauder all having their TMall stores.

Overseas Purchase - HaiTao

Over the past two years, another new group of Taobao merchants called "HaiTao (海淘)", meaning "Overseas Purchase" emerged. Due to high import duties, as much as 50% on luxury items, smart Taobao merchants started to source products overseas and ship directly to China. Even after the logistics expenses, the product is still cheaper than buying in China. Some Taobao merchant even broadcast their shopping overseas via a live show on Taobao, sending real time product and price info to its audience for instant buying! The merchant, usually a young girl studying overseas, would walk into a store, and show the audience what she sees in the store. If the audience sees something interesting, the transaction can be done online real time through the internet technology. The buyer will charge a small markup as service charge. In case you want to try out HaiTao, be cautious that there is actually risk of China Custom holding up your product and requesting you to pay import duty before releasing it. Also the fake HaiTao products industry, including fake overseas receipts, is emerging.

11.11

One cannot not talk about Taobao without mentioning 11.11, the highest sales day in online shopping in history. It is equivalent to the online version of the Black Friday in the US. 11.11 refers to the date Nov 11. Because that date is made up of four '1's, people in China also referred it to as the Single's Day. When Single's Day was first started, it was supposed to be a day where single people all go out and celebrate being single instead of staying at home and feel pathetic. But Taobao re-branded Single's Day to be the day you should stay at home and shop online, since you don't have a date to go out with anyway. Taobao worked with many of its merchants to offer deep discounts that is only valid on 11.11, sometimes as deep as 90% off! In order to get a good deal, many people would stay up all night and place their orders at midnight of 11.11! The deepest discount items are usually gone by 6am. On 11.11.2016, Taobao transaction volume reached a record high of US$ 17.8 billion (RMB 120.7 billion) of sales on that single day! To share with you my personal experience: this year's 11.11, my husband and I together spent US$2000! We bought two air purifiers, plane tickets to Hong Kong, clothes for kids from Gap and Uniqlo, and running gears for ourselves. We were never crazy online shoppers (at least I don't think so), yet because the discount was so deep, we shifted our purchasing schedule to take advantage of the sale. Now 11.11 has become the biggest online shopping day in modern Chinese history. Taobao even created a TV show on 11.11 to broadcast online shopping that night and brought in international celebrities like David Beckham.

Gallery 2.8 TMall sales on 2016 11.11 Single's Day

You would often hear your friends complaining about buying too much on impulse after 11.11. Some said they had not finished using items bought from last year, yet they were at it again this year. Courier delivery that usually took 2-3 days would take more than a week. In fact, because people spent so much money on this single day, they needed to cut back their spending in the following weeks. Many retailers' sales in their physical stores actually dropped dramatically after 11.11 for quite a few weeks.

Gallery 2.9 Street corner turning into courier distribution center to handle large volume of goods post 11.11

Everything offline can be done on your mobile phone

With the rapid growth of mobile technologies in China, mobile applications have expanded into many facets of everyday lives beyond basic communication needs. There is a mobile application for almost every task in real life. Mobile phone has now become inseparable for many Chinese. Let me take you through a typical day of my colleague, Susan's life, and you will be amazed by how much can be achieved on a smart phone.

Susan woke up in the morning realized her son had a fever. She quickly sent me a WeChat message to ask for half day off to take her son to see a doctor at a local hospital. She knew she needed to get to the hospital as soon as possible to wait in line for an appointment with the doctor in person, which is common at a large hospital with reputable doctors. Instead of dragging her already sick son through the long line, she opened an App called "Lin Qu (邻 趣)" which for a small fee offers an assistant service where a stranger would do any chore such as lining up at the hospital for the doctor's appointment. The assistant arrived at the hospital within 15 minutes, and lined up for Susan for two hours for the appointment. When it was almost Susan's turn to see the doctor, the assistant called Susan to come. The assistant would be paid by the hour, and for a total of three hours of service, Susan paid him RMB 35 (US$6). After the doctor's appointment, Susan came back to work. She felt the hunger as she forgot to eat her breakfast, but now she had no time to dine out and finish the piled up work for the day. Again she opened another App called "Eleme (饿了么)," which is an online food ordering and delivery application. She browsed through a few choices and ordered from a Sichuan restaurant she never tried before but seemed to have good reviews. Deliver charge was only RMB 5 (US$0.8). The food arrived within an hour and she paid for it using WeChat Pay. Later that day, Susan made a video call using WeChat video to check how her son was doing at home. Finally it was 6pm and Susan was eager to go home for the obvious reason. Normally she would take the subway but today she had to go home fast. She ordered a car and driver from "Didi (滴 滴)," the local equivalent of Uber. (In August 2016, Uber China decided to sell its China business to Didi.) With all the subsidies on Didi, she only paid RMB 20 (US$3) for her ride home which a normal taxi would cost double that amount. To Susan, her biggest concern is her mobile phone's battery life. That's why she carries a charger and battery pack with her all the time.

Susan's mobile phone usage is a common sketch of the daily life of a white collar worker in China. Almost anything can be accomplished on your mobile phone: you can check if there is a bike nearby for you to rent using a bike-sharing app; you can book a masseuse to go to your home to give you a massage and manicure using a beauty app; you can subscribe to a weekly flower delivery service with pre-arranged flower bouquet delivered to your home or office on WeChat store; you can find a tutor to help with your kid's homework problem using a tutor app; if you suddenly remember today is your wife's birthday, you can still quickly order a birthday cake and have it delivered to your wife's office by the afternoon from an online cake shop in the Taobao app! The list can just go on and on.

An American friend of mine who recently moved back to the States from China complained to me that she had a hard time adjusting. One example is money transfer: she was trying to transfer money from her bank account to her PayPal account for an online purchase. It took ten days for the money to successfully show up in her PayPal account, whereas in China, a similar transaction would only take no more than 5 seconds. That totally drove her insane. Another example is grocery shopping: now she has to drive 30 minutes to the nearby supermarket, and carry everything home herself. While in China groceries are bought online and typically delivered for free, not to mention many online grocers like YiHaoDian.com offered delivery within 24 hours. She said she was completely spoiled by the convenience offered by all the mobile applications in China. Now she has no choice but to learn how to do everything in the old fashion!

The widespread of mobile app usage is not only limited to top tier cities in China. It is estimated that there are over 600 million smartphone users in China in year 2016. [11] Approximately 1/3 of the smartphone users come from rural areas. You must be wondering, as a family from rural China makes less than US$500 a month, how could one afford an iPhone or Galaxy that cost nearly a month's income? Remember from Chapter 1.4 that there are always local manufacturers who would come up with low priced products to meet the needs of low income segments? There are quite a few local manufacturers who launch smartphones at very affordable price. One can get a simple smartphone with 3G capability for as low as US$15 (RMB 100)! So now farmers in rural area and small merchants in lower tier cities are using their smartphones to procure materials from suppliers, conduct sales with customers etc.

In summary, large smartphone user base, low logistics labor costs coupled with ease of mobile payment are key enablers to many mobile business models in China. Today startups and corporates only focus on developing mobile apps and company WeChat accounts. If you can find a service that does not offer on any mobile app yet, that could be your opportunity. And the VCs are listening.

Gallery 2.10 Low priced smartphones (quoted price in RMB, US$1 = RMB6.9 as of Dec 2016)

What internet sites do Chinese people visit?

The China internet space is dominated by local players. None of the big internet companies in the US is able to duplicate their success in China. One main reason is the Great Firewall setup by the government to block uncensored contents. But more often the failure is due to a lack of local knowledge and understanding consumer behaviors.

Instant messaging – QQ

Instant messaging has the highest usage among all internet users in China at 91%. [10] QQ instant messenger, offered by the WeChat provider Tencent, is the second most popular after WeChat. While MSN was a fairly popular competitor by Microsoft, it only had about 1% market share in China. QQ focuses on the younger demographics while WeChat is more popular among the grown ups. Almost everyone around me has an QQ account from their college days. QQ is also used by many Chinese corporations and government offices for business-related communications. If you want to better connect to your Chinese clients, especially understanding the young ones, you should sign up for a QQ account. QQ with its Q-Zone discussion forum remains to be a strong product for the next generation youth.

Search engines – Baidu

Search engine has 82% usage rate among Chinese internet users, third highest after instant messaging and internet news. [10] Unlike in many other western countries where Google is the dominant search engine, here it is Baidu, the locally-developed technology similar to Google. As Google services are mostly blocked in China, Baidu has

90% market share, essentially a monopoly. Back in the US where we say "google it" here it is "Baidu Once (百 度 一 下)." You will be surprised that a lot of people are not aware of Google at all. I often remind my analysts to look for information using Google, not just Baidu, as these two search engines actually provide quite different search results.

Given Baidu's near monopoly status in search, many companies would purchase keywords on Baidu as part of their digital advertising effort. As the "Google of China," Baidu has replicated many of the applications offered by Google, like cloud, map, translate services etc. Over the last few years, Baidu has also ventured into other areas like food delivery, Chinese version of Groupon, BBS and Q&A. Despite Baidu's attempt to diversify into other businesses, it still makes majority of its revenue from online advertising, accounting for over 95% of its revenue.

Video-sharing websites

There are a greater variety of video-sharing websites than search engines in China. Youku-Tudou, iQiyi, PPTV, PPS just to name a few. According to studies by CNNIC and Nielsen, there are more than 430 million users of video sites. That means there are same number of video-sharing websites users as television viewers in first-tier cities. One key reason is that TV programs are streamed on these sites and programs are downloadable for mobile phone viewing. In addition, many of them provide foreign movies and television dramas in their original recordings or dubbed in Mandarin as well. A vast majority of the content is free, whether it is legal or illegal copies. One of the key

GOOGLE IN CHINA

As we all know, the relationship between Google and the Chinese government is not at its best; therefore, Google shut down its China site in 2010 and all traffics were re-directed to Google Hong Kong if you access Google from China. Since 2014, Google website and Gmail became inaccessible in China as blocked by the China firewall. So if you have a Gmail account, you might consider redirecting your emails to another email account, like Hotmail, Yahoo, QQ, Sina, 163, etc otherwise you will not be able to receive any email. But if you already have your VPN (virtual private network that reroutes you to servers in other countries to avoid the firewall of China) set up, then you have nothing to worry about.

insights to the China internet market is that the majority is not willing to pay for contents, as there is always a competitor offering it for free. Protecting intellectual property rights is always a top concern among foreign companies operating in China. For example, one can always easily find bootleg version of newly released movie online and in DVD stores, an illegal industry that has always existed and flourished.

However, due to copyright infringement issues overseas, most of the content of these websites are disabled when accessed from outside of China. What about Youtube? Unfortunately, Youtube is banned in

Hao123.com

It is reported that on an average day, ten million people go to Baidu (the dominant local search engine) to search for the word Baidu. Why? Because many people, especially those in Tier 3 and 4 cities and villages, do not know how to input the URL of websites. To meet this basic need, a brilliant entrepreneur created a website called hao123.com in 1995 and listed the links to all the popular Chinese websites, much like the first version of Yahoo directory, except it is only one page. The URL Hao123 is extremely easy to remember, meaning Good 123 in Chinese. You would be shocked to see the traffic. Its popularity resulted in Baidu acquiring it in 2004 for RMB 50 million (US$8M) plus stock options. Lesson learned? Internet flattens the society and brings in a huge amount of potential consumers previously unreachable. Meeting their needs could be more profitable than targeting the savvy consumers in top tier cities.

Gallery 2.11 Front Page of hao123.com

China, and you can only access it if you are using VPN (and if you can tolerate how slowly the contents download). There are far fewer peer-created viral contents in these Chinese video sites compared to Youtube.

Today many of these video sites took on the shape of a mobile app, and installed on an Android based set-top-box for TV sets. Fewer people turn on TV for the broadcasted signals over air or cable, now it's all streamed on demand.

A lot you can do online, also a lot you cannot do

Local server for local business

Linda, a friend from Singapore, started a retail business in Shanghai. Like many other businesses, she set up an official website for the company and launched a customer loyalty program. At the beginning, Linda did not want the customer data and company activity to be censored by local authority, so she put the server in the US. Soon she learned her lesson. Her foreign website was suddenly blocked as the traffic started to increase. Many of her customers complained the service was down. On a lucky day, the block would be relieved briefly, and the loading time slowed to a crawl. She had to connect to a VPN service to access her own site and it became painfully frustrating. In the end Linda had moved the site back to China. Linda told me that if she had known the troubles, she would have placed the server in China in the first place.

In early 2016, the Chinese government introduced a new rule that all customer information databases must reside within China for Internet Security reasons. If Linda had not moved the server to China, she would be violating the law by now. For many foreign businesses, whether yielding to this level of censorship is a critical issue one should consider prior to entering the market. A common solution is to separate the global database from China database, which would certainly increases expense and management costs, but satisfy the legal requirements.

Be careful of what you search and what you write

A friend Tim from Hong Kong owns a small business in China. Even though he was quite into politics, he tried to keep a low profile and not create unnecessary attention from the government. Once he was curious about activities in Hong Kong on June 4th in memory of the Tiananmen Square Incident, he did a search on Baidu using his company computer. Nothing came up from the search as it is considered a highly sensitive keyword and results were closely censored. Two days later his company server was mysteriously hacked with contents accessed and deleted. It took a week for his IT to get everything running again. While it is difficult to draw the causal conclusion, it wouldn't surprise any locals who is familiar with the censorship control. After the incident, Tim published a new company policy that no employees should conduct search on any sensitive words (敏感词) using the company's computers.

More serious than knowing what not to search, you should know what not to write in public and online. Today social network sites are closely monitored by the government, including all conversations on WeChat and Weibo. Sensitive posts would be automatically blocked and worse, your account could be frozen. If you were lucky, your account may be released in a few days. As a guest in this country, you should be aware of the local regulations and laws.

The Behaviors of Chinese Netizens

The internet means much more than entertainment to the netizens, it is an integral part of life to the local Chinese. Part of the reason is human's universal addiction to online contents, but more significantly it created space for an alternative identity away from the real life.

One prominent phenomenon is the ever more popular netizens. Their popularity originates from being "experts" or "opinion leaders" in particular areas, such as child rearing or skincare by publishing on WeChat or Weibo. They are often referred to as "Big V" because their identity is verified. Since many celebrities start to get verified, they tend to get large followings. Any verified account with more than half a million followers is consider Very Important, hence the Big V. If the Big V can accumulate half a million followers, brands are willing to promote their products through their feeds. A "Big V" is a profession for many, and frankly, if writing a review or a blog about a product could earn you a few thousand to ten thousand dollars, why not?

Big V's popularity online is directly measured by the number of followers or "fans." It is a source of pride for many people to have a large fan base, and it is also a source of competition among peers and colleagues. To acquire a larger fan base, some people would pay for zombie followers. As the cost of recruiting real people tend to be high, there is an entire industry where "zombie fans" accounts are created, maintained and sold for as little as a couple of cents. "Zombie fans" are even great gifts ideas. Small internet advertising firms may give tens of thousands of these "zombie fans" to its clients to help cheating digital marketing managers report to their bosses how great a job they have done. I once had an advertising firm wanted to send me fifty thousand fans as a gift! I refused because I didn't want inactive followers on my online networking account to make me look good. In general, the existence of the industry shows the level of simplicity of digital marketing has been, but the trend is changing quickly as firms are focused on more sophisticated metrics such as conversion rate rather than a simple follower count.

Not only is becoming a KOL or Big V a real profession, there is even a new term called "Fans Economy" to describe this whole new industry. The number of fans in a WeChat or Weibo account has now become a due diligence KPI for investors to judge a startup. If you have a large number of followers, companies want to pay you to deliver marketing messages to your fans. Among my friends from the investment circle, I always hear urban myths of VC funding big KOLs. For instance, a girl born in 1987 received RMB12 million (US$1.9 million) funding in 2016 because her first 30 minutes live broadcasting was viewed by 20 million viewers. Whether these are real fans or zombie fans, it would be very hard for an investor to verify. Unfortunately her program was shutdown by the government one month after the investment due to "vulgar content." Yet many investors continue to look for the next big hit.

As brands and investors look beyond the number of followers and focus on the amount of replies on the feed, another phenomenon occurred: paid content writers, or "the internet water army" which will be explained later. These troops were paid by companies and organized by digital marketing firms to create news, praise or bash certain service providers, or simply post irrelevant postings to occupy space to cover real contents on the screen, and all in a short period of time. In Chinese slang, creating posts for the sake of occupying forum space or to appear popular is called "filling with water or guan shui (灌水)," thus the term "water army." Don't underestimate the power of the mob if you are involved in internet sales and marketing, as they can easily sway public opinion. A suggestion is to hire the service of an internet media consultancy to manage its impact, rather than getting your own hands dirty as the water is deep.

Based on the opinion of many internet experts, majority of the opinions and information found on the Chinese internet tend to be negative. As the official media channels are completely controlled by the Communist Party, the rise of social media such as WeChat and Weibo provide a grassroots channel to express discontent and social issues. Before the government figures out how to censor effectively, these new media are offering "freedom of speech" that this generation of Chinese has never seen before. This has led to the surfacing of angry youth, constant complainers and nitpickers. Their watchful eyes help the public monitor government activities and increase the social transparency. They also put on a lot of pressure on brands' corporate public relations. Next we will discuss a case that was handled particularly well, apart from the mountain of other ill-handled cases.

March 15th, 2012 – the McDonald's Incident

On March 15th, 2012 Consumer Rights Day, CCTV "315 Gala" put McDonald's in the spotlight and said that the fast food giant had failed to follow protocol to discard apple pies that were not sold within 90 minutes of production (more on "315 Gala" in Chapter 3.6). In fact, the pies were put out for two hours before being removed from the shelves. If you were the management of McDonald's, you should have every reason to be concerned as tremendous amounts of effort will be needed to rebuild the brand's tarred image. The CCTV show is extremely influential in forming public opinions and a signal that government will take actions against the firm quickly. In fact several large consumer companies, including MNCs, were targeted in the past with their public image and sales damaged subsequently.

However, after McDonald's issued an apology on its official Weibo account at 9:50pm that evening, it generated 14,000 comments and 19,000 forwarding, an excellent marketing activity as a normal post usually generates only a hundred comments and a thousand forwarding. What's interesting is that the majority of the comments were supporting McDonald's. Most people felt that they didn't know McDonald's had such stringent quality control, and its pies, even after two hours, would still be much fresher than almost every other restaurant in China, which could keep them for days. As someone started a "let's go eat McDonald's tomorrow" movement on Weibo, many online celebrities joined the grassroots campaign. Amidst the potential PR disaster, McDonald's reacted promptly, i.e., an apology statement was sent within 2 hours of the show, and thus handled the situation very well. They were able to turn it into a brand-enhancing opportunity. Some of my colleagues even had McDonald's for lunch on the next day to show support.

The Statement from McDonald's Official Weibo on March 15th, 2012 (excerpt from Sina Weibo):

"McDonald's China has well acknowledged the incident reported by the CCTV "315" event, where the restaurant in Beijing's Sanlitun has allegedly failed to follow official protocol. We will start investigation into this incident immediately and show customers our commitment to providing quality products through actions that will be taken. We will also use this opportunity to improve our management and to ensure that protocols are rigorously followed in order to serve quality and safe products to our customers. We thank and welcome the monitoring provided by the government, media, and consumers."

Skyrocket Housing Prices

Traditionally, owning a property is a basic Chinese mindset. It is such an important aspect of Chinese lives that even on matchmaking TV shows, one of the first questions the female participants ask the guys is whether they have a property and how big it is. Thus buying houses and housing prices are some of the most discussed topics among the Chinese. You may be curious why? Chinese government initiated an SOE reform campaign in late 1990's to streamline state owned assets. Millions of labors were forced to leave comfortable state factory jobs, immediately losing job security and pensions. As a compensation, a lump sum is paid out, and state housing were transferred to private ownership before the commercial constructions permeated the entire country. Until today, people can longer count on the government for their old ages, such as big disease insurances. What is more secure than an apartment or a house to ensure the stability of the entire family through ups and downs. So in this section we will discuss the general housing prices in different cities and the affordability of property in China.

From Government-provided to Self-helped

China has only seen its economic boom in the recent decades, and we will discuss some aspects of contemporary Chinese history here to paint a more comprehensive picture of the real estate market in China. In the 1970s and 80s, one could not just buy much of the daily commodities such as sugar, flour, rice, meat, eggs, coal, cloth, but with vouchers under a strict quota system. Everything was assigned by the government, such as your job, your apartment and even your child's daycare service! At that time if you didn't like your job, you could pay the government and buy yourself out. If you did not have money, you didn't have much of a choice. This arrangement continued onto the mid-1980s when the nation began to open up to the international market. With the influx of foreign influence, the more adventurous young people started to look for their own jobs instead of joining state-owned enterprise, and preferred to join foreign companies where pay was a lot more descent. Also around that same period of time the sale of private housing began. As the nation's growth accelerated, certain segments of the population grew rich, and commodities became increasingly expensive. The Chinese government could no longer take care of everyone and started to reduce social benefits. People started to realize that they have to work on their own in order to get what they need. The property market started to take shape as the economy opened up. The ones who were able to take advantage of the property market as the nation was opening up and invested in real estate thus became very, very rich.

The Expensiveness of Beijing and Shanghai

Before we discuss property prices, we should paint a general picture of the standards of living in Beijing and Shanghai. We will compare everyday prices among Hong Kong, Beijing and Shanghai, as Hong Kong has always been considered one of the most expensive world class metropolitan cities. In Hong Kong, a pastry bread roll typically sells for USD $ 0.5-0.8 in a local bakery, and a loaf of bread costs about USD $ 1.9. In Beijing and Shanghai, the same pastry bread roll would cost at least USD$ 1.0, and a loaf of bread would easily cost USD$2.4-3.7 at the same bakery chain, nearly doubled the Hong Kong price.

General consumption are definitely not cheap in China. What about property prices? As of August 2016, the property prices of central Beijing (within 4th Ring) and central Shanghai have skyrocketed to US$16,000-19,000 per square meter! An overview of the property prices in some of the major cities of the world are listed in Illustration 2.2. From the statistics, you can see that Hong Kong has become extraordinarily expensive, but you may also notice that the unit prices of Shanghai and Shenzhen are on par with the prices of New York and San Francisco! Unit housing prices in Beijing are around the same level as Taipei and Paris. In fact, they are more expensive than many cities in the developed world.

Even though the unit property prices of Beijing and Shanghai have not reached the level of Hong Kong and New York, you may end up paying the same amount for a house in China. This is because houses in China tend to be bigger than their counterparts in many

Gallery 2.12 Real estate listing of US$1.5M+ apartments at street corner in Shanghai

other Asian countries. In Hong Kong and Tokyo, an apartment that is 60 square meters (650 square feet) is considered above average size; while in China, any apartment that is below 100 square meters (1,100 square feet) is deemed as small. In the Chinese property market, the majority of the houses are above 100 square meters. If you calculate the total price of an apartment in central Shanghai with the unit price, it could easily cost you US$1.5 million or more. That is enough money to purchase property in Hong Kong, Tokyo, San Francisco, and even Manhattan. Furthermore in most western countries the property sits on a permanent freehold, meaning buyer owns the land and the structure on top forever. However in China, the land belongs to the government and is not for sale. The property is sold on a 70 year leasehold contract since the date leased out by the government. Commercial property has a leasehold of only 50 years. It is pretty ironic that you are paying a million or two on a property yet you do not really own it. If you buy second hand, your potential usage timeline is even shorter.

We have established that buying a house costs a lot of money, but what about how affordable houses are in different cities? For comparison, we will use the case of a typical middle-class three-person household living in a flat with one living room, one dining room, and two bedrooms to see how the family will fare when residing in different cities.

If a family living in Shanghai or Beijing plans to purchase a 100 square meter (1,077 square feet) flat in the city center, how long will it take them to save the entire amount? In 2015, the average household income in Shanghai and Beijing are both around US$ 2,100 (RMB 13,000), making the total payment USD$ 1.25 million (RMB 8 million). In Shanghai, it will take them 49 years and in Beijing 43 years! Compared to the other major cities, these figures are quite alarming.

Since not everyone could afford these ultra-expensive flats, or even the ones that cost several million dollars, developers have begun to tap into the market for smaller flats in cities such as Beijing and Shanghai. As the name suggests, these flats are considered "small", but they still range from 60-80 square meter (650-860 square feet) in size. These flats are very popular with the younger "post-80's" generation (Chinese slang for describing people born in the 1980's. More on post-80s in Chapter 2.7) for their special layouts. They usually have a smaller living room and bigger bedroom, which caters to the younger generation's preference for going out instead of inviting guests over. Usually these flats are farther away from the city centers but are still located along the metro subway lines. These properties generally cost about USD$ 4,800-6,500 (RMB 30,000-40,000) per square meter. Therefore, the flats would sell for USD$ 320,000-480,000 (RMB 2–3 million), and for many young couples, the 10-30% down payment is affordable with free financial aid from parents. For these younger generation, this is often the only way they can afford their first home.

It is already a thing of the past when living in Beijing or Shanghai can be money-saving compared to Hong Kong or Tokyo. The standards of living in these major Chinese cities are just as high, or even higher than that of many developed nations.

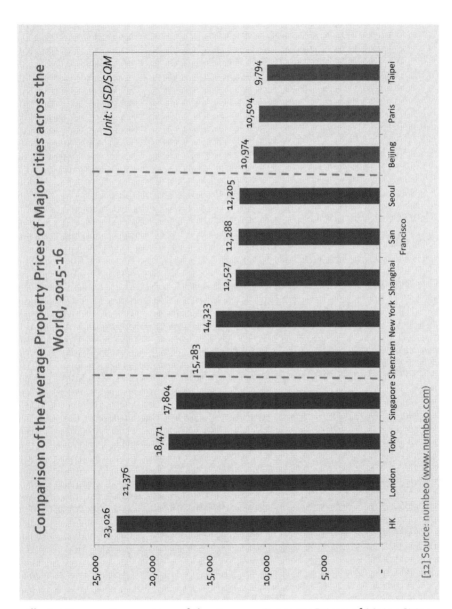

Illustration 2.2 Comparison of the Average Property Prices of Major Cities across the World, 2015-16

Analysis of Affordability of Real Estate in Big Metropolitan Cities Worldwide, 2015-16

CITY (CITY METROPOLITAN AREA)	SIZE OF A TWO-BEDROOM, ONE LIVING & ONE DINING ROOM FLAT (SQM)	PRICE OF FLAT (IN USD)	COST PER SQUARE METER (IN USD)	THE AFTER-TAX MONTHLY INCOME OF A 3-PERSONS FAMILY (USD)	HOW MANY YEARS' WORTH OF SALARY IS NEEDED FOR PURCHASE OF FLAT
Shenzhen	100	$ 1,528,299	$ 15,283	$ 1,788	71
Shanghai	100	$ 1,252,663	$ 12,527	$ 2,121	49
Beijing	100	$ 1,097,381	$ 10,974	$ 2,119	43
Hong Kong	60	$ 1,381,535	$ 23,026	$ 3,194	36
London	60	$ 1,282,541	$ 21,376	$ 3,384	32
New York	60	$ 859,363	$ 14,323	$ 3,435	21
Tokyo	60	$ 1,108,285	$ 18,471	$ 5,809	16

[12] Source: number (www.numbeo.com)

Illustration 2.3 Analysis of Affordability of Real Estate in Big Metropolitan Cities Worldwide, 2015-16

The Prices of Real Estate in Different Tier Cities

Illustration 2.4 shows the comparison among Tiers 1-4 cities in the Jiangsu Province as an example. However, keep in mind that Jiangsu is a relatively wealthy province, so even its villages are comparatively rich. Once I spoke to a Jiangsu native who was working in Shanghai, and she said that her home in rural Jiangsu costs RMB 5,000 (USD$ 800) per square meter, which is the same price as tier 4 cities in the province. On the other hand in the poorer provinces of western China, real estate prices may not reach RMB 5,000 (USD$ 800) per square meter even in tier 2 cities.

So how much would you have to pay to buy an apartment in different tier cities? Illustration 2.4 uses a 100 square meter flat to draw the comparison. As you can see, the price differences between various tier cities are quite large. Key cities have always been very expensive. Now that Tier 1 cities' real estate prices are almost catching up to the Key cities' level. The high standard of living in big cities is why many migrant workers cannot afford to live in the cities where they work. In tier 4 cities, for example, the cost of buying a house is 1/10 of key cities, while the salaries offered are 1/2 - 1/4 that of key cities.

Forever Changing Housing Policies

The Chinese real estate market is experiencing a bipolar phenomenon. There are markets, particularly Tier 2 and 3 cities, with over supply of housing due to over investment to drive GDP and increase land sales receipts as revenue to local governments. In these cities, the local governments are even encouraging college students to

Comparison of Real Estate Prices by City Tier in Jiangsu Province, 2015-16

CITY TIER	REPRESENTATIVE CITY	UNIT PRICE (USD/SQM)	PRICE OF A 100 SQUARE METER FLAT (USD)	AFTER-TAX MONTHLY INCOME OF A FAMILY OF 3 (USD)	NO. OF YEARS' INCOME NEEDED TO PURCHASE A FLAT
Key City	Shenzhen	$15,283	$1,528,299	$1,788	71
Key City	Shanghai	$12,527	$1,252,663	$2,121	49
Key City	Beijing	$10,974	$1,097,381	$2,119	43
Mega City	Guangzhou	$7,137	$713,710	$1,884	32
1st Tier City	Nanjing	$6,452	$645,161	$1,859	29
2nd Tier City	Yangzhou	$1,452	$145,161	$1,328	9
3rd Tier City	Gaoyou	$968	$96,774	$1,170	7
4th Tier City	Baoying County	$726	$72,581	$998	6

[12] Source: interviews with real estate agents, numbeo (www.numbeo.com)

Illustration 2.4 Comparison of Real Estate Prices by City Tier in Jiangsu Province, 2015-16

purchase real estates using their parent's savings and by offering these students attractive mortgage rates. In order to avoid the housing bubble burst and maintain near term stability, local governments would rather drive up current demand in the expense of future consumption. Over supply of real estate development is also one of the key reasons of low housing price relative to large cities as shown in Illustration 2.4.

On the opposite end of the spectrum, there are markets like Shanghai and Wuhan where real estate prices have sky-rocketed over the past few years. It is becoming extraordinarily difficult for average citizens to purchase homes, which in turn breeds a lot of resentments. In order to maintain social order and harmony, the Central Government had instructed municipal governments to regulate property prices, and one of such measures is the house purchasing limit. As the policy name suggests, the government places a limit on the number of houses one can buy. However, the fine prints of the ordinance differ from city to city; for instance, some city may limit housing purchases to residents with local registry account Hu Kou, while others like Shanghai may limit one housing purchase per family, which fueled the spike in fake divorces. As a couple is divorced, the husband and wife can each purchase one apartment. There are other restrictions to foreigners purchasing real estate as well: some require the foreigner to be living in the city and paying taxes for at least a year before the purchase, and in some cities singles are not allowed to purchase property. If you would like to purchase property in China, it is advised to first check with the latest local regulations, since they may be updated from time to time. Even my local friends find it hard to keep track of local regulations, as a foreigner you should pay extra attention.

2 . 5

Guanxi in Everyday Life

Guanxi literally means the relationship between people which is highly important in daily Chinese life. With 1.3 billion people, resource allocation becomes highly uneven given the top-down command and control structure. To complement the rigid system, guanxi comes into the picture to adjust the rules of the system where oftentimes resulting in rent seeking activities and wasteful spendings. This concept is less applicable to foreigners, unless the foreigner needs to tap into local resources such as visiting a local hospital, applying for local private schools for your kids or bootstrapping a startup. Since many locals have established a network of guanxi from living in a city for generations, most are reluctant to leave their hometown, especially after having kids. In this section we will primarily talk about how guanxi impacts the daily life of ordinary citizens.

Hospital Visits

Knocking on wood, if you have to pay a visit to the local hospital and don't know any doctors or hospital staff, you will have to go early and wait in line. Remember Susan's story of hiring a "personal assistant" to wait in-line for her? With some luck, you should be able to see the doctor in the afternoon. But if you have the guanxi, you can walk right in and complete your hospital visit in an hour. At this point you may frown or even feel upset: why would you cut in front of hundreds of other patients just for a checkup or receive medication for flu? But imagine a life-threatening disease such as an emergency surgery? If you observe the rule of the queue, while nobody else does, you will always be the last in the queue and never receive any medical attention. You will find more often than not, local Chinese would tap into all of their guanxi network if they have a family member who needs hospitalization. Lining up at the hospital for a doctor's appointment would be the last resort for people who don't have the network. Unfortunately the lack of medical resources, especially the top doctors at top hospital facilities such as beds and expensive imported machines, are highly sought after by hundreds of thousands of patients from all over the country.

Wedding Banquets

Guanxi can also be helpful if you want to secure a wedding banquet at a nice five-star hotel on a lucky date according to rules stated in the traditional Chinese lunar calendar. Because the number of these lucky dates falling on the weekends are limited in a given year, knowing someone at the hotel would increase your chance of getting the spot. But if not, you may still be able to make the booking, but probably pay a higher price, and you will have to reserve way in advance. Additionally, if you want to make sure that there is no skimming in the preparation of the food, having friends in these places may also help. A friend of mine once held a wedding banquet in Shanghai, and she was able to find someone from the Commission of Health to visit the hotel to request for good quality ingredients (or at least ask them to not use fake stuff) and to offer a reasonable price to my friend. If an inspector from the Commission of Health comes knocking at your door, as a restaurant owner you would do what he asks, right?

Education

For Chinese parents, it is the highest priority task for the entire family to send their only child to a good school, more so than parents' own career advancement. The latest popular phrase that captures this mentality is "you cannot lose on the starting line," to express the parents' eagerness. For instance, the competition starts at getting your child into the best possible kindergarten. Good kindergartens usually come at a cost, and that can start with tens of thousands of "sponsoring fee," in addition to the necessary red pockets "hongbao" to the teachers and guanxi with the school staff. However, the game just started when your child enters the prestigious kindergarten. It is imperative to maintain good guanxi with your child's teachers as well. A few years ago I was in Seoul for a business trip with my colleague. We went to a cosmetics store and she bought a whole bunch of cosmetics sets at once. As I was about to ask her why, she told me everything she bought was for her son's teachers and the ayi's (helpers) at school! I didn't understand at the time, but my colleague explained that the gifts were for the teachers and ayi's to take better care of her son in a class with so many children. For instance, if her son doesn't eat lunch as quickly as the others, maybe the teacher can give extra attention to help him or at least wait until he is finished before cleaning up the dishes. When her son is napping, maybe the teacher or ayi would be more inclined to tuck him in. Therefore, gifts to the teachers cannot be skimmed, and many companies are taking advantage of that to sell products such as gift cards for the teachers. Unfortunately the parents' behavior is turning the teaching profession into a profitable business and putting all the parents in a prisoner's dilemma.

Since a person's own network is limited, people tend to seek external networks when making a big purchase, such as buying a house or a car for an additional discount. While the person with the guanxi may be able to save you some money, you owe them a favor in return. Chinese people take giving and returning favors very seriously, and this is also how guanxi is maintained in the society. But be sure not to cross the fine line of bribery and corruption, which tend to be blurry.

Gallery 2.13 Cash gift card specifically targeting teachers

2 . 6

Your single child cannot lose on the starting line

China implemented its one-child policy from 1978 to 2015 to limit city registry residence "city-hukou holders" to have one child and village registry residence "village-hukou holders" to have two children at most. Virtually all the post-80s and 90s generation in China are the only child in the family, and this policy has had tremendous impact on the Chinese society.

The 4+2+1+1 Model

Since most families only have a single child, these families tree follows the "4+2+1+1 model:" four grandparents plus the parents for a total of six adults looking after one child. If you think having six adults taking care of one child is not enough, some families hire domestic help as well. So the single child will be in the center of attention of seven adults. Both the parents and the grandparents will provide the best they can afford to the only child, and treat the child as if he/she is the Little Emperor, who is so spoiled and not unable to complete any task independently.

Grandparents as Primary Caretakers

Given most young parents are in the work force, the grandparents tend to volunteer for the child care during the week. It is not uncommon for some young couples leave their child with the grandparents and only pick them up over the weekend. Even though domestic help is affordable, grandparents are insistent that they can provide better services to their only grandchild. The kids are often spoiled by the grandparents during the week, while parents live a DINK lifestyle. During weekends, to compensate for their schedule away from the child, parents take the turn to spoil the kid. As a result, a child growing up "Little Emperor" tend to demand instant gratification and unconditional obedience from all family members. No is not a vocabulary in their dictionary.

Not Necessarily the Best but Definitely the Most Expensive

It is only natural for the parents and grandparents to shower the only child with a big portion of the family expenditure. From my previous job at a diaper company, I interviewed families with young children. While their monthly income was around US$650 (RMB 4000), they could easily spend half of that on their only child! The parents would save up anything they can to provide the most expensive clothes, toys, food, kindergarten education, etc. This is all because of the phrase we mentioned before, that "you cannot lose on the starting line," the extreme and extremely unhealthy way of expressing their love. To cater to this general sentiment, many baby product brands quote it as part of their marketing messages. For example, a local baby formula brand uses "our baby formula cultivates the nobility in your baby" as its slogan in its advertisement. As parents and grandparents are overwhelmed by the huge amount of brands: domestic, imported, fake imported (local brands with a convincingly foreign sounding name), all of which they have never heard of before, they resort to price as a proxy for quality. The common behavior is to buy the most expensive items without really checking if it is indeed the best quality. If you have a chance, you can stop by the shops selling children's items in the Grand Gateway Mall in Shanghai. A piece of baby clothing could easily cost US$65-80 (RMB 400-500), and parents still flock to these shops.

Every year about 16 million babies are born in China, which is roughly equivalent to half of the population of Canada. With the large number of newborns, parents are more than willing to spend, thus making the market for children's goods a gold mine.

Split Pants

Illustration 1.11 indicated that only 50% of babies in China wear diapers. You may be asking what do the other 50% babies wear? They either wear cloth diaper or they simply wear nothing! While it is understandable not to wear anything during the hot summer, what about winter? It is not uncommon to see children wearing pants with an opening at their buttocks so they can go to the bathroom whenever and wherever. It is called the "peeing pants" or "split pants." This originates from the belief many elderly and parents hold that diapers are bad for the child since it doesn't allow for proper air circulation.

That raises an obvious question: if the child goes to the bathroom anywhere he wants at home, wouldn't it be a nightmare to clean up? The parents we interviewed simply replied that with so many people looking after the child at home, even if he makes a mess, it would be easy to clean up! This is a pretty big culture shock for someone from Hong Kong like me, let alone foreigners. With so many watchful eyes from the grandparents, this is a partial reflection of the level of pampering in Chinese families.

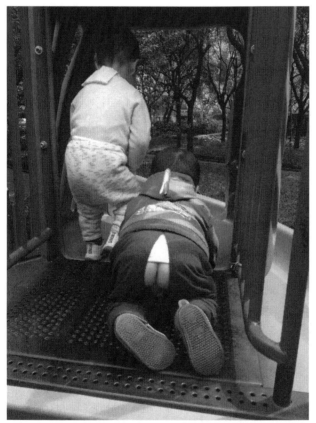

Gallery 2.14 Young toddler in split pants in Shanghai

The Generation that Never Grows Up

One of the major concerns about these pampered kids is that they are too well-protected and do not fare well in the face of hardship. As these kids leave college campuses and head into the real world, many find it difficult to handle the stress from work and choose to stay home and live off of their parents. For most parents, they have been babying their only child their entire lives and often have no choice but to continue to support. In fact, I know someone in my extended family doing exactly this, well into his 30s and married and even after having a kid of his own.

Having a Second Child

As aging population and gender imbalance problems surface, there has been an increasing pressure for abandoning the single-child policy. The Central Government has finally responded by passing a law in 2015 to allow every married couple to have a second child. Many of my Chinese friends say that they will definitely have two kids because growing up as a single child themselves, they feel that their childhoods were missing the sibling dynamics. Therefore, don't be surprised if a Chinese person tells you that he has two kids as the one-child policy has now changed to two-children policy.

2 . 7

Generation Gap

By now you have read about how companies in China segment the consumer market by city tier, income group, and even taste profile. Another important dimension that is popular among consumer product companies and the media is by age group. When talking to younger friends or listening to consumer research, it is very common to hear people label themselves as post 80s, post 90s etc., which is classified by the decade in which they were born. Similar to the American term "Millennials" describing the similar age group, the Chinese terms are even more specific in that they believe people born in different decades have different attributes. Due to different socio-economic conditions associated with different time periods, each generation seems to exhibit different values, beliefs, and needs.

To provide you with a snapshot of each generation, I interviewed a few friends who represent the post 70s, post 80s, and post 90s generation, and present to you their true stories. I primarily interviewed the middle-income class group, since they represent the key consumption power of the future. By reading through their stories, I wish to provide you with a demographic background of each generation, their main concerns, and their view of the other generations.

POST 70s: Wendy, age 43, married with one son, living in Beijing

Wendy and her husband John are both senior executives at multi-national companies. They have been living in Beijing since they graduated from university in 1995.

Wendy grew up in a small town in Shanxi province. Her family was very poor, like many other families, back in the 1970s. She still remembered sleeping on top of the stone stove with the family to stay warm during cold winter nights in her childhood times. To get herself and her family out of poverty, Wendy studied hard and got into one of the top universities in Beijing. After graduation, instead of joining a SOE (State Owned Enterprise) for a stable job, she joined a US consumer goods company as she saw more career advancement opportunity with international companies. With all the years working at multinational companies, Wendy has risen to a senior position. She was also lucky to catch the first wave of real estate market growth by investing in properties in Beijing. Her family now owns two apartments in Beijing, which gives her family a net worth of at least US$3 million.

Wendy and her husband love to travel. The family makes one long haul and one short haul trip every year. After their recent trip to France, Wendy and John both developed an interest in wine. They would take wine tasting classes along with a few other friends. Besides wine, Wendy also starts to invest in contemporary artwork after her friend took her to an international photography exhibition a few months ago. She was thrilled that she finally found an art piece that can fit the decor of her living room, even though it cost her RMB 20k. While she seems to be quite willing to spend on wine and artwork, she is not a big spender on luxury goods. Wendy would occasionally buy herself a handbag or a scarf from luxury brands to reward herself for her hard work. But when it comes to her son, she is willing to write big checks. For the last few years, she had sent her son to prestigious summer camps in US and UK. Those programs can cost US$10,000-15,000 easily.

She believes western education will give her son a competitive advantage over other kids. She also admitted that she did not want her son to go through the same pressure as she did in the Chinese education system. She already decided to send her son to the US to attend boarding school next year. To prepare for this, her son had been taking English tutorial classes every week since he was seven years old. In fact, she is thinking of moving to the US within the next five years. Wendy and her husband are both very fed up with the air pollution and traffic in Beijing. She estimated that the money she will receive from selling the two apartments would be enough to pay for a very nice house in the US. And there would still be plenty of cash left to support their retirement.

How Wendy sees the other generations:
A lot of her team members are from the post 80s generation. Somehow Wendy felt that the post 80s are not as driven as those in her generation. She attributed it to their growing up without hardships. She also found the post 80s are very sensitive to criticism, probably because they were all "Little Emperors" growing up. She had to be very

empathetic when giving them feedback and worrying about hurting their feelings.

The new recruits at her company are mainly from the post 90s. While Wendy views these young people as creative, they are also very hard to manage. She could never guess what's in their mind. Once she hired a fresh graduate as trainee. The young man quitted the job after three days, and over WeChat, told his supervisor that this is not what he wanted to do. She found his behavior completely unprofessional. She thought these post 90s kids had completely different sets of values and beliefs which she would never understand.

Post 80s: Cissy, age 33, married with two children, living in Shanghai

China's economy started an upward growth trend under Deng Xiao Ping's leadership in the 1980s. Benefiting from the economic growth, Cissy's parents both held nice jobs with decent pay in Shanghai. Even the apartment she grew up in was given to her parents by the SOE her father worked for. Her family was considered to be well-off middle-class family in Shanghai. Unlike those who were born in the 70s, Cissy was never lacked material goods growing up. Since she was the only child, her parents would give her anything they could afford. However, she also felt quite lonely growing up as the only child. After she was married, also to an only child, her husband and her both agreed they wanted to have two kids. Now she is a proud mother of a boy and a girl.

Her husband works at a bank, while she works at a multi-national company in Shanghai. When they are at work, Cissy's parents take care of her kids. As a result, a lot of the child rearing decisions are made by her parents. Even though there were times when she did not agree with the grandparents' parenting methods, she had to let go to avoid arguments, especially when she and her husband enjoy the freedom with the grandparents' help. Sometimes Cissy still felt like she is her parent's little baby herself, even though she is now a mother.

A big part of her family's income goes to the monthly mortgage payment. She was glad that her family already owns an apartment. When she got married five years ago, her parents and in-laws helped with the down payment. Without their help, they could not afford this apartment, especially when apartment prices have gone up so much in recent years.

During weekdays, Cissy and her husband's focus are on work and social life. During weekends, they try to spend more time with their kids. She has enrolled her children in early education classes, like baby gymnastics, English, music classes etc. Lately she also enrolled her 4 years old son in Chinese pinyin and "logic mathematics" class, in preparation for his primary school interview in a year. Cissy wanted to make sure her children do not lag behind other kids, as in a popular Chinese term "not to lose at the starting line." Every weekend, Cissy and her husband become drivers, busy taking their children to attend different classes around the city.

Lately she also started to worry about the health of her parents and her in-laws. As she and her husband are both the only child, they must take care of the four elderly parents. A few months ago, Cissy's mother went through a surgery. She had to take a week off from work to take care of her parents and the kids at home. Cissy was stressed and even fell sick after her mom was discharged from the hospital.

In the long run, she plans to send her children to school overseas. Cissy and her husband are working hard to save up for their children's education. Last year, they made a trip to Hong Kong to subscribe to a life insurance plan with savings component to fund for their children's college education in the future.

Gallery 2.15 Post 80s Family

How Cissy sees the other generations:

Cissy finds the post 70s take things too seriously. They like to lecture others. And the post 70s always think of themselves as superior than the younger generations. They are also somewhat conservative in decision making. But she admits that the post 70s tend to be hard working, and better team players compared to the post 80s generation. She also envied the post 70s who have accumulated a lot of wealth from buying properties.

Post 90s generation are giving her a real headache, as she is directly managing one at work. They don't listen to orders and tend to insist on their own ideas. They always come up with the most random ideas that are typically unrealistic. As a supervisor, Cissy felt like she was a jockey riding a wild horse. How to keep her post 90s subordinate happy and motivated poses a real challenge. She does admire the post 90s as being spontaneous and adventurous.

Post 90s: Max, age 24, single, living in Guangzhou

Max grew up in Xiamen, Fujian, where his parents run a small business. He is the only child in the family, or to be exact, he is the crown jewel of the family. He had his first computer when he was 14. He is also quite knowledgeable of many international brands, as he has been a consumer of products like Nintendo Wii, Microsoft Xbox, Nike shoes, Levi's jeans, Starbucks Frappuccino and JanSport backpack etc. since he was young.

Always aspired to live in a big city, he chose to attend university in Guangzhou. After graduation, he decided to stay in Guangzhou and found a job at an advertising agency. With less than RMB6,000 salary a month, Max is frugal. He rents a small room in an apartment building in an old residential district. There are three other young people sharing the same apartment, but he does not know them. It seems like they do not have any interest to know each other even though they share the same roof.

He does not like the mundane 9 to 5 jobs at large corporations. He chose to work at an advertising agency because he finds it more interesting to work for different clients and on different projects. It also makes him sound cool telling others he works for an ad agency.

In his leisure time, he meets up with his friends for dinners and movies. Given the limited budget, he always searches online for bargains from Nuomi (Chinese Groupon). He also does most of his shopping online. He is very proud that he has achieved "diamond buyer status" on Taobao. Even though Max is not a big spender, he still outspends his monthly income. He is thankful that his parents continue to give him a monthly stipend to support his living in Guangzhou.

He loves microblogging. When he is not working or sleeping, he would be on his iPhone, a birthday gift from his parents, updating his status on WeChat and Weibo. Though he does not talk to his roommates, he talks about almost anything online: social issues, work, personal beliefs and feelings etc.

He yearns to travel around the world one day. He traveled with his parents overseas a few times, but always with the guided tour group which he found boring. He wants to explore the world on his own. His latest life motto is "Drop everything behind and go travel (说走就走的旅行)." He believes by the time he can realize his motto, he should be quite accomplished at work and earn a lot more.

It is very important to have fun in life. He finds his parents have worked too hard all their lives. He truly believes one can strike a balance between enjoying life and having a career. While some of his friends are worried about not able to afford an apartment, that does not seem to bother him. He is confident that he will be successful one day. By that time, he will be able to afford anything he wants. Moreover, he knows his parents will help him out if he wants to buy an apartment in Guangzhou. They offered to buy him one after he graduated from university but he turned them down. He enjoys living with strangers. It is more fun for him.

How Max sees the other generations:

Post 70s are old schools and too traditional. Probably because they came from the old education system. While he thinks of himself as being very individualistic, the post 70s tend to group-think, as that was what the Communist Party advocated back then. They also do not seem to understand the trends of the 21st century. He finds it very hard to communicate to these aunties and uncles alike.

The post 80s generation to him are practical, and predictable. For example, his line manager Steve always orders the same drink from Starbucks, while Max always like to try something new on the menu. Max also feels that the post 80s are very suppressed inside, and not quite capable of expressing their feelings. As they are the first generation of single child in China, he believes they are under a lot of pressures from their family and from the society.

Gallery 2.16 Trendy Post 90s

CHAPTER 3

Unspoken Business Rules

This chapter describes the workplace. It includes "soft" knowledge like etiquettes for business meetings, drinking and dining, and to some extent "unspoken" business rules. It is meant to quickly bring you up to speed on the most critical and useful local knowledge to avoid some of the mistakes through my personal experience. Knowing these rules will put you in a step closer to your goals, and not viewed as a foreigner who knows nothing about China.

Navigate the Chinese Organizations Maze

Different Types of Chinese Enterprises

In most western countries, the classification of enterprises is straightforward. The most common types are sole proprietorship, partnership, and corporation. In China, the classification is a bit more complicated due to historical and political reasons. Companies can be classified by legal entity, by economic type, etc. To make it easier to understand, the table below illustrates a simplified version of the most common types of enterprises used in China:

A **stated-owned enterprise (SOE)**, as the name suggests, is directly owned and controlled by the government. There are two types of SOEs: Central Government Owned Enterprises (CGOE) and SOEs.

Central government owned enterprises (CGOEs): While the term state-owned already conveys superiority to normal companies, when an organization is owned by the central government, it is even more important and prestigious. There are a total of 114 of them in China. Owners of CGOEs include powerful government agencies and regulatory bodies like the SASAC (State-Owned Assets

Supervision and Administration Commission of the State Council), central financial institutions like CBRC (China Banking Regulatory Commission), CIRC (China Insurance Regulatory Commission), CSRC (China Securities Regulatory Commission) and other ministries from the State Council. Central enterprises typically own businesses in state monopoly industries: energy, natural resources, telecommunications, finance, tobacco, airline, railway and certain strategic industries like auto industry. Moreover, CGOEs generally get to use "China" in their names, like Petro China, China Life, Bank of China and China Mobile. It is simply impossible for private companies to use the word "China" in the company's official registered name.

Despite the fact that some of the companies are listed in overseas stock exchange with non-state equity owners (such as China Mobile), the senior executive and board appointments are done directly by the state council. The top executive leaderships, chairmans, of CGOEs are usually equivalent to the ranking of vice minister in the official system (which is just one level below minister and governor of province). As a result, you can often observe the rotation of one CGOE chairman to another CGOE, or a government post without much notice or discussion with the public. Chairman is the highest executive officer in China, not the CEO or GM. For instance, on the morning of August 24th, 2015, the Organization Department of the Central Committee of the Communist Party of China announced the chairman change for the top (and only) three mobile carrier companies (China Mobile, China Netcom and China Telecom). The chairmen of China Netcom and China Telecom swapped jobs, and a vice minister took over the China Mobile chairman job. Can you imagine the US senate

Different Types of Chinese Enterprises

Source of Capital	State Owned		Private Owned - Domestic			Foreign Owned	
Classification	Central Government Owned	State Owned Enterprise	Large Local Enterprise	Small Medium Enterprise/ Sole Proprietor	Hong Kong/ Macau/Taiwan Owned	Wholly Owned Foreign Enterprise	Joint Venture
Examples	Petro China	Beijing Capital Airport	Metersbonwe	Mom & Pop Stores	Ding Tai Fung	Starbucks China	Shanghai Volkswagen Automotive
	China Telecom	Quanjude Peking Duck Restaurant	Huawei		Watsons	Walmart	Carrefour

Illustration 3.1 Different Types of Chinese Enterprises

majority leader Mitch McConnell (as of 2016) announcing effective immediately AT&T and Verizon swap CEOs? You may complain that CEOs of listed companies manage the company strategy by the quarter, how do you think these chairmen manage their companies based on this level of unpredictability?

A friend of mine who studied at a popular MBA program in China a few years ago told me that in his class, students from CGOEs would emphasize that they were from central government owned enterprises, not state-owned enterprises. They proudly pointed out the difference in superior status and distinguished themselves from SOEs. This is not difficult to understand, as people usually perceive SOEs as being backward and pedantic, while CGOEs have made great progress in terms of management and business performance, and of course receiving preferential policies and financial support from the central government over the past decades.

The Chinese government used to sponsor government officials and executives from state-owned enterprises to attend MBA/EMBA programs. However, as Xi Jinping, the current Chinese President and General Secretary of the Communist Party, launched the anti-corruption campaign in late 2012, these programs are banned to government, military, stated-owned company officials, as guanxi network was built to profit particular private companies. A friend from a famous EMAB program in Shanghai last year told me that there were a few SOE students enrolled at the beginning but forced to drop out soon after. It is sad to see the baby thrown out with the bath water.

State-owned enterprises (SOEs): They are mainly owned and controlled by local governments. If the SOE's asset is very large then it is likely that it would be under SASAC's direct supervision. Top leaderships in SOEs are appointed by the local government. These companies are in all sorts of industries, not just monopoly. SOEs, in general, are named after local towns or cities at where they are based, like the Beijing Capital Airport, Beijing Cigarette Factory, Lanzhou Petrochemical, etc.

CORPORATION REGISTRATION

You can tell if a company is an SOE based solely on its name. As mentioned in the previous section, if the name contains the word "China 中国", "Zhong Hua 中华" (which all mean China), or is named after a place in China, it is highly likely that the company is a stated owned enterprise. Also, if you plan to set up your own company in China, company registration no longer allows words like "Zhong 中," "Hua 华," "Guo 国" (country) or "Dang 党" (communist party) in the name since these words imply the company belongs or is related to the government. Beware that there are a small number of companies and brands out there with the legacy name "Zhong Hua", but they are not state owned. These company names were grandfathered since they were registered many years ago. For example, Zhong Hua Toothpaste is actually owned by Unilever in China and is not a state-owned brand.

Privately owned enterprises: the biggest of them are called Large Local Enterprises (LLEs). CEO or President of LLE is usually the founder of the company, while the senior management of LLE is family members of the founder. Business owners of LLEs tend to trust their own relatives much more than professionals from the outside when it comes to money. The other two types of privately owned enterprises are Small and Medium Enterprises (SMEs) and Sole Proprietors.

Foreign-Owned Enterprises: There are three types of Foreign-Owned Enterprises, (1) Hong Kong/ Macau/ Taiwan Owned Enterprises; (2) Wholly Owned Foreign Enterprises (WOFE); (3) Joint Venture (JV). In the early history of China's reform and opening up, many cities offered tax incentives to attract foreign investments, like "Three Halves, Two Free," meaning first two years of tax exempted, next three years tax rate halved. As the Chinese economy grew more mature and local firms became stronger, local governments reduced incentives to attract foreign capital. If a local government needs foreign investment to meet the KPIs set by the central government, such as GDP, registered capital, key technology transfer, employment, etc., then foreign companies can always negotiate with the local governments to receive preferential treatments such as tax exemptions or free land to build manufacturing plants. Remember, you can always negotiate with the local government to reduce your initial investment and risk. There is one differentiation between WOFE and JV though. WOFE, as the parent company has 100% ownership, is technically not eligible to be listed in China's stock exchange. On the other hand, joint ventures and private enterprises are not allowed to be listed in an overseas stock exchange unless you change the company to a WOFE by restructuring ownership. The only exception is SOEs, as long as the government approves, they can be listed in either/both domestic and overseas stock markets. China Mobile, an A+H share listed company in both Hong Kong and China, is a good example.

The following section will focus on three types of enterprises that are most relevant to our everyday business lives in China: SOEs, LLEs, and WOFEs. How do they differ in terms of business operations and corporate cultures? Comparisons will be drawn based on the following five dimensions:

CORPORATE TAX TIPS

Wholly Owned Foreign Enterprise (WOFE) is usually first registered in an offshore region such as BVI, Cayman or Hong Kong, followed by registering a subsidiary in China. If structured through Hong Kong, the investors of the company only need to pay 5-10% capital repatriation tax based on a treaty with Hong Kong. If the parent company is not registered in Hong Kong first, then like most joint ventures, the capital gain tax rate when exiting China will be at 20-25% and subject to negotiation and interpretation by the local tax officials. The difference in tax payment is quite substantial! So if you want to structure a WOFE in China, do your research on corporate tax in addition to other policy limitations.

1. Decision making

2. Management style

3. Risk taking

4. Strategy

5. Pay and benefits

SOEs (including CGOEs): Party and Government Co-op

Since SOEs are owned by the government, they combine both state administrative culture and elements of the commercial market. In SOEs, the boss is not just the boss, they are also senior government officials. You do not report to only one boss, but to the entire government! Therefore, there is a common saying that dictates how SOEs are run in China:

党政工团，齐抓共管
"Dang Zheng Gong Tuan, Qi Zhua Gong Guan"

which means **Party-Government-Union-Youth, joint efforts and manage business operations as one team.**

- **Party** refers to the Communist Party
- **Government** refers to the PRC Government
- **Union** refers to the All China Federation of Trade Union
- **Youth** refers to the Chinese Communist Youth League

So if your company is working with a SOE on a large commercial project, you need to first find out to which state ministry this SOE reports. They (or you) must get approval from the supervising state ministry before you can proceed with real projects.

Many economists criticize the SOE model as an inefficient way to allocate resources, since SOEs need to bear both political and social responsibilities in addition to seek profits. Unlike normal public companies where most if not all business decisions are made in the best interest of shareholders, that is not the case for SOEs. Profit is only secondary as senior management reports to the government, which is not always the same as its shareholders. The government's interests are top priority to SOEs. For example, Guizhou Maotai, the most prestigious Chinese white liquor producer based in one of the poorest province of Guizhou, is an A-share listed company. Every year its largest shareholder, the Guizhou government, takes out a portion of the profit from the company coffer to subsidize the poor regions of the province instead of managing through taxation and a formal provincial budget process. If in US, it is considered criminal offense for one shareholder to siphon off capital for its own use, but it is accepted in China as the CSRC (SEC equivalent in China) has the same minister level authority as the provincial government.

Take another example of China Mobile, who was tasked to develop and deploy a Chinese 3G standard called TD-CDMA, incompatible with WCDMA or CDMA2000 used by the rest of the world and adopted by Apple, Nokia and Samsung. Yet China Mobile had to deploy the new network at great costs to its shareholder. Within a few years before China Mobile could fully roll out its base stations equipped with this proprietary standard, 4G developed by the western companies took over.

WHEN GOVERNMENT ORDERS, THERE IS NO MISSION IMPOSSIBLE

In general, mobile network coverage can never reach 100% even in a large city like Beijing. That is why when you make a call on New Year's Eve, you have to dial a few times before the call goes through. A friend at a leading mobile carrier said that during the 2008 Beijing Olympics Games, a senior government official requested the mobile operator to showcase the best service and the most advanced technology to all visitors to the Olympics. To accomplish the task, the mobile operator ended up spending millions of dollars to achieve the mission impossible: 100% first time call going through, zero call drops, and zero complaints. In other words, if everyone of the 80,000 audience at the Bird's Nest (the main Olympics stadium in Beijing) made a call on their mobile phone simultaneously, all 80,000 calls must be connected! If the same request went to other countries, telecom companies would probably find the government's request unreasonable and refuse. But this leading mobile operator went ahead and installed so many frequency transmitters (mobile communication signal processing instrument) on mobile trucks outside the stadium than all transmitters in Hainan province combined! Of course, the extra capacity was immediately disassembled after the game was over.

When central government decided to consolidate polluting industries such as coal mining in 2015, large state owned mines benefited from the policy by forcing private coal mines to shut down or sell to SOEs at a steep discount. The property rights is not quite as enforced as in the developed countries when facing competition from SOEs.

The senior management of SOEs is typically state-appointed government officials who carries the official rank status. Because of their background and experience, SOEs are bureaucratic organizations and filled with rigid protocols in official meetings. Some SOEs are run like a military outfit because of the chairman's background. A friend at a large state-owned food company told a story that nobody is allowed to mix English words with Mandarin in the office, a common practice in many private companies for convenience. English was not even allowed inside the office. Employees were assigned specific paths and entrances to get to their workstation; they were required to yell out slogans every morning before start of work. There were even rules on what personal items can be placed on the desk.

In terms of decision making, regardless of how much progress is made by way of research and team discussions, one person in senior position makes the final call. An important implication for dealing with these organizations is to receive written confirmation from the decision maker before you breakout the champaign. And pray they don't change the decision maker before your contract is carried out. Nevertheless, a few progressive SOEs have begun to adopt some modern management styles, such as setting KPIs for employee performance assessment. Of course, flattery and playing office politics with your boss is still a key factor for promotion.

In terms of risk taking, strategic planning, and employee benefits, we need to separate the reformed SOEs and the ones that have not been reformed, as not all SOEs are created equal. Again, this is a result of whether an open-minded top official is put in charge.

To improve the performance of SOEs, the government selected a number of them to undergo restructuring and reform to incentivize the management. Over the past two decades, the government has given extra resources to these reformed SOEs such as subsidized land, bank loans etc. At the same time, these reformed SOEs have also been requested to grow rapidly in assets to meet with the government's growing financial needs. Some of the reform measures include:

1. Share reform to allow the SOE to be listed on domestic or international stock exchanges to attract private capital;

2. Convert civil servant employment contract and pension system into private company employment system;

3. Compensation system is adjusted to meet market condition.

As a result, these SOEs are also willing to take risk in order to achieve the high growth target set by the government, which is typically a total asset based target. Despite the reform, local banks (mostly SOEs themselves0) still treat these SOEs having the same credit risk as the government, i.e, no default risks. In many cases the local banks would actively pursue SOEs to take out more low interest rate loans. As nobody gets fired for buying IBM, nobody at the bank can be fired for giving loans to SOEs, even if they go bad. But if you issued a bad loan to a private company, people may question the motive or integrity of issuing the loan in the first place, which will affect the bank staff's promotion opportunity or bonus. In the extreme cases of the banks themselves, the government bails out the banks when the bad debt got out of hands. Without the capital constraint, SOEs tend to take extra risks to generate high returns by taking on extremely high leverage.

Unlike the old SOEs, some of the reformed SOEs are more than willing to engage international strategic consulting firms to help them with long term planning, like drawing five-year strategic roadmaps. However, reformed SOEs' strategies are still highly dependent on the government's policy. First, SOEs are required to submit 10% of profit to the central government to fund social security, with the latest policy raising the requirement to 15%, therefore financial forecasting is pre-determined. Secondly, corporate strategy may need to take into account central government's development plan. For instance, a policy stated "Connecting Every Village in China" where by 2005, at least 95% of all administrative villages in China must be wired with land lines. As a result, China Telecom's strategy must align with the central government's goal even though the project returned a negative ROI.

In terms of pay and benefits, employment by these large reformed SOEs has become a dream job for many university graduates. In the old days when the entire economy was state run, children followed their parent's footsteps to work in the same company or factory. Today working for SOEs is still similar to working for government agencies, where there are many hidden fringe benefits and job stability. But unlike the government agencies, these large SOEs and CGOEs do require their employees to work very hard, as least by the amount of hours a day. It is also admirable if one tells his or her relatives and friends about the SOE job. But unfortunately the culture of these organization also tends to be bureaucratic. Job promotion is slow and must follow internal policies. First you need to be a member of the Communist Party to get the promotions beyond certain level. Then there are glass ceilings, unless you are backed by a senior government official or you have strong family connections. Oftentimes, working hard at a SOE means meeting the whims of one senior manager's random idea and not executing a well-planned and thought-out strategy.

Wages in SOEs are likely to be lower than those in multinational companies, but employee benefits are more comprehensive. In many cases household expenses are covered from a subsidized apartment, to gas and phone bills, laptops, prepaid spending cards and even groceries. My friend Lisa worked at a CGOE that trades food and household products. I visited her home in Beijing which was filled with detergents, cooking oil, sugar, vinegar, etc. It turned out that her employer regularly gave away its traded products as benefits. Even though her salary level was average, she actually saved a lot on groceries. Sometimes she received so much goods from the company that she had to sell and turn them into cash on Taobao (the Chinese version of eBay). Some SOEs build their own apartment complexes in prime locations and sell or rent to employees below the market rate.

The SOE is able to get favorable land allocation at next to nothing, sometime an annex to its office building. In today's lucrative housing market, this kind of obvious subsidy is too excessive and attracts jealousy and hatred from the society in general. Recall that a nice apartment may take a family 40+ years of salary to buy. Trading the first 5 years of a fresh college grad's life for such a property would totally make financial sense.

Smaller and unreformed SOEs are typically run like a government agency. The senior management teams never take any risks for their shareholders in return for a safe career, totally opposite to a hedge fund. The incentive system determined the type of talents and predicts their behaviors. Long term planning is irrelevant since the government policy dictates company strategy. The central government does not have high expectations except a vehicle for stable employment. As long as they can meet basic financial targets set by trading or servicing other SOEs, they will do just fine. Overall, small SOEs are not well managed, and employees' pay is low. Young people working at small SOEs based in the Midwest are particularly vocal online about their low pay and the mundane job.

Local & Taiwanese Owned Enterprises - Short term focus, high risk high return strategy

Taiwanese entrepreneurs are among the first to enter the China market, even before the western companies. They have developed a very deep understanding of the local market through practicing basic western management principals and adapting them to the local market. The shared cultural and language between Taiwan and mainland China added to their advantage. The Taiwanese model of doing business in China, such as focusing on localization and sales distribution is very similar to local enterprises founded by mainlanders. Thus in the following section, LLEs refer to both Taiwanese-owned and Large Local Enterprises.

Today almost all the private enterprises are built by the founders one brick at a time. Even if a company is quite sizable today, its founder tends to be very hands-on on every detail and every decision. They remain a one-man show or family business with little space for professional managers. Only the founder's word is final. Once a friend working for a Taiwanese company told me that the CEO must approve every advertisement and packaging design before it can hit the market. The company has over 100 products, and you can only imagine the level of detail the founder has to attend to! Because of this level of work load, the founders are typically very hard working and work long hours.

Collaborative decision making is not common within LLEs. As the founder makes all the decisions, the rest of the team, no matter how senior they are, executes the order. This is very different from western enterprises with modern management style where important decisions are often discussed thoroughly within the management team before rolled out. LLEs do not spend too much time on market analysis or internal discussion. LLEs demand speedy execution – every decision needs to be carried out fast, whether correct or not. Given the China market is constantly changing and growing, speedy execution actually becomes a competitive advantage for LLEs to fend off competitors and seize market share quickly. LLEs are able to take advantage of market opportunity before it disappears, while MNCs spend months or years gathering data and performing researches. Due to the pursuit of rapid growth, the CEOs of LLEs do not pay much attention to establish corporate culture, such as employee retention. Wei, a friend working in a LLE based in Shanghai, once told me that the founder CEO of his company conducted sales meeting every two weeks that run from early morning until midnight for 20 consecutive hours! During the sales meeting, the CEO was the most energetic one despite being sixty years old. Recently the company started the business planning process for the next year, and the CEO even required these meetings to be held once a week! This time, the CEO wanted to meet with each sales manager individually to talk about next year's plan. One week, Wei made an appointment with the CEO at 5pm. As all his previous packed meetings ran over time, he had to wait until 3am when they started the meeting, a total of 10 hours beyond his schedule time. During the 10 hours, he never dared to interrupt the CEO or leave, fearing the CEO get the impression that he was not as dedicated as the rest. When he walked into CEO's office, he had to pretend he was not tired and full of energy! Wei was joking that if he talked to his boss about work-life balance and the need to establish good corporate culture, the CEO would probably fire him on the spot!

LLEs' willingness to take risks is probably the highest among all types of enterprises in China. Founders of LLEs tend to be natural gamblers and opportunists to navigate in a market with no clear rules. They are constantly looking for opportunities to make quick money. They are not afraid or even aware of high risks because they are confident that high risk means high return (one sided). Jake, a friend who is the general manager of a Hong Kong-based real estate developer based in Zhejiang province, told me that when he worked with LLEs on local development project, LLEs usually add very high leverage to achieve high return. Leverage ratio sometimes got so high that the slightest market downturn could threaten the company's survival. That is exactly what one would call "throw a sprat to catch a whale!" He was also amazed by how these LLEs were able to secure financing from the local banks. This is partially caused by the fact that Chinese banks have yet to establish a sound risk control and credit rating system. Loan issuance is non-transparent, potentially involving briberies. And if the loan fails, the entrepreneur could walk away without any damage to his credit history (non-recourse). It is this "I win, you lose" mentality and a social and legal system that does not punish bad behaviors that has been fostering this extreme risk-taking culture. It is nearly impossible for Hong Kong and foreign investors to adapt to this type of high leverage model when doing business. Mary, a friend who is in charge of a famous CEO class at Chinese business school, told me another interesting story. Owners of LLEs are often enrolled in expensive part-time executive EMBA or CEO programs to build "networks." Often they gathered at dinner or bars to talk about investment opportunities. Once they spot a potential investment opportunity, they could quickly call tens of millions of dollars to complete the deal. Despite the EMBA program taught western management skills, which their secretaries attended on their behalf and completed the homework, they did not evaluate the deal from a professional investor's perspective such as thorough diligence. As long as they saw an opportunity, especially those in the grey area and perceived as a private club deal, they would put money in it and rolled the dice! Since the economy had been growing rapidly, many deals were very profitable indeed. But as the economy stabilized and the market became more efficient, this wild-wild-west way of investment would inevitably see its own demise with massive and spectacular failures. Chinese media uses the term "barbaric growth" to describe how LLEs grow aggressively without any consideration for rules and regulations.

Other friends who work at LLEs also mentioned that the company would never discuss five-year or ten-year plans. The founder would view the effort as a waste of time and money (which is out of his own pocket). Again, owners of LLEs are opportunists who look for short term gains. When performing business planning, they only plan for the next year. To them long term means three years at most. Anything beyond three years is pure speculation, as they understand how quickly the markets and government policies can change. Thus brand building and R&D investments are scarce amongst the local companies. Intellectual property protection does not exist either, or at least the part of execution of protection, which makes five-year planning meaningless. Local entrepreneurs are very decisive in making investments as well as cutting losses. For any project, they can tolerate up to two years of losses at most. They will not hesitate to cut off after two years of unprofitability. Wherever the founder CEO spots a business opportunity, he will immediately gather resources and execute on the idea at breakneck speed to gain first mover advantage! This is why you rarely find LLEs talking about long-term investment plans, such as brand building, market analysis, R&D investments etc. Some high-margin products, such as liquor, would rather spend half of the previous year's profit on this year's advertising on CCTV (China Central Television - the predominant state television broadcaster in China) to achieve rapid but short term sales growth. Does that sound familiar? You can find like-minded people trading stocks on the Wall Street.

LLEs are probably the worst in terms of employee benefits compared to SOEs and foreign enterprises. LLEs are generally viewed as stingy and do not provide sufficient employee welfare. To LLEs, they tend to pay more attention to an employee's ability to execute rather than his or her education qualification and long term potential. They are not willing to pay high salary to attract the best talents. Once a CEO of a listed LLE said, in my face, that he would never spend money to hire the so-called MBA students because he finds them useless! He would rather recruit those who are not well educated, but are obedient and hardworking! Even Jack Ma, the founder of Alibaba had a saying: "Hire three people, pay wages for four, and have them do the workload for five people." [13]. LLEs also tend to invest little in training their employees. This is in direct contradiction to a company's long-term development.

On the other hand, most LLEs follow an inheritance system where the CEO would rather transfer the company to one of their own children instead of hiring more capable professional managers to run the company. They would never trust an outside manager to take over the business. Many high-level positions, especially in finance and accounting, are often given to the owner's family members, so an outside hire may never get promoted to a senior position. If you want to join a LLE, no matter how international the company may seem, you should take extra precaution. Without talents and a professional management team, a family business will quickly run into transitional issues when the first generation of entrepreneur reaches the old age and the next generation is not interested in the business. That is why there are very few long lasting private firms in China today. There is an old saying in China "wealth does not pass through three generations" meaning the first generation builds wealth, but the next two will squander the wealth for sure.

So if wages are low while workload and pressure are high, how do LLEs attract talents? For one, LLEs account for the majority of job opportunities in the market. Another reason is that you can get promoted fairly quickly from an entry position if you can prove yourself. In SOEs and foreign enterprises, job promotion is based on a career path set by HR policies, and hence it could take a long time to reach. In an LLE, if you work hard and demonstrate results that are recognized by the senior management, you can be promoted quickly. Pay also improves quickly with rising ranks. In addition, how LLEs conduct business is more flexible than foreign companies, which allows young people to learn and perhaps have a higher sense of accomplishment. LLEs are willing and love to play in the grey areas to gain an unfair advantage over competitors. Wei, from the LLE mentioned earlier, told me that there was a merchandiser from a European hypermarket retailer asked for RMB 120,000 (about US$20,000) in red pocket (i.e., Chinese way of gifting, or in this case, bribery), otherwise, he would not allow the new product from

Wei's company to go on shelf. My friend told his supervisor about the merchandiser's request, and without a word, his supervisor gave Wei RMB 120,000 in cash and asked him to get the problem fixed! Situations like this would never happen in a foreign company with proper corporate governance. Even if money needed to be paid, it would be through the distributor's or consultant's account, not directly from the company. Unfortunately the British pharmaceutical giant GSK was investigated by the Chinese government for such offense paying directly to the doctors using extravagant conferences overseas. [14] For those who are comfortable working in the grey areas, results and job promotions comes quickly.

Multinational Companies: Thriving by following rules to the letter

When it comes to decision making, MNCs tend to be more cautious than its Chinese counterparts by taking their time to conduct proper analyses and research, taking a page out of its developed country strategy book. While the founder CEO is the only one making decisions in LLEs, important decisions are usually discussed among the senior management team until general consensus is reached in MNCs. Sometimes, even the regional head office and the global headquarter may need to approve the decision before any execution can be carried out. As a result, the decision making process becomes quite slow. I remembered in a consulting project where I interviewed several senior executives from MNCs, they all cited slow decision making and execution as being one of the key barriers to MNCs' growth in China.

Management style and corporate culture are mainly determined by the MNCs' global headquarter. MNCs are usually seen as more open minded and employees are encouraged to make decisions in a collaborative manner, which is different from SOEs and LLEs' where only the most senior managers' words count. In LLE, even if an employee has a brilliant idea, he or she has to make the boss look good by crediting the decision to the superior. MNC's corporate culture highly depends on the proportion of expatriates in the company's senior executive level, who in turn hires and trains people who also endorse the same culture. MNCs with a high number of expatriates run more like a western company since these expatriates will also bring the headquarters' culture to China, with the down side of sometimes not adapting well to the local market and culture. Whereas for other MNCs where the majority of senior executives have been transitioned to local hires, there will be more Chinese cultural elements injected. Examples like the establishment of labor unions, election of "Worker's Class Role Model" — which is very common among SOEs and LLEs, etc. In this case, the MNC can better adapt to the local market and talent pool, but may deviate from the global corporate culture. Again, for a MNC that answers to its public shareholders, there is a fine balance between profit targets and consistent culture.

Risk control by MNC is done in a more systematic way, with an emphasis on balancing risks and returns to achieve sustainable growth. Most investments by MNCs in China are done relatively conservatively. There may be two reasons. First, many MNCs are still not profitable even after entering China for ten to twenty years, and the headquarters may not be willing to increase investment in the unprofitable China operation. But as a strategic market and manufacturing base for global markets, they cannot afford to exit China. Secondly, high investment is required in marketing, sales, and even R&D in order to grow business in the China market. The headquarters simply cannot invest a lot of money into one single market. It needs to take into account other markets' needs as well. Nevertheless, MNCs must maintain a good looking balance sheet with reasonable asset/debt ratio. MNCs will not be able to grow like LLEs by taking very high leverage.

MNCs generally have more long-term strategic planning. In addition to the annual business planning process, MNCs also conduct longer term strategic planning like five- or even ten-year business plan. MNCs tend to care less about short term gain, and focus more on long term growth in China. Otherwise those who have been losing money in China would have exited China long time ago. However, China's development is just going too fast. Usually the market size calculated in the five-year plan no longer makes sense in one to two years' time. Sometimes, these five-year or ten-year plans are simply unrealistic for the fast moving China market.

Many university graduates view working for MNCs as their dream jobs given MNCs' favorable management style and established processes, particularly among the middle class segment. In cities like Shanghai, family members would be very proud to tell their friends and relatives if their kids get a job at large MNCs! Since MNCs tend to put more emphasis on acquiring local talents to help develop the local business, salary levels and employee benefits are typically higher than SOEs and LLEs. Back then there may still be glass ceilings in MNCs where only expatriates can get promoted to senior executive positions for the fear that the locals cannot communicate well to the global senior management. Nowadays, MNCs understand that they need local talents to help grow local business from a reasonable cost perspective, and glass ceilings no longer exist. In fact, many MNCs in China are actually run by mainlanders, many of whom received higher education in Western countries and spent years working in large corporations there. These Chinese returnees are typically called "Hai Gui (海归)," which pronounces the same as sea turtle in Mandarin. So next time if someone tells you he is a "Hai Gui", that means he is mainland Chinese returning to China from overseas.

Key considerations when dealing with different Chinese organizations

Among SOEs, LLEs and MNCs, MNCs are probably the most straightforward to work with. As mentioned in previous sections, MNCs have established transparent processes and management styles. Every project starts with clear objectives and expected outcomes. In order to ensure fairness and prevent corruption from happening, MNCs usually source suppliers using open tender so that the entire bidding process is generally transparent and fair, whereas a SOE or LLE project's open tender sometimes rigs requirements to favor a particular bidder. Once a contract is signed, MNCs typically follows through. This is why a lot of my friends doing business in China prefer to or only work with MNCs that play by the rule, even though the payment terms of MNCs may be a bit long. In contrast, local companies' contracts may not worth the paper they are printed on, and very difficult to enforce even through the court system. The only challenging part of serving MNCs is that the vendor needs to have a relatively good level of English communication, as the vendor may need to be patient and communicate with the MNC's headquarters.

SOEs may seem to have a laid back culture from earlier description, but working with one is definitely not laid back at all. A friend Xu who runs an online marketing company in Beijing told me his first and bad experience working with SOE. The project was to design and run a digital marketing campaign for one of the SOE's brands. The contract was signed with the project objectives and scope defined. However, problems emerged at the beginning of the project. First, the SOE client kept changing the objectives of the project. For instance, one day the boss said they needed to focus on word of mouth advertising on Weibo, and then the entire project scope had to steer towards the Weibo platform. Next week the boss said the campaign should not omit online video channels. Then the campaign changed its emphasis on online video sites. Since that was the first large SOE client for Xu's company, he could not refuse the client's endless requests. Finally the project was completed and way above budget, resulting a heavy loss for Xu's company. But that was not the end of it. Payment collection became the next problem despite of what is written in the contract. The brand team from the client side claimed that payment request has already been submitted to the finance department when the project was delivered. They did not know why the payment did not go through. So Xu had to physically send an employee to the

SOE's finance department every day, trying to figure out the cause for delay. After some digging, Xu finally found out that it was one of the finance managers who did not approve the payment because the brand director once had an argument with him and therefore holding a grudge and letting it out on Xu's company. Poor Xu had no choice but to take the finance manager out for dinner and sent him gifts, hoping that he would approve the payment soon. After all the wine and dine, the finance manager finally approved the payment. According to the contract, the SOE client should pay Xu's company thirty days after the project delivery. The reality is that Xu's company did not receive the payment until four months later. So I asked Xu why he chose to work with an SOE client given all the troubles, there are many MNCs he could serve as well. Xu then gave me a wry smile, and told me that SOEs tend to ask for client references of another SOE before they are comfortable signing a contract with a new vendor. Everyone in China knows SOEs are difficult to serve and very critical when selecting vendors. If a company managed to serve a SOE client, it gives confidence to other SOEs: "See! My company survived from serving a SOE! That means my company has solid financial strength, so you don't need to worry about working with us." Moreover, SOEs are somewhat loose in terms of price negotiation. SOE projects can usually earn a higher profit margin than MNCs and LLEs projects, if you can manage the cost by managing the relationship with the decision maker.

LLE clients may be the toughest to serve among the three. They are similar to SOEs who are indecisive and change their minds all the time. Every decision is based on what the founder chairman says, and nothing is final unless you get the nod from the boss. My friend Alice was the creative director of a 4A advertising agency, and working on a TV advertisement production for a LLE. On the day of shooting, her client "Wang Zong" (in China, you address your client or your boss using the suffix "Zong" to show respect) showed up to supervise the entire shooting. During the whole process, Wang Zong did not raise any concerns and let everything go smoothly. Alice felt relieved and thought it had gone well. Well, later she found out that she was celebrating too soon. When she presented the first cut of the TV advertisement to the LLE client, Wang Zong's boss rejected the copy and said that was not what he wanted. To make matters worse, Wang Zong also told his boss that he was not happy with the shooting and blamed the advertising agency for being unable to deliver results. Alice was very upset but there was nothing she could do but to re-edit all the footages. After many revisions, the LLE client finally approved the copy. After this incident, Alice said she would never work for another LLE client! The experience was too frustrating and devastating! So next time if you have to work with a LLE client, first you need to find out who the key decision maker is and make sure all decisions are approved by that person. Nobody else's approval counts.

While decision making is a headache, price negotiation is another big headache for working with LLEs, since they are known to be extremely cost sensitive. If a LLE does not bargain on price, it probably means the employee of the LLE wants a kick back. A friend Lei who runs an internet advertising company told me his experience of working with a famous LLE in Beijing. He sold a project to this LLE for US$160,000 (RMB 1 million), under the condition that he has to pay one of the staffs from the marketing department US$80,000 (RMB 500,000) as kick back, which is half of the contract value! Lei just started his company so he desperately needed the business. Even though he understood that is not right, he had no choice and had to agree to the ridiculous request. Moreover, LLEs tend not to honor contracts: words on paper are never binding and there is always room for negotiation. LLEs are like SOEs who like to delay payment to their suppliers. If you really need the payment from LLE to support the company cash flow, the LLE may squeeze you and ask for up to 50% discount! If you take the case to court, it will cost you more money and time, and may even cost your company's reputation! So if you have to do business with a LLE, it is important that you establish a good personal relationship with the decision maker, and perhaps a big portion in pre-payment if you can. That would save you many troubles down the road.

SOE DRESS CODE

If you are about to attend a meeting with a SOE, particularly with senior level personnel, you should learn about the proper SOE dress code. Basically SOEs follow the same dress code as government officials. For formal meetings held in the government, men usually wear a white shirt and dark blazer, where the zipper is zipped all the way up to the neck line. Still don't know what that looks like? Turn on the CCTV news and take a look at what government officials wear during internal meetings. You will see that everyone dresses in the same way. In formal external meetings, staffs are required to wear dark color suits. If the leader wears a tie, then everyone in the meeting also needs to wear a tie. Even if the leader does not wear a tie, but if the meeting is a very formal one, then all the subordinates should also wear ties. You should not assume you are at the same level as the leader, but instead, your dress code should reflect your respect to the leader. For instance, in March 2013, when the Chief Executives of Hong Kong and Macau visited Beijing to meet with President Xi, they both wore a dark blue tie in order to match President Xi's. Later in the same day, when they met with Premier Li, they changed to a light blue tie to match with Premier Li's. So next time if you get to meet any senior government officials in China, make sure you bring along a few different colored ties for change if the occasion occurs! The western saying of "imitation is the highest form of flattery" applies in China as well. If you want to tell your boss that you are a loyal employee, you may want to have the exact look of your boss, meaning not only the way he dresses, but also his hair style! This is why in CCTV daily news it is not surprising to see most Chinese government officials sharing the same hairstyle as the government leaders!

3 . 2

Uniqueness of Chinese Government Policies

PRC Government Structure

There are many different committees and congresses in the Chinese Central Government, and you can't really tell what their functions are sometimes just by looking at their names. The following section will outline the posts and duties of the top officials in the central government in ways that you can better understand and relate to.

As I repeat myself again and again, you must understand the fact that the Communist Party ("the Party") is the highest authority above the government. In China, various branches of the government, including the legislature and the military, all report to the Party. Therefore, the Party's General Secretary usually becomes the President of PRC, which is the case with the current President Xi Jinping, who was first the General Secretary before being appointed as President.

Besides the President, the center of power lies within the Politburo Standing Committee (the PSC) of the Communist Party of China. Every major governmental division and organization is headed by a member of the PSC, and one must be a member of the PSC in order to be nominated for the positions of President or Premier of PRC. Therefore, everyone pays close attention every four years when members are added or removed from the committee. In addition, the number of members in the PSC is always an odd number, currently 7, previously 9, to avoid deadlocks. The rankings within the 7 members of PSC also varies, observable by measuring each person's seating distance to the president in public meetings, and order in which names are presented in the media.

The next level of authority is the Member of the Political Bureau of the CPC Central Committee, including the 7 standing committee members, currently there are a total of 25 members.

The Communist Party of China Central Committee (CPC Central Committee) is another organization frequently mentioned by the media. The PSC is at the center stage of the center of power, while the Central Committee is the group behind the scene that influences the PSC. This committee of more than 200 members is responsible for nominating the members of the Politburo itself.

Second is the concept of the People's Republic of China. The National People's Congress (NPC) is stated to be the organization holding the highest level of power in the country. The members of this 3000-strong congress are, technically, voted into office by the public, and they are meant to be representatives of the people. They are supposed to have the power to elect and approve the country's leaders, as well as the power to pass legislatures. The NPC, like the PSC, is headed by a standing committee. Basically, members of standing committees are higher ranked than other members. Besides the National People's Congress, every province and town have their own municipal congresses to monitor local policies and regulations, but they are far less influential and powerful than the NPC.

The Premier: the Premier holds the top position in the government officials' hierarchy as the head of the State Council. The State Council is responsible for the execution of the nation's policies, and naturally the Premier oversees its operation. The Premier is also responsible for an annual report to be evaluated by the NPC.

The National Committee of the Chinese People's Political Consultative Conference (CPPCC): it is one of the most elusive of the Chinese political organizations; frankly, after reading the description on the official website, I had a hard time understanding what it is that they actually do (or perhaps I just lack political savviness). Afterward I found some online reviews that provided insight – the CPPCC is an organization that offers membership to influential people in the society, for instance successful businessmen or others who have big social impacts, who are not members of the Communist Party. These chosen people tend to have substantial influence in society, but the Central Government does not want them to hold actual political power, so this exclusive club is formed for them to voice their opinions. In addition, in case the opinions are too lopsided at the NPC, the situation could be somewhat mitigated by the opinions of the CPPCC. Similar to the NPC, the CPPCC has local chapters, but of course their influences are far less than that of the national CPPCC.

If the structure of China is compared to that of a business organization, the President is the CEO, whose main responsibilities are to establish the mid- to long-term development plan and to manage external relations, while he is not too involved with the organization's day-to-day operations. The Premier is the COO overseeing the organization's daily operations. The NPC is like the Board of Directors in that it is usually not too involved in how the organization is run, but decides on the next CEO appoint or large investment projects, etc. Last but not least, the CPPCC is like the company consultant where it does not have actual decision-making power, but it would still be consulted before an organization makes a decision.

Last, there are many conferences held by the Chinese government and Communist Party. For instance, often in the news you would hear about the Third or Fifth Plenary Session of the CPC Central Committee. The CPC Central Committee holds a number of conferences in a year, in which many positions, such as the Chairman of the Party or the Politburo Committee members, are nominated for election. The first conference in the year is labeled as the first session, the second is the second session, etc., with each session discussing different issues.

The NPC & CPPCC Annual Sessions are held every year in Beijing. Since the two meetings are usually timed to be back to back, they are often referred in one term.

Members of the 18th Central Politburo Standing Committee of the Communist Party of China

Member	Holding Titles
Mr. Xi Jinping	General Secretary of the CPC President of People's Republic China Chairman of Central Military Commission of the CPC
Mr. Li Keqiang	Premier of People's Republic of China
Mr. Zhang Dejiang	Chairman of NPC Standing Committee
Mr. Yu Zhengsheng	Chairman of CPPCC National Committee
Mr. Liu Yunshan	First Secretary of the Central Secretariat of the CPC
Mr. Wang Qishan	Secretary of the Central Commission for Discipline Inspection
Mr. Zhang Gaoli	Vice Premier of People's Republic of China

Illustration 3.2 Members of the 18th Central Politburo Standing Committee of the Communist Party of China

Central Government policy

It is important to recognize the serious impact of Central Government policies on daily business in China. There is no clear difference between policies, regulations and laws when they are executed and enforced. The only difference is that policies and regulations don't need to be passed through due process in China.

SOEs are undoubtedly the first to follow the government's policy by the book. For example, real estate prices in China have risen out of control over the last few years due to excess liquidity, which attracted many SOEs to the industry no matter what their original businesses were. The government introduced different measures aiming to cool the market, one of which is banning SOEs from real estate projects unless they have explicit approval. Once this policy was out, only the Central Government approved SOEs remained in the real estate sector, while the smaller SOEs obediently exited the market. Another example is the steel industry. A few years ago, the Central Government realized there had been an overcapacity in the low-end steel market. Again the government forced a consolidation in the industry and banned private sectors from entering. Since 2005, all new steel projects must be approved by the Central National Development and Reform Commission. Even SOEs had difficulties obtaining approvals.

Government policies could also affect wider industries that are seemingly immune. In 2010 the Central Government mandated local governments to reduce energy consumption and emission as part of local officials' KPIs for future promotions. As a result, local officials executed quickly by cutting electricity supply to manufacturing plants to three days a week, resulting in reduced production capacity by 40% over night. One of my OEM suppliers at the time simply could not deliver products as scheduled, causing large scale stock shortfall all over China. Fortunately the OEM had their own backup generators, which is more costly to operate, and our orders were eventually filled. Despite the increase in cost, we were unable to pass the cost to our consumers by raising the prices. To add insult to injury, we had to pay penalty to the tough retailers for our failure to keeping our shelves stocked. At the end, as a law abiding MNC, we took all the losses. As a relatively large global company, we had the financial strengths to weather the storm. Smaller business may not be able to survive due to cash flow issues. The only alternative is not to follow the rules, which is the grey area a company needs to carefully consider before stepping into. Someone out there could be gathering these evidences and use them when needed.

The 2008 Beijing Olympics presented the strength of an emerging super power to the world. To accommodate the athletes and millions of visitors to Beijing without suffering from horrible air pollution, the Central Government shut down all factories within 150 km (90 miles) radius of Beijing 6 months before the games started. For an entire month during the game, many companies within Beijing were ordered to give vacation days to employees to reduce traffic. Local cars cannot get on the public roads during the day, and there was even a special lane for vehicles carrying Olympic-related personnel. The game went on without a glitch, with clean air and no traffic for a city with over 20 million people. The Central Government officials prided themselves for the incredible achievement, but the pollution and traffic returned with a vengeance shortly after the games. Today, Beijing remains one of the top cities with the worst air pollution and traffic congestion in the world.

In order to protect local companies and strategic industries, the government often introduces specific policies favoring local companies, such as banning foreign companies from entering the industry, or restricting joint ventures (JV) with local partners. To avoid issues with the World Trade Organization, rules often appear in the form of a set of conditions for entry so that only certain favored local players are qualified. A blatant example is the importation quota system for foreign films. To promote the development of the domestic film industry, starting in 2011, China introduced a policy that allows no more than twenty foreign films to be imported into China each year, whereas before only a smaller number was allowed. Furthermore, two-thirds of the domestic cinema screenings must be given to domestic films. Fortunately, by 2012, the quota for foreign films importation increased to 34. Moreover, foreign movie producers are limited to 25% of total domestic box office revenues. Because of the import limitation, piracy is rampant online and in the black market for DVD as there is no legal mean to access foreign films otherwise. Chinese films were also given better and longer dates in theaters compared to the imports, such as summer and Chinese New Year.

Similarly the Chinese auto industry required foreign manufacturers to form JV with weak local partners to ensure technology transfer. Cars with engine size of over 1.6L are subject to a higher tax rate, which specifically targets bigger import cars and protects the small local manufacturers. Fortunately, or unfortunately, large foreign manufacturers were able to keep the knowhow such as engine and automatic transmission, AC compressor, and started manufacturing smaller cars to win the market under these policies.

While the examples above illustrated the negative effects of government policies, positive examples do exist. One such example is the healthcare reform in China, where the government increased the number and type of drugs covered by the Medicare program. As a result, both local and foreign pharmaceutical companies have benefited.

PRC National Development and Reform Commission (NDRC)

If you work for an MNC or work in the food, construction or energy sectors, you probably have heard of NDRC – National Development and Reform Commission, which was established in 2008 by the State Council. Its responsibilities include: medium and long term planning of China's economy, approving major national construction projects (like the subway or high-speed railway), major foreign investment projects, and overseas resource excavation projects (such as offshore oil fields) and even gas prices at the pump. The State Administration of Grain, National Energy Administration both report directly to NDRC. Foreign capital invested projects that are less than $300 million require approval from the local Development and Reform Commission. Projects over the limit must seek approval from the central NDRC, which could take months to complete. In addition, foreign companies and companies in food, construction and energy sectors need to pay close attention to policies issued by the NDRC, because new policies could lead to major upheavals in the industry! Some people also say that reporters will look at the queue at a local printing shop outside of NDRC office to determine the intensity and strength of the government's investment into the country. It is a pretty good proxy to forecast China's future economic growth. Thus NDRC acts as the central planning arm of the Chinese government, and has earned a nick name of Mini State Council in China with higher authority than many provincial governors.

Provincial Level Authorities

Just like China is not one China, each province has its own policies in addition to the central government. This is similar to the US concept where each state has its own set of laws, before the interstate commerce law was passed. Take China Mobile, the largest wireless carrier in the world with 740 million subscribers, as an example. Each provincial unit of China Mobile operates as an independent subsidiary and owns its separate P&L. Each subsidiary can only conduct business within the province. For my first year living in China, I had a Beijing mobile number. A year later when I relocated to Shanghai, I had to change to a Shanghai mobile number. Using a Beijing mobile phone number in Shanghai not only meant an expensive roaming bill every month, but people in Shanghai would have to pay long distance charges to reach me by dialling a prefix '0' in front of my number. Moreover, I could not obtain the official receipt for my Beijing phone bill from the China Mobile office in Shanghai for reimbursement by my company. But switching is not straightforward either as the number is not transferrable. To terminate my mobile contract in Beijing, I had to physically be present at the China Mobile office in Beijing, while Shanghai China Mobile office had no access, nor authority to make changes to my Beijing account. If a mobile phone number within the same carrier can get this complicated, imagine running a small business trying to navigate the cross-province maze!

Since each province has its own policies, setting up a business operation in one province means you can only do business and sell products within that province, but not in other provinces. For instance, if you produce cookies in Shanghai it does not mean you can sell them in Suzhou, which is merely a 45 minutes' drive away. The reason, of course, is tax related. Each province is seeking rent from businesses through tax. My friend Jenny opened a candy company in Shanghai, and she also opened a few representative offices in the neighboring provinces to deal with local customers. Her representative offices were not allowed to take customer orders. All business orders must be processed by the headquarter office in Shanghai. If a local customer needed to place an order urgently, and the representative office for some reason had to take the order, they needed to hide the paper trail so that it was recorded properly as if the sale was done in Shanghai headquarters. If the local commerce bureau officer suddenly performed an inspection at the representative office, and found the order paper trail, the company would be fined.

Ever-changing Policies

While many Westerners admire how quickly Chinese government implements and executes new policies, the reality is that mistakes are often made and carried out quickly without due process. While living in China, we often hear locals complain about rapid changes in policies. Locals made fun of it with a rhyme: "Communist Party is our sun, wherever it shines wherever bright; Communist Party policies are our moon, beginning of the month and middle of the month are different."

That explains why LLEs are short-sighted since no one can afford to plan for the long term. Let's use the housing policy as an example. A few years ago when the Chinese government wanted to promote economic growth, it introduced policies to stimulate real estate investments including tax refund for down payments and made banks provide subsidized mortgage rates. Then all of a sudden the government realized the property market was turning into an overheating bubble. It immediately halted the old policies and introduced new ones to suppress the property market. Chapter 2.4 already talked about how the big cities kept changing its housing policy and purchase restraint order. Even locals do not know if they are allowed to buy a property or not in the city they reside.

Beijing encouraged residents to buy cars one day, but started to limit license plate with an auction, with 2% success rate the next day, increased parking rates all over the city, and limiting even-odd plate number to drive only half of the weekdays. Traffic rules also change every year. If you drive in China then you had better pay attention to the latest rules. Streets that are two-way one day may turn into one-way streets the next day. Don't trust your GPS or Google Map blindly.

The same phenomenon applies to public holiday schedules. The State Council announces the official public holiday schedule for the entire following year in mid-December, 15-20 days before the turn of the New Year. If you want to arrange travel plans for New Year and

Chinese New Year holidays, you will not be able to confirm on the exact date until mid or late December.

I was once the victim of changing policies. In September 2009, I received notification from my media buying company that the government had just announced a new policy starting on January 1, 2010, TV advertising of feminine hygiene products was not allowed to be aired during "meal times," or times for breakfast, lunch, and dinner. I was responsible for next year's TV advertising spot plan for Kotex (a feminine hygiene product). This sudden change really turned our original plan on its head. Since the government had already announced the new policy, there was no point of arguing. We quickly changed the plan to ensure compliance, which meant added cost and delay to our execution.

To businesses in the western world, the government is usually there to ensure a fair playing field and enforce the market conditions and contracts. In China, the government directs the businesses as their more senior leaders. I could not stress enough the importance to know the policies and maintain a close contact with the government so that you know what's to come. Don't fall victim to an oversight of changing policies.

3 . 3

The Unspoken Rules

Unspoken rules, we all know that means they are not written down anywhere, but people know that these cultural rules exist and must comply to be part of the society. What do they actually mean? How do they apply to everyday life? All the scenarios and examples mentioned in this section happen in China's business world every single day. Your company's employee guidebook will not talk about them, but everyone knows. If you are able to internalize these points, your colleagues and business partners in China will be very impressed. No doubt they will think you really know how to do business in China!

Face - "Mian Zi (面子)"

Face is a very important concept in China, it means maintaining the most basic mutual respect that forms the fabrics of the society. There has been many books on the topic, but the true meaning still eludes people from different cultures. What does it actually mean by giving face? What does it mean by not giving face? Here we will cite a few real-life examples to better illustrate the point.

Ms. Xu used to be a sales manager at an international medical device company in China. A few years ago, she accompanied her

American colleague, Global Sales Vice President, who flew to China from the headquarter to visit a few local 3A hospitals and their senior management in Beijing (3A designates the highest grade hospitals in China). As they were wrapping up the meeting, Mr. Sales VP shook hands with everyone on the hospital management team who were present. Since there were quite a lot of people at the meeting, Mr. Sales VP missed one of the department heads before he left. A few years later, that very head of department was promoted to the head of the hospital. Since his new appointment, all business with Ms. Xu's medical device company was put on hold. Ms. Xu did not know what had transpired, but later discovered the story where years ago the head of the hospital lost face in front of all his colleagues and felt ignored and belittled by the visitor. Unfortunately for Ms. Xu's company that a grudge was held for so long. Multiple requests to meet in person and amend the situation were coldly rejected. Not knowing the intricacies of giving face at the right moment made Ms. Xu lose a large account. Since then, Ms. Xu paid extra attention and prepped people before important meetings. She carefully made note of everyone who attended the meeting including their titles, and made sure she shook hands with everyone before and after the meeting. She would go as far as acknowledge the secretary or office helper who served her tea. When greeting and shaking hands, she would always start from the most senior person and work her way down. If the order was messed up, the senior folks would feel that they "lost face" as well.

Since face is such an important social element, it applies to both government SOEs and private companies. Ms. Yang, a sales manager at a multi-national consumer product company had a meeting with the buyer of a local retail chain store before Mid-Autumn Festival. This local retail chain sold its own branded mooncake and pre-paid mooncake vouchers. The buyer told Ms. Yang that his boss had given every buyer a sales quota on these vouchers. The buyer directly told Ms. Yang to give him face by purchasing vouchers to meet sales target. When asked point blank, Ms. Yang must comply and bought 20 mooncake vouchers on the spot. Helping the buyer met his sales quota at that moment of desperation really gave face. To reciprocate, an equally important concept, the buyer offered to give Ms. Yang's company free exposure on its flyer without any sales commitment. It is obvious to many that the short-sightedness of the local firm's owner made them lose the potentially more profitable advertising revenue in exchange for a few boxes of mooncakes. While the short term revenue increased, the long run pricing power of its key displays and weakness shown to its customer could be multiple times more damaging.

Giving face to internal team members is just as important when facing external clients. What happened to my friend Ken serves a very good lesson to those who need to deal with colleagues in China. Ken, a senior management executive at a MNC, was attending an internal global conference in Shanghai. Senior executives from many other countries were present. At the cocktail party, Ken was chatting with a group of his peers, and out of nowhere, one of his American colleagues criticized Ken's subordinate in front of everyone, complaining about the staff's capability. Ken was upset and felt that he was losing face in front of everyone, particularly with his direct supervisor present! Suppressing his emotions, Ken defended his subordinate with a smiling face, which is a cultural practice not to show in public. Ken admitted privately later that he'd be very happy to listen to his American colleague if he had voiced his complaint one-on-one. Criticizing his subordinate in front of everyone was the same as criticizing him for mismanagement, a professional context of a slap on this face. Ken was still mad when he told the story.

It is easy to make the mistake of giving feedback to an underperforming employee's manager in an unplanned setting where the topic just jumped into mind. But it is more important to remember not to openly criticize someone in public, particularly because nepotism is very common in many local companies. The one you criticized could be related to the manager personally, which may jeopardize your relationship with the manager. So if you have to give negative feedback next time, better check the background of the person and make sure not to put your foot in your mouth.

Give Face by Calling Someone with the Suffix "Zong (总)"

Giving someone face can be as simple as the way you address him or her. The most common way to address someone senior is by calling someone's last name followed by the word "Zong (总)." For example, Lin Zong for Mr. Lin, Zhang Zong for Mr. Zhang. Zong means head of a department, organization or superiority. It is similar to calling someone Doctor, Sir, or Professor in the western world. If you find it difficult to pronounce the word Zong, it is perfectly ok to address someone as Mr. or Mrs. + his or her last name. On the other hand, your Chinese counterpart will surely be very impressed and flattered if you address him or her with the title Zong.

FACE IS BIGGER THAN ANYTHING

I was taking the subway in Shanghai one afternoon, and there was a couple from outside of Shanghai with a 4 year old boy. They were dressed nice and clean, typical of first time visitors to Shanghai trying to blend in to the mega metropolitan. Out of nowhere the mother pulled down her son's pants and told him to pee in the subway car! It is not uncommon for uncivilized people to do their business in public. Many passengers and I rushed over to stop the couple, trying to explain to them that this was not acceptable to pee in the car and that they should take their son to the station's washroom. Realizing their lack of knowledge in big cities, the couple gave excuses of an emergency so as not to lose face. All of us insisted that it was unacceptable behavior. In the end, the couple felt embarrassed, yet not quite ready to give in and lose faces in front of their first trip to Shanghai. The mother then took out a thermos cup and said "Son, just pee inside the thermos! We will go buy a new one later! So is that ok now?" And the boy obliged! The rest of the subway passengers were so stunned speechless. This is a great example of how having face is more important than having good reasons or logical behaviors!

"Ling Dao (领导)" = Leader

Another common term people use to address their supervisor is "Ling Dao," which literally means leader. Its usage is very similar to the western term boss. It is particularly common in governments, SOEs and LLEs, as a more personal but equally respectful title as Zong. You will see that throughout this book, the term Ling Dao is used interchangeably as boss.

A Show of Extravagance (排场)

A show of extravagance means displaying the best of your possessions to others to elevate your status or strength, much like a peacock in a mating dance. This is particularly important in business settings, to ensure that you don't lose face. It functions as a credit score mechanism to disclose one's own financial strength and credit worthiness for subsequent business dealings. For western companies, you rarely pick up clients or internal team members from the airport and accompany them to their hotels unless they are VIPs. But in China, it is almost mandatory to have your staff, if not yourself, do the pickup and welcome dinner in person. It is considered rude to leave your guest or boss figure out their way to the hotel and eat by themselves. Worse, they may think the company is not willing or unable to spend the money to hire a driver or pay for dinner. Next time when you get off the plane in China, pay attention to all the people waiting at the arrival gate with name signs for their guests. Pick up and drop off are the most basic display of extravagance and hospitality to your guests.

NO SHOW OF EXTRAVAGANCE = NO FACE

A few years ago the company I worked for was responsible for hosting the annual conference for its industry association, whose participants included the CEOs and top management of all the industry players. The PR Director responsible for organizing the conference picked an extravagant five-star hotel in the suburban Shanghai for the event. Unfortunately in an effort to save money for the company, the PR Director picked a small but modern restaurant located next to the hotel to host the evening banquet. The restaurant was nicely decorated and was very cozy. Normally a great choice for family and friends gathering, but it was far from extravagant for a business banquet. When the PR Director's boss arrived at the restaurant, his face turned half black, a term for anger that is often used by Chinese. To make things worse, the PR Director did not budget enough for wine that went with the dinner. To save money, she only ordered two bottles of wine for each table of ten guests. Given the way people drink in China, two bottles were emptied in the first five minutes. When the PR Director's boss realized there were not enough wine for the guests, his face turned completely black! He even showed his dissatisfaction to the PR Director in front of me, criticizing her for being too stingy, and now other companies probably thought our company was in financial troubles, etc. One must know that criticizing someone publicly really makes the person lose face! After this incident, I learned that it is not always right to help company to save money in China. It really depends on the situation!

Another example is when commencing a large scale project jointly with SOEs or LLEs, there must be a formal staged contract signing ceremony, stone laying ceremony or ribbon cutting ceremony. If there isn't one, your local partner probably consider this project trivial. Today many private companies also picked up the ritual when launching their products to stage an Apple product launch style event to invite all the government officials, media and business partners to witness the glorious moment.

An investment banking friend once went to a lower tier cities to meet with local entrepreneurs for a potential deal. He stayed at the most expensive hotel in the city, which was paltry compared to the investment banks travel policy. To go to the client office, he hired a black Audi A6L, since this is THE standard issue by most senior government officials in China. It gave the superficial impression to be related to the government! It is important to show extravagance here because a lot of the local entrepreneurs could not tell if your company is credible. Given a lot of swindlers in China, one of the best ways to judge a person's financial strength was based on these external traits. There was an old Chinese saying of "salute to one's expensive outfit before salute to the person," and it is still true today.

Extravagance is not only important among SOEs and LLEs, it is equally so among smaller businesses. If your company needs to host a distributor sales conference, then the conference should be set at the best hotel you can find in that city, and your guests have to dine at the best restaurants in the hotel (Chinese food only, paired with French red wine). That way, your distributors will feel that they are being respected and having face. Most importantly, these shows act as reassurance to your distributors about the financial strength of your company. They are more likely to feel confident and less likely to bargain on prices and terms in reciprocation. In a nutshell, in China one cannot lose face, and one also cannot afford to lose the extravagance!

Company annual dinner party usually takes place before Chinese New Year. Annual dinner is undoubtedly the most important event of the year for the company and is definitely a show of extravagance! Leadership and management team would walk on the red carpet, sign on a wall like Hollywood stars. Professional film production house would be hired to design the stage design, year-in-review video production, TV anchor as master of ceremonies, and professional show run-down, etc. Nothing short of the Oscar ceremony. Employees are also dedicated to the performance, since it is a rare chance for employees to perform. And if the subordinates perform well in the annual dinner, the supervisor will earn face too! On the other hand, the supervisor will lose face if the subordinates do a lousy job. Certain large SOEs have dedicated teams in the union whose full time job is just to organize a successful and entertaining annual party! So plan your next China trip around the same time as the annual dinner to get a taste. You will be amazed by the hidden talents of your colleagues!

Ranking (级别)

Ranking is another important way to separate people into different classes in the Chinese society or businesses, where hierarchy is more strictly observed than western countries. As a guest, you will need to pay extra attention to people's ranks, especially dealing with SOEs or government organizations. Knowing people's ranks is a prerequisite to giving face by knowing exactly what to do and the order in which they should be performed. Sounds complicated, let see a few real life examples.

Same Rank to Same Rank

One of the key principles in Confucius's teachings is the respect of ranking. In the ancient times, the emperor was on the highest level of the social hierarchy and was at the same place as God, naturally everyone must respect the Emperor. Government officials are above ordinary citizens, and teachers are considered at a higher level than merchants, etc. The concept of rank is deeply embedded in the Chinese culture. As a result, this hierarchical thinking is transferred into today's business world. If you are at the manager level, your Chinese counterpart will only send another manager level employee to do business with you. It is likewise for staff at all other levels.

In business meetings, you need to know in advance the rankings of the other side, since you need to have representations of the same ranking at the meeting. A friend of mine in the local real estate development business told me that every time when he arranged a meeting with the government office, the person in contact always asked him for a complete list of participants including name, title and department. The government side then would, based on this list, arrange officials of the same ranks to attend the meeting. In case there was a change in the participant list, the government side must be notified promptly so that adjustments could be made. If the most senior person from the business side did not show up in a meeting due to last minute changes, the government would consider this company highly unprofessional and disrespectful by not giving face to their highest official. As a consequence, the government office would likely turn down any proposal after the meeting and refuse any future meetings. At the same time, it would also be inappropriate if the company arranged a more senior person without notifying the government side. This move would make the government attendees uncomfortable, as it is beyond their pay grade to have meetings with Lingdao's counterpart, equivalent to not giving face to the Lingdao. Your kind consideration sometimes does more harm than good by surprising the government officials. The only accepted and appropriate way is to maintain the harmony and balance consistently.

In my previous job as a marketing director for a consumer products company, I was asked by the sales manager to attend a meeting with a European retailer because the other side also planned their merchandising director to attend. Subsequently we needed a director level person to show respect. Similarly, when I made a request to attend a sales meeting, the sales team refused because the customer did not plan to have a director at the meeting, and it would be inappropriate for me to join.

Similarly in the private equity world, the partner of the fund meets with the CEO and chairman, the director interviews the VPs and the associates would talk to all the other team members at the company. No line should be crossed despite the obvious drawbacks of information transparency and flow, otherwise the the target company would consider the fund not respectful and trying to dig out the dirt behind their back. Clearly the rank-matching activity for meetings is common for all business and government offices.

Next time when your Chinese client asks who on your side will attend the upcoming meeting, you know exactly what he is trying to find out: whom on their own side should attend and whether the meeting is important.

Discussion Topics by Government Ranks

My local real estate developer friend also emphasized the importance of discussing only the appropriate topics as they should be relevant to the ranks of the government officials:

- Provincial- or City-Level Party Secretary: Party secretaries are more senior than the governor or the mayor. As a result only the top macro-level topics or topics directly related to the KPIs set by the central government should be discussed. Contribution to GDP is usually the most important metric used by central government to measure their work for promotion purpose.

- Municipal Level Government Officials: Benefits to local city, e.g. tax revenue a project can bring to the municipal government; total number of newly registered companies, particularly the "in fashion" industries promoted by the municipal or provincial government, like e-Commerce, modern logistics, bio-tech; total amount of registered capital (capital density).

- District Level Government Officials: Total number of newly registered companies; total amount of registered capital (capital density); development direction of the district, whether the business is setting up headquarter or branches, opening a new development project, building a new landmark in the district, etc.

No Rank Skipping

If an SOE employee encounters a problem at work, he must first report it to his direct supervisor. Only when the direct supervisor finds it necessary to elevate the matter, the issue can go to the next level. Employees are not supposed to skip his direct superior and report to the more senior levels. This is very important to maintain the order within the SOE. The same principle applies to external parties as well. If you are doing business with an SOE, you should only speak with your counterpart who is at the same rank as you. Even if you encounter a problem, you can only ask your boss to speak with your counterpart's boss. If you bypass your counterpart and approach his boss directly, you will either be ignored, or if you are lucky, his boss will ask his subordinates to follow up, and it will only be one-time. Moreover, your counterpart will find you not giving face and consider him incapable. By now you probably have ruined relationship with your counterpart. Good luck with the next step or next project.

In any province, the provincial-level city (Tier 1 city) always has priority in resource allocation as mentioned in Chapter 1. Second priority goes to the prefecture-level cities (Tier 2 cities), then county-level cities (Tier 3 cities), and so on. Even if a Tier 2 city has higher GDP contribution than the Tier 1 city, resource allocation still follows this order. For instance, in Jiangsu province, GDP of Suzhou (a Tier 2 city) is higher than Nanjing (Tier 1 city). However, Suzhou government could not build its subway system before Nanjing does. Only after Nanjing started to build its subway then Suzhou and other Tier 2 cities could have approvals for subway constructions. This is a way Suzhou officials observing the ranks and giving face to Nanjing officials.

Order of Giving Speech

The rituals of rank-following goes all the way to the order presentations are given in SOE meetings: after the most senior officials arrive and announce the start of the meeting, the most junior person first presents the report, next the second most junior person gives his comments, then the people next level up give their comments, and so on. After hearing the comments from everyone in the meeting, the Lingdao finally gives his comments and draws the conclusion. Once Lingdao finished his speech, no one else in the meeting can give further comments. No debate, no discussion, and decisions are made. Even if someone forgets to present an important piece of information, it was not appropriate to speak up after Lingdao finishes. Once the Lingdao makes a final decision, it cannot be challenged or changed. As you know, the Lingdao are always correct and firm, thus it is unnecessary to make any changes. Don't dare to play devil's advocate with Lingdao, even if when asked to, unless you wanted to be fired. After each meeting, a formal meeting minute is written, and every participant of the meeting must read and ensure nothing is left out and Lingdao's words are captured correctly. Once proofread by everyone, the meeting minute is printed out, stamped with an official seal, and became an official document.

Government Officials Ranking

Given the importance of rank-matching when meeting with government officials, you should first understand the different government official ranking levels to avoid any mishaps. Illustration 3.3 shows the ranking and titles of government officials of China. Director-General and above are all considered senior government officials (the highlighted ones).

PRC Government Officials Ranking

LEVEL OF CIVIL SERVANTS	RANK	EXAMPLE
1	总理 Premier	总理 Premier
2-3	副总理 Vice Premier	副总理，国务委员 Vice Premier, Member of State Council
3-4	正部级（正省级） Minister (Province Level)	部长，省长，直辖市市长 Minister, Governor of Province, Mayor of Centrally-Administered Municipality
4-5	副部级（副省级） Vice Minister (Vice Province Level)	副部长，副省长 Vice Minister, Vice Governor
5-7	正厅级（地市级） Director-General (Prefecture Level)	省、直辖市里的局长 Director-General in Province or Centrally-Administered Municipality
6-8	副厅级 Associate Director	
7-10	正处级（县团级） Division Chief (County Level)	
8-11	副处级 Associate Division Chief	
9-12	正科级 Section Chief	
9-13	副科级 Associate Section Chief	
9-14	科员 Officer	
9-15	办事员 Clerk	

Illustration 3.3 PRC Government Officials Ranking

It is important to note that the Communist Party leads the government in China, not the other way around or even parallel. Remember the term Party-Government-Union-Youth League? The Party always comes first. In Illustration 3.3, the most senior official is the Premier. This is only referring to the government's executive branch. In terms of real power in China, the General Secretary of the Party, the President and Chairman of the Military, typically the same person in recent years, is above the Premier. In a given province, the Party Secretary of Province is of higher rank than the Governor of the Province. Likewise, the Party Secretary of City is of higher level than the Mayor. This is an extremely important fact. If you mess up the titles, you are surely asking for troubles.

FIRST COMES THE SECRETARY, FOLLOWED BY THE MAYOR

A real story told by my friend Andy, head of legal department of a foreign owned high-tech company. A few years ago, Mr. Yu Zheng Sheng, then Party Secretary of Shanghai, and Mr. Han Zheng, then Mayor of Shanghai visited his company. The company's head of Asia Pacific and head of China was accompanying Party Secretary Yu, and the CFO and COO to accompany Mayor Han. You probably guessed that Secretary Yu is more senior in ranks than Major Han, which is important to remember when receiving government guests. Andy happened to be walking right behind them, and noticed that during the entire visit, Mayor Han was always walking precisely 3 steps behind Secretary Yu, with the rest officials following further behind. Despite the Mayor title, Mr. Han constantly paid attention to ensure these unspoken rules were followed. We were convinced that with Mr. Han's political savviness, he could go places.

Note: In the 18th National Congress of the Communist Party of China that took place in Nov 2012, Mr. Yu Zheng Sheng was promoted to the Standing Committee of the Politburo, while Mr. Han Zheng was promoted to be the Party Secretary of Shanghai - Mr. Yu's old post as the most powerful official in Shanghai.

Relationship "Guanxi (关系)" in Business

Chapter 2.5 discussed the guanxi elements in daily life, and it is equally if not more important in business deals. In business operations, there are two facets of Guanxi. One side of Guanxi is about establishing a good relationship with your business partners on a regular basis. Chinese always believe in building strong personal ties before business deals, partly to mitigate the weak legal protection. You are not only building a relationship with the person, but also building trust for doing business together. This is particularly important to the older generation where they don't expect much protection by the conventional legal system. So how do you build relationship? It is not necessarily through red pockets or gifts, most of the time it is through frequent visits and sharing similar interests. This is similar to sales representatives meeting with merchandisers, medical sales representatives visiting doctors and nurses on a regular basis etc. It all goes back to the basic principle of doing business: in a highly competitive world, how do you ensure your customer will remember you, and think of you whenever a business opportunity comes up? Recall, recency and repeat. A friend who is a sales director for hospital channels told me that she requested that every sales staff must visit assigned hospitals at least once a month. The important ones must be visited at least bi-weekly or more often! The frequency of visit is in everyone's KPIs. In fact, Chinese people also believe in the phrase "out of sight, out of mind." It is very common in the western world of maintaining good relationship with your customers through frequent visits, so this should not be surprising to anyone.

Another facet of guanxi is about receiving benefits through the established relationship. It could be as simple as shortening the normal procedures to speed things up. As mentioned earlier, Chinese focus on matching rankings and following procedures when it comes to getting things done. You will have a competitive advantage if you can get things done faster than your competitors. Just like my friend who is a sales manager of a B2B business in China told me, if you have good relationship with the purchasing director of a large corporation, you can bypass all his junior staff and go directly to him to discuss business opportunities. People under the purchasing director will also probably process faster to get the deals done. But the relationship with the purchasing director needs to be a strong one, otherwise, as mentioned in the previous section, skipping ranks to get things done may anger the junior staff to delay things and make things worse for you.

For serious offenses such as building relationship through bribery, there are plenty of news on caught officials. Given the serious consequences, it is important to steer clear of the legal line to avoid long term damage to the business.

I have been living in China for almost ten years, and I have never encountered a case where I needed to use guanxi to solve a problem. A lot of my local and foreign friends who are doing business in China also told me that they never needed to resort to guanxi. So unless your business or job requires you to deal with government organizations (particularly the licensing approval departments), SOEs, or LLEs, building guanxi will then become important. If you only need to deal with MNCs, things are much more straightforward.

Gifting

The Chinese culture places a lot of emphasis on reciprocation. If someone gives you a gift, you must do them a favor in return. Thus, gifting becomes an important tool for building guanxi: you gift when you meet someone, you gift when you say farewell to someone, you gift when you want something done, you gift when you want to get business, and you gift if you want to thank someone for a favor performed. As a result, gifting accounts for a very high proportion in the country's total consumer spending, especially in luxury goods sales. There has been a study estimating that gifting accounts for nearly 30% of the country's sales of luxury goods. In my opinion, the proportion should be even higher. Luxury products in China are selling at 30% to 50% higher price than in Hong Kong or Taiwan, thanks to import duties, value-added tax, sales tax, operation tax, etc. This is why mainland Chinese go crazy when shopping in US, Europe and some parts of Asia. So why so many luxury product stores are opening in China despite the fact that prices are cheaper overseas? There are two reasons: first, these stores are for government and military officials who are not allowed to leave the country for national security reasons. They can only shop in China and they have very strong purchasing powers. The second reason is attributed to gifting that cannot wait for overseas purchases.

Whenever you need help from someone, you gift. Gifting is also seasonal in China. It usually starts around Mid-Autumn Festival and continues until Christmas and New Year's Eve, finally peaking at Chinese New Year. Everything cools down after that. But over the last few years, the time around Dragon Boat Festival sees another spike in demand for gifts. The impact of gifting can actually affect people's livelihood as well. Since there is a large number of gifts to be hand delivered to Beijing's central government officials before Chinese New Year and Mid-Autumn Festival, traffic becomes highly congested. In case you need to travel to Beijing before these gifting seasons, you should be prepared for heavily congested traffic conditions. Accompanying peak seasons for gifting, there are also peak seasons for returning gifts. On the e-commerce site Taobao, people put their excess gifts for sale, creating a liquid market. So if you want to find some bargain sales, go on Taobao right after Chinese New Year.

Now that you know when to gift, how about the kind of gift that you should give? By default, you give rice dumplings for Dragon Boat Festival, and mooncakes for Mid-Autumn Festival. Hairy crab has become another popular gift idea during the fall season. What if you want to give something more expensive? Hard liquors and French wines are also popular gift ideas. Remember there is a saying among IT managers that "you can't go wrong buying an IBM," there is a similar saying for gifting in China "you can't go wrong giving Mao Tai (茅台)," the most well-known white liquor which we will talk about in Chapter 3.5 Drinking Etiquette. Besides Mao Tai, Lafite has become a highly popular gift item in China recently. The key point here is not about the taste, it is about popularity and scarcity of the gift items. High end Mao Tai are expensive ($200 for a 500mL bottle), yet they have high demand but limited supply, which makes them hard to find. So the rationale behind giving Mao Tai is this: "See! Mao Tai is so expensive and hard to find these days, but I still got it for you!" You really give face to your Lingdao or client by giving them Mao Tai as gift! But before you go buy Mao Tai or Lafite, you have to know that there is an industry of fake producers targeting these products. We all know that there are limited supplies of high end Mao Tai and Lafite in the market, yet demand is high and the profit margin is huge! Be very careful where you buy these products in China. You will look bad if you get your Lingdao or client the fake stuff! In case you receive Mao Tai or Lafite as gifts, I suggest you do not drink it, since the majority of what is selling in the market is fake. You may consider selling them to stores. There are a lot of mom-and-pop style liquor stores who are willing to buy back expensive liquors and wines, usually at 50% of the market price.

China has a huge market for gift cards and prepaid cards driven by the gifting culture. This is because by giving gift cards or prepaid cards, it is like giving out cash but in a more discrete way and untraceable. In the high end supermarkets in every major city, if you pay attention at the checkout counters, you can always spot shoppers paying with these prepaid cards, but obviously those shoppers are not your stereotypical customers who shop at these places. You will notice the same thing happening in high end department stores as well. I was told that in one of the high end department stores in Shanghai, over 50% of sales come from prepaid cards! That tells you the importance of prepaid or gift cards in driving consumer spending in China! It is also very easy in case you have received gift cards and want to turn them into cash. You can sell them online or offline. Online is of course through Taobao. For offline selling, you may notice there are always some "mysterious" people hanging outside of high end department stores or shopping malls. These people make a living by buying and selling the prepaid or gift cards. They usually buy back at 90% of the face value, and sell out at 95% of the value; making a 5% margin on every transaction. In fact, the second hand prepaid or gift cards market is well established in China! But note that at the end of 2012, the Ministry of Commerce announced a new rule: personal ID information is required with the purchase of gift cards valued over RMB 1000 (~USD $160). As a result, most of the gift cards in the market only offer maximum face value of RMB 1000. Of course, you can always buy multiples of RMB 1,000 gift cards to circumvent the rule.

Gallery 3.1 Man buying and selling cash cards outside of a high end department store in Shanghai

Other great gift ideas include luxury handbags and watches. My friend's husband works at the overseas branch of a large Chinese enterprise in Munich, Germany. He said that a lot of the European branches of the large Chinese enterprises have VIP status at most of the luxury goods stores in Europe. His company often asks him to buy a large number of luxury goods and bring back to China as gifts to officials and clients. As a VIP, these luxury goods stores will give his company 30% off all year round. Last time when my friend's husband came back from Munich, he brought back 12 luxury watches as gifts for his clients and his VIPs. But in late 2012, the Weibo media exposed a case of a few government officials wearing luxury watches in public, and they were subsequently expelled from the Party and relieved of their administrative posts. Afterwards, many government officials are wary of wearing luxury watches in public or even receiving them as gifts! Another friend working at a European luxury goods conglomerate told me that after the press exposure incident, luxury watch sales in China dropped by 30% in the second half of 2012 compared to the first half of the same year!

If it is not a good idea to give luxury watches as gifts, what about luxury cars? Well, it is certainly less common to give luxury cars as gifts, because it is hard to justify the price. Even if you are a senior government official, it is not likely that your salary is high enough to afford a luxury car, particularly when luxury car price is 50-90% higher than that in the US. So what happens is that the luxury car is usually generously lent to a friend. A European luxury car brand has estimated that 40% of their car buyers are not the drivers of their cars. I also personally know a 2nd Generation of a government official living in Shanghai who told me that the Maserati he drives every day is borrowed from a friend. He also has a Ferrari in his garage that is also borrowed from another friend! Well, I wish I had friends like his.

Some people do not want to be seen as materialistic, which leads to a new culture trend of arts and antiques. Many people in power who are used to receiving gifts are unimpressed by cash or common luxury goods. Antiques and artworks have become another popular gift idea. Not only because artworks and antiques usually appreciate over time, it is also hard to put a current value on them even when the receiving end is accused for bribery, but also the receivers will feel special and cultured for receiving such unique gifts. If you think antiques and artworks are not special or powerful enough, you may also consider getting "Doctor Honoris Causa" or "Emeritus Professor" title to someone as a gift!

So we have talked about what you can give as gifts. There are also a lot of items you cannot give because of implications from the Chinese culture. For instance, clock sounds like going to someone's funeral in Chinese, and giving shoes and books sounds the same as bad luck. Green hat or cap is also bad because wearing one means that your wife has cheated on you. So if your company logo is green, no matter which shade of green, you can forget about making hats when designing souvenirs. Also in the western world, people like to un-wrap gifts in front of the givers to show appreciation. In China, it is the opposite. People find it impolite to open gifts in front of the givers. So if you give a gift to your friend in China, do not expect that he or she will open it in front of you.

Please bear in mind, this section is not encouraging the act of excessive gifting to build relationships. But you must understand that gifting is an important part of the Chinese business culture. Giving your clients rice dumplings and mooncakes during the traditional Chinese festivals, or small and meaningful souvenirs at conferences are appropriate and common practices in China. In fact, people I interviewed for this book realized that many foreigners or employees of MNCs do not know about gifting, or they do not take or give gifts due to company policy or Foreign Corruption Practices Act, yet they can still conduct business as usual. The influence from the west is changing the common practice of gifting in China. Some of them actually asked me not to mention gifting in my book, or else foreigners will get the wrong impression and get into the gifting practice. But it will be wrong for me not to mention the gifting topic, given its prevalence and importance. On the other hand, President Xi Jinping is strongly against corruption and advocated clean government and business practices in his inaugural speech as the leader of the Communist Party. Shortly after that, the State Administration of Radio Films and Television also announced a new rule which bans the word 'gifting' in all advertisements! The Chinese government is also working towards a clean business environment by discouraging corruption and gifting.

Receiving Gifts

In the last section we talked about giving out gifts, so what happens if you are the one receiving the gifts? As long as you are doing business with Chinese companies, you will have your chance of receiving gifts

'PRE-DETERMINED' LUCKY DRAW?

Li is the owner of an online marketing company. His company needs to give gifts to his clients all year round, and the most popular gift items these days are Apple products. So whenever his employees went abroad for business trips, he would ask his employees to get the latest models of iPhone or iPad if they were not yet available in China. How did he give out the stockpile of gifts? Usually his company would organize conferences and invite clients to attend. At the end of every conference there would be a "lucky draw." Even though it was called a lucky draw, every draw was predetermined. Who got what was all planned out in advance, so that the smaller client account would get an iWatch, while the large client account would receive an iPad. I asked Li why he would go through all these hassles to give out gifts? Then he reminded me that a lot of companies had policies in terms of employees receiving gifts. But you could somehow "legitimize" the gift giving by calling it a gift from the lucky draw. Also, some people might turn the gift down if you gave it to them directly. But people usually wouldn't turn down a lucky draw prize.

for sure. So what if someone, your supplier for instance, gives you a gift? What should you do? Well, we all know that there is no free lunch in this world. Once you receive a gift offered by someone, you must do them a favor in return. As mentioned earlier, Chinese culture puts a strong emphasis on reciprocation. If you accept someone's gift, you are sending a signal that you are willing to help.

When I started my first job in China, I was offered an expensive gift within the first six months on the job. That was the time when I took over a brand's operation. Since I had the say on how to spend the budget on advertising, a lot of media companies wanted to set up meetings and sell their products and services to me. One day, I got a call from a sales manager of a media company, let's call her Ms. M. Ms. M asked me out for dinner that night, saying that she wanted us to get to know one another better. Since I was somewhat new to living in China, I thought it doesn't hurt to make a new friend, so I agreed to meet her for dinner (when you read the section on dining later, you will know you really should not agree easily to have dinner with someone work related in China). So I picked a casual Cantonese style restaurant near my home. Once we were seated, Ms. M took the menu and wanted to order all the expensive dishes like shark fin, sea cucumber, etc. Fortunately I was able to stop her by telling her that I do not eat those things, so we ordered a few simple dishes and started chatting. Towards the end of the dinner, Ms. M took out a large Hermès paper bag. She told me that she just traveled to Europe, and since we were good friends, she bought me a Hermès scarf as a gift! I was puzzled about when we became good friends given this was the second time we met? Even if we were good friends, since I could be her potential client, it was not appropriate for me to take her gift, particularly an expensive item like that. So of course I turned her down. She insisted she wanted to give me the scarf, and I insisted that I could not take it. We pushed the scarf back and forth literally for about five minutes, and I almost gave up (imagine someone begging you to take a Hermès scarf - it is not easy to turn down)! Luckily the rational part of my brain won over my emotional part, and I firmly rejected Ms. M's gift. I remembered Ms. M mentioned that she bought a lot of chocolate from Switzerland, so I suggested her to give me chocolate instead. Ms. M knew I was the stubborn type who would not take the gift, so she finally gave up and took back the Hermès paper bag. I was relieved. No wonder why Ms. M was the top sales of her company! A few days later, Ms. M did send a few boxes of chocolate to my office, and of course I shared them with my colleagues. When I told my local friends about this incident later, they all laughed at me and said I should at least check out what was inside the Hermès paper bag! Maybe there was a stack of cash inside! After my dining experience with Ms. M, I became very selective when suppliers or clients invited me to business dinner.

So how do you decide whether to take a gift or not? First of all you should check your company's policy. Most companies, particularly MNCs, have very strict rules on the maximum face value of gifts which employees can receive, as part of the FCPA compliance rules. In case you are unsure whether it is appropriate to receive a certain gift, the best way is to report to your supervisor. Of course you do not need to be that cautious when it comes to receiving rice dumplings or mooncakes during the festival seasons, as long as they are not made of expensive ingredients like abalone, bird nests, caviars, etc. What I usually do when I receive these goodies is to share them with my colleagues, which also turns into a good team bonding opportunity!

Let me share another case on gifting. The previous company I worked for was going through renovation. One of the HR staff was in charge of the renovation work. He was fired after the company found out that the construction team doing the renovation work also renovated his home for free. So after that incident, his name was most likely be black-listed by most MNCs in China and it was unlikely that he would be able to find another job within the MNC circle. But how did the company find out about the side deal? Obviously the HR staff didn't tell others. Most likely it was the renovation company who leaked the information. So don't think under the table deals are secrets. Always think twice before you take someone's gift. I have heard plenty of cases where people got fired by their companies because of receiving gifts from suppliers or agencies.

Driver

What is so important about drivers in China? On multiple occasions, I was told not to underestimate the impact a driver can make. By drivers I mean the Lingdao's personal driver, or company car chauffeurs. Within LLEs or SOEs, the driver of the CEO is usually the most trusted person other than his secretary. Sometimes, the driver may even be more influential than the senior management of the company. There is one case where a driver of the CEO of a listed LLE was also in charge of the company's raw material procurement, quite interesting to most people. We all know that procurement usually involves large amount of the company's capital and cash flow. As a result, the senior management of that company also needed to give face to the driver. Later, the successor of this LLE was struggling to wring back the power from this driver as the CEO stepped down. There are also many real life cases in China where the senior government official's driver got promoted to become the department head of a government organization or the head of a county, etc. One of the most well-known examples is that the CEO of Ping An Insurance Group, Ma Ming Zhe used to be the driver of Yuan Geng, the Chairman of China Merchants Group (Ping An used to be a subsidiary of China Merchants Group). [15]

One should always respect others regardless of one's occupation. Nonetheless, you should pay extra attention when dealing with your Lingdao's driver. My friend who works at an SOE told me that whenever there was a large company dinner event, he would pre-arrange seating, meal, even souvenirs for the Lingdao's driver. During major festivals, he would also give gifts to the driver. Besides, a lot of juicy gossips and rumors usually are leaked from corporate drivers as well. So if you want to know the latest gossips in the company, make friends with the corporate drivers. At the same time, be careful of what you say in front of them. Even if you speak in English, the driver may actually understand.

Significance of Dining

Food is an integral part of the Chinese culture. Dining and drinking are important occasions for the Chinese to establish friendships and relationships either socially or for business. An entire book can be dedicated solely to the topics of dining and drinking alone, since there are so much subtle and intricate customs involved. The following sections will introduce you to some basic etiquettes so that you will not unintentionally offend the locals by assuming western customs.

No Such Thing as Casual Meal

In most western cultures, meals, particularly dinner, are considered personal and private affairs. Business is often conducted during office hours in a professional setting. Very rarely do you conduct business over lunch or dinner unless it really requires the intimacy and privacy. In China it is just the opposite. If you want to close a deal, you usually will ask the person out for lunch or dinner first so that you can establish mutual relationship in a relatively casual setting. If the meal goes well, then you can move on to talk about business cooperation.

Rule number one - do not easily accept lunch or dinner invitations with your clients or suppliers, especially if the meal is paid for by the other party. (It is ok if it is your local colleague inviting you to his or her home for a home cooked family dinner.) If you don't think there will be an opportunity to work together, it is best to turn down the invitation politely. If you agree to meet with someone for a meal, it sends a positive signal. There are also different implications to having lunch or dinner. Andrew, an American, was responsible for finding a new headquarter location in Shanghai for a US high-tech company. After he reviewed a few industrial parks in Shanghai, one of the industrial park developers extended an invitation for dinner. Andrew was inclined to accept the invitation, thinking it might be a good opportunity for him to make some local friends. Fortunately, his real estate agent reminded him that if he was not serious about the particular deal, he should not accept the dinner invitation. But if he had narrowed down to a few before the final decision, he could meet the developer for lunch because it would signify his seriousness without a commitment. Having dinner delivers a higher commitment than having lunch! After hearing what the real estate agent said, Andrew was shocked at the subtle complexity that he turned down the dinner politely.

Even though lunch is more relaxed than dinner and may not necessarily send a signal for commitment, you should not overlook its significance. Small local companies, especially those from the northern region, have the tradition of drinking alcoholic beverages with guests at lunch while drinking at dinner is a must. There was a time when my friend, who was a financial auditor, went to Shandong to conduct an auditory review on a local company that was recently acquired by his client. The management team of the acquired company insisted on taking the audit team to lunch right after they landed in Shandong. The team did not think much and agreed to go along. After they were seated at the restaurant, the management team ordered half a dozen of Chinese white liquor and started toasting (as a gesture to welcome the guests) before the food arrived. Shandong people are known for their hospitality and high tolerance of alcohol, so before lunch was done almost all the auditing team was drunk. The only member who was still sober was so concerned that he called back to the head office in Hong Kong and asked for help. Be mentally and physically prepared to drink the next time when you have to meet with your local client for lunch in small cities. If you have a physical condition or religious belief against alcohol, most people would understand and not force upon you. However the rest of the team may not be so lucky. It is important to have someone on the team who can take the bullet.

Organizing a Business Dinner

When it comes to organizing a business dinner, there are more rules and etiquettes than lunch. First, you need to book a private room for dinner, so that your guests can drink comfortably and feel secured to talk about sensitive topics, and sometimes avoid being seen. This is why many high end restaurants in China would have separate areas for private dining. Some of them have no publicly shared seatings at all, signifying its target clientele and price points.

Secondly, you need to know the number of guests attending the business dinner. It is important to have an approximately equal number of people from the guest side and the host side to attend, particularly when we talk about drinking in the subsequent section, you will understand the importance of having the same number of people from both sides.

Thirdly is the seating arrangement. Seating must reflect seniority so do not walk in and take any seat available. Always wait for the guest to show you. In most business dinners in the west, hosts and guests usually like to mix up so that people have the chance to get to know one another. In China, you should not mix the seating of your guests with the host side. There are specific rules for seating based on the attendees' seniority. Remember three major principles: (1) Facing the door to respect; (2) Facing East to respect; (3) Left side is superior than right side.

- The middle seat, usually facing the door, is called the "Guest of Honor" seat. It should be given to the most senior person from the host or guest side. In the event that the top host is higher ranked than the guest, such as a government official, this center seat is reserved for the highest ranked host.

- The seat on the left side of the Guest of Honor (or Head of Guest) is usually given to the most senior person from the host side, called the "Head of Host" seat.

- The seat to the right side of the Guest of Honor is given to the second most senior person from the guest side.

- Then dinner participants should be seated based on seniority. Basically, the closer the person sits to the Guest of Honor, the more senior the person is.

- If it is the same distance to the Guest of Honor, then the seat on the left side is of higher ranking than the seat on the right side.

- Usually it is the most junior person from the host side who is responsible for ordering for everyone and paying the bill. This person should be seated closest to the door so that he or she can easily communicate with the restaurant staff on guests' needs.

Formal Business Dinner Seating Arrangement

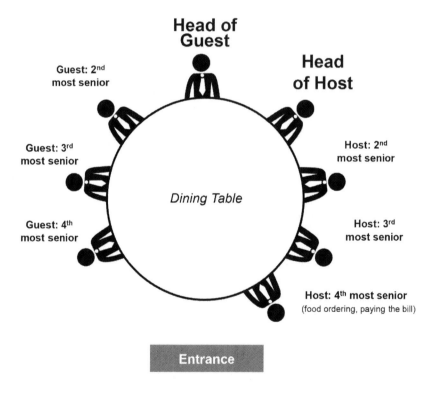

Illustration 3.4 Formal Business Dinner Seating Arrangement

These rules mainly apply to round dining tables where Chinese cuisines are served. In some modern Chinese restaurants or Western restaurants where the dining table is in a rectangular shape, these rules can be applied too with small tweaks. For example, the center of one of the long side table should be reserved for the Guest of Honor (ideally the side facing the door), with his host counterpart sitting across, much like a formal meeting between government officials from two nations or royal banquettes. If you still find the above rules hard to apply, just remember to give the seat facing the door to your most prestigious guest. If there is no door because you forgot to book a private room so that you have to eat in the big dining hall, then have your guest face the east or the open area of the restaurant. Next seat every attendee based on seniority. The most senior ones sit closer to the Guest of Honor, while the junior ones sit further away from the Guest of Honor. Still don't understand? Please take a look at Illustration 3.4. Or you can always wait or ask the host to show you.

When it comes to ordering Chinese dishes, you should first circulate the menu among the guests and ask them to order whatever they like. If you are worried that they may order something out of your budget, pick a restaurant that is within your budget to avoid any awkward situations. But, generally speaking, guests will ask the host to take charge of the ordering. At this time, the host should find someone to take care of the task. This person should not be the most senior person in the host group, unless he volunteers. The most senior folks should focus on socializing with the guests instead of spending time on ordering dishes. In fact, before everyone arrives for dinner, you should have assigned someone to be responsible for ordering.

The person can be the most junior staff, or someone who is a gourmet eater. Also, before you start ordering, it is important to ask your guests if they have any dietary restrictions (like Muslims do not eat pork). Do not try to impress your guests by ordering exotic dishes and find out later that your guests could not or do not enjoy them. That will make your boss lose face in front of his guests. If you are a guest, make sure you let your host know what kind of food you do not eat. Don't be shy to reject the host's recommendations politely.

There are also rules about the types of dishes and number of dishes to be ordered in a business dinner. It is not appropriate to order whatever you want. It is also not appropriate to cancel any courses because of budget concerns. A good rule of thumb is to order one cold dish (appetizer) and one hot dish per person. A standard Chinese business dinner should include appetizer / hors d'oeuvres, main course / restaurant specialty dishes, common dishes, vegetables, carbohydrates / dim sum, soups. Dessert is not mandatory, order only if the restaurant has featured desserts that you would like to recommend to your guests. Finally a fruit platter is served, often complimentary of the restaurant. In short, the meal should be like having a big feast!

When the food is served, don't dive into the dishes or pass the whole plate to the next person after you take your share like the western style. There are rules as well. As the table top rotates, the guest of honor should be served first. If it is an internal team dinner, then the boss should be served first. If the restaurant staff makes a mistake and serve someone else first, you will need to tell the restaurant staff the correct order of serving. Typically, there is a lazy-Susan rotating plate on the table. Rotate every new dish to the guest of honor's seat to start. If your guest of honor or boss does not start, you should not lift your chopsticks or fork! Typically the plates are not lifted for serving, and you can always ask the waiter to help serve everyone or separate into individual plates. These rules apply not only to the first dish, but also every dish including the fruit plate!

SAMPLE BUSINESS DINNER MENU

If there are eight people at dinner, you can refer to the following ordering as a guideline:

6-8 Cold Dishes: Half vegetarian, half with meat.

2-3 Entrees: Expensive dishes like seafood, abalone.

1-2 Specialties: Local or the restaurant's signature dish.

2 Common Dishes: General household dishes like braised pork, poultry etc.

2 Vegetables: Vegetables, tofu and the like.

1 Soup: To make your guests feel warm.

2 Staples/ Dim Sum: Rice, noodles, dumplings etc., to fill up the stomach.

Dessert: Optional.

Fruit Plate: Some restaurants give out free fruit platters while some do not. Need to check with restaurant staff.

Time for Opening Up

Lunch and dinner are important occasions to build personal relationships with clients and suppliers. They are also good times to talk about sensitive business issues. How to approach the topic? Ming was a distributor of baby products in China. When Ming had meeting with sales representatives from the manufacturer in the office, they may speak for long hours but only on trivial matters. He would wait until they were in a restaurant. After some alcohol was served, then Ming would bring up topics that were not appropriate to openly discuss in formal meetings. For instance, Ming might mention that since sales were doing quite well, the outstanding payments from the past months should be settled as soon as possible. Or maybe Ming heard rumors that the manufacturer was planning to sign up an additional distributor to cover the same area, etc. He would not talk about these sensitive matters in meetings because he would be worried that the sales rep found him too aggressive and not sensitive, which could make him lose face in front of others by discussing money issues. Also if the two sides started to disagree, it would be hard for the two sides to cooperate going forward. But during lunch or dinner when both sides are relaxed, either one of them could bring up these topics casually. They could even bring up sensitive topics by saying "your company has not paid me for four months! Come on. You have to finish this glass of wine for me!" By bringing it up in a half-joking way, the sales rep acknowledged the matter without hurting each other's feelings. In that case, both sides would not feel embarrassed. This is also an example of Chinese people not liking to accuse someone directly because of face saving.

You may be puzzled as to why these issues were not codified in contracts clearly and enforced by China's commercial law, which clearly protects rights from both sides. In reality, enforcement is rarely efficient or cheap. The notion of strictly following a contract is weak in China, even among government officials, the highly educated and business communities. Instead, people depend on personal relationships and trust for repeat business.

Serving Chopsticks

Western culinary culture encourages the use of serving utensils for hygienic reasons. On the contrary, Chinese culinary culture does not consist of the concept of serving utensils. In fact, the Chinese find it more intimate if everyone eats from the same dish using his or her own chopsticks, which is not the most hygienic! As a result, there is a high percentage of people with hepatitis and tuberculosis. If you ask your co-workers in China to use serving chopsticks whenever you eat with them, no one will want to eat with you. If you ask your clients to use serving chopsticks, your client will probably get mad as he believes you think he has diseases. He may feel that he is losing face in front of everyone and will be very unlikely to conduct any business discussion! So what should you do? Let me share with you my personal experience:

1. It is best for you to take both hepatitis A and B vaccine shots, since you can never tell if someone is a hepatitis carrier. For your own protection, hepatitis vaccines are strongly recommended.

2. Budget permitting, take a client out to a high-end Chinese restaurants where the waiters would serve food for everyone using serving utensils. Many upscale restaurants offer two sets of chopsticks (black and white) to each guest. Just remember which pair is for your mouth and which pair is for the common plate. If your clients don't mind western food, then going to a high-end western restaurant is also a good option.

3. If you have lunch or dinner with your colleagues, you can't go to high-end restaurants for every meal. In that case, you will need to act fast! Whenever a dish is served, quickly get some for yourself using the serving chopsticks. If you do not want to look too voracious, then help your colleague who sits next to you to get some as well. Your colleagues will probably think you are a very nice person. But this trick only works if you are eating with close friends and colleagues. You will look bad if you do that in front of your clients or your boss. If you did not get enough from the dish, well, eat more rice to fill up your stomach!

4. Before the dishes arrive, ask the restaurant staff for 4 to 5 spoons to be used as serving utensils and place them on every dish served, particularly the ones that are not easy to pick up using chopsticks, like tofu, steamed egg, etc. This can also encourage your colleagues to get used to using serving utensils, instead of using the spoon where he or she has just licked to pick up food!

If nothing works, just say you feel a cold coming up and you don't want to give it to the others by sharing. Start with your shared chopsticks and hope the others will follow.

Saying No to Eating Wild Animals

"You can eat anything with its back facing the sky!" This is an old Chinese saying reflecting wisdom on exotic food. Today, most foreigners or people from Hong Kong and Taiwan could not agree with the old way. What if your colleague orders a wild animal? My former boss was from India, and many years ago he went on his first business trip to Guangzhou. While at dinner with his local colleagues and several foreign colleagues, someone ordered wild animal for every single dish. Whether this was a practical joke or naïve hospitality to showcase local dishes, no one knows. Some foreigners felt obligated to stuff the food down as a sign of respecting the host despite the disgust deep inside. But my Indian boss could not stand eating them, and asked for a vegetable dish and ate all by himself. The incident did not affect his relationship with his colleagues. As a guest, you can definitely tell others what you do not eat, and your wish will be respected.

Similarly, it is not wise to mention you want to try these exotic foods, since the host will be more than happy to honor a guest's request. A Taiwanese friend once traveled to Chengdu for business and mentioned that she heard locals love to eat rabbit heads. Sure enough, her colleagues took her to dinner where they served rabbit heads, six of them in total! She freaked out at dinner and had many nightmares afterwards. So if you are not ready for it, don't mention it even as a joke.

3 . 5

Drinking Etiquette

When it comes to Chinese business dinner, drinking is inevitably a critical part. Before you attempt to take your first sip, you should know rule number one: if you cannot drink or prefer not to drink, don't start, not even a sip! Instead you should make your preference clear, use tea or water as a substitute. Business people dislike those who say they cannot drink, but then have a few sips as a display of insincerity. Thus you don't drink at all, or you drink until you drop! There is no such thing as controlled and civilized drinking at most business dinner tables. Even if you are not drinking at all, you still need to pay attention to the following rules on giving toasts. You should drink tea to substitute for alcohol when you give or receive a toast. In an extreme case, I have seen people drinking vinegar instead to show their respect to the host's hospitality.

Types of Chinese Liquors

Before we talk about drinking etiquettes, we should first understand the various types of popular alcoholic drinks in China. Unlike western dinner wines, there are a wide variety of local liquors with high alcohol content, some of which you should avoid. There are five types of locally brewed Chinese liquors:

White Liquor - "Bai Jiu (白酒)"

Even though the Chinese name Bai Jiu literally translates to white wine in English, do not mistake it for the Californian white wine Chardonnay, which is referred to as white grape wine by the locals. White wine is distilled liquor similar to whiskey. Bai Jiu contains the highest alcohol content among all Chinese liquors, usually at 50-60%. Even the so-called low spirits Bai Jiu contains 30-40% in alcohol content! Therefore think twice before you give a toast using Bai Jiu! The most famous Bai Jiu is the previously mentioned Kweichow Moutai (贵 州 茅 台), which is also known as the national liquor of China. You may not get to drink Moutai in casual business dinners because of its price tag, since a bottle of regular Moutai costs about US$160-300. Moutai is usually served during important government banquets and business dinners or given out as gifts to VIPs. If your host provides Moutai, they think you are important, and you should try to savor its pureness and smoothness! Besides Moutai, there are many kinds of Bai Jiu. Below are the more common ones:

1. Sauce-Fragranced Type: Moutai (茅台)

2. Intense-Fragranced Type: Wu Liang Ye (五 粮 液), Jian Nan Chun (剑南春), Yang He Da Qu (洋河大曲), Lu Zhou Lao Jiao (泸州老窖) etc.

3. Refreshing- Fragranced Type: Er Guo Tou (二锅头), Fen Jiu (汾酒), Xi Feng Jiu (西凤酒) etc.

4. Rice-Fragranced Type: Guilin San Hua (桂林三花酒)

Bai Jiu is probably the most popular type of drink at business dinners, particularly in the northern region. Among all Bai Jiu, Wu

Liang Ye (五粮液) and Yang He Da Qu (洋河大曲) are the most popular ones. These two brands are among the top three best selling brands. Bai Jiu is usually consumed using small shot glasses, with each shot about 10-15ml. Each toast requires all participants to drink bottoms up, and there will be many toasts during the dinner process. What if you do not know which one to pick at a restaurant or shop? Just remember the five big brands in China: Moutai (茅台), Wu Liang Ye (五粮液), Lu Zhou Lao Jiao (泸州老窖), Jian Nan Chun (剑南春), Yang He Da Qu (洋河大曲). Pick one out of these five brands and you will be fine.

Gallery 3.2 Bai Jiu "Moutai (茅台)" and shot glass

Yellow Wine – "Huang Jiu (黄酒)"

Yellow Wine "Huang Jiu" is also known as "Lao Jiu" (old wine). One of the most popular kind is the rice wine. Yellow wine is produced using the pressure filtration method, therefore its alcohol content is generally around 15-20%, which is much lower than that of Bai Jiu. Yellow Wine is usually consumed together with local specialty dishes. The most common and widely advertised ones are Shaoxing Yellow Wine "Hua Diao (花 雕)," "Zhuang Yuan Hong (状 元 红)," "Shikumen Shanghai Yellow Wine (石库门上海老酒)," "Shandong Jimo Lao Jiu (山东即墨老酒)." Every province in China has its own brew of yellow wine, and here is a list of the most common types:

1. Zhejiang-brew Yellow Wine: Shaoxing Yellow Wine, Ala Old Wine etc.

2. Suzhou-brew Yellow Wine: Wujiang Taoyuan Yellow Wine, Jiangsu Baipu Yellow Wine etc.

3. Shanghai-brew Yellow Wine: He Jiu, Shikumen Shanghai Yellow Wine etc.

4. Anhui-brew Yellow Wine: Qingcaohu Yellow Wine, Gunanfeng Yellow Wine etc.

5. North Region-brew Yellow Wine: Shandong Jimo Lao Jiu

6. Fujian-brew Yellow Wine: Minan Lao Jiu, Fujian Lao Jiu etc.

Since Yellow Wine is considered to be less prestigious as Bai Jiu, business people usually do not drink Yellow Wine at formal dinners. Yellow Wine is sometimes consumed at home or at dinner with friends. At business dinners, you can order the local yellow wine to pair with local specialty dishes. For example, some people like to pair hairy crab with yellow wine. Some locals also like to add a piece of preserved sweet plum into the warm yellow wine to enhance the flavor. If you are a guest at dinner, you can also request to try the locally brewed yellow wine. You should drink it with a traditional Chinese ceramic bowl in order to taste the true, authentic flavor.

Gallery 3.3 Yellow Wine, Western Wine, and Cigarettes Served at a Wedding Banquet in Shanghai

China-Made Western Wine

China has started to manufacture its own red and white wines over the last ten to twenty years. The consumption of western wine has become popular in business and government banquets as the western practice of pairing wine with dinner influenced China. But the way red and white wines are consumed is quite different from western countries. In the western world, sophisticated drinkers prefer to savor the wine by slowly drinking it. Wine is typically poured to one-third of a glass full, allowing the wine to be swirled and aired properly to demonstrate the full range of fragrances. In China, people like to pour a full glass of wine, as pouring 1/3 of a glass is a sign of stinginess on the host's part, and then finish in one shot during toast. Just when you think you can get a bit more civilized and less likely to get drunk by ordering a bottle of sophisticated wine, you are wrong again. In some extreme cases people add soda to the wine, such as Sprite, to the wine to make it taste "better" or more acceptable to the local pallet. Similarly some people add sweetened green tea to whiskey at clubs and bars. Actually, if it is an inferior wine to begin with, it may not be a bad idea to dilute the taste. At least you will not get drunk as easily and quickly!

Beer

While Chinese wine has been consumed in China for thousands of years, beer was only introduced around a hundred years ago. Because of its unique taste and low cost, beer has become one of the most popular alcoholic beverages in China. Besides the famous national brand Tsingtao Beer, there are actually many breweries in China producing locally branded beers. For example, Yanjing Beer from

Beijing, Harbin Beer from Harbin, Shancheng Beer from Chongqing, Zhujiang Beer from Pearl River Delta etc. And locals always believe local beer pairs better with local cuisine! So don't forget to try out local beers when you are visiting different parts of China. Beer drinking is also the same as wine drinking. Some people like to pour a full glass of beer then bottoms up! Some people also like to add soda into beer, like in some parts of Germany.

Medicinal Wine

Medicinal wine has a strong Chinese heritage, but as the name suggests, it is mainly for medicinal purpose rather than for daily consumption. It is typically made from Chinese herbs, or traditional Chinese medicines such as ginseng or other wild animal parts, soaked in liquor for a long time. If someone offers you medicinal wine, think twice before you drink or accept it. You may be surprised or even offended by the ingredients they use, like the genitals of wild animals. It is totally understandable if you refuse to drink it. It is better to be safe than to be brave.

Western hard liquor, like whiskey and vodka, is still not as common in Chinese business banquets. Brandy and champagne are even rarer, and they are usually served at night clubs or KTVs.

Gallery 3.4 Chinese Medicinal Wine

Drinking Traditions

People from different parts of China have different drinking habits. For instance, the Henanese tends to make their guests drink more to show respect. On the contrary, people from Jiangsu and Zhejiang drink more than the guests to show respect. Shandong people like to play fair on the drinking table, meaning the host and the guest would drink the same amount.

One common drinking habit is universal in China – people like to fill the glass full, regardless of the size of the glass and regardless if it is red wine, white wine, yellow wine, Bai Jiu, or beer! What's worse, they like to drink it bottoms up every time when they toast! If you only drink a few sips, your local host will look down on you. This rule applies to both male and female. At the beginning of this chapter, I mentioned that if you do not want to drink, do not start the first sip. However, this tactic only works in large cities. When it comes to small cities and rural areas, people do not care. If you do not drink, your local host will feel that you are not giving face, or showing disrespect to him. My friend Annie is a senior executive at a LLE. She often travels to small cities to work on mergers and acquisitions projects. If she did not drink with the local host, her local host would get angry. They would look down on her and gave her a hard time during the deal negotiation. She had no choice but bit the bullet and joined the drinking with everyone else.

What typically happens, as shared by Annie, is the following. First, after people leave the office and move to the restaurant's private room, they start drinking around a designated drinking table two to three hours before dinner starts, while socializing. Hopefully by then people from both sides already know each other better and certainly tipsy. Next everyone moves to the dinner table where food is already served, and this is where round two of drinking starts. Everyone continues to drink with increased vigor and waves of toasts, typically one-to-one to avoiding group toasts. By now, it is hard not to get drunk after five to six hours of drinking!

If you find yourself stuck in this situation, follow the tips shared by Annie. Tip number one, stay with one type of alcohol for the entire time. Mixing wines, liquor and beer means you are testing the limits of your tolerance, and the result will be disastrous. Tip number two, drink beer if you can. Since beer has the lowest alcohol content among all alcoholic beverages, it is not as easy to get drunk. A few trips to the bathroom could alleviate the pressure. Also, remember that people like to fill the glasses up? Gulping down a full glass of beer is better on the stomach than gulping down a full glass of hard liquor or wine! Also it is less likely to get fake beer than fake liquor to avoid handovers the morning after. Your local host would not mind if you drink beer or liquor, as long as you are drinking. Tip number three, which is also very controversial, is to get drunk first to show respect. Given that you will likely be wasted at some point during the night, you might as well show the bravery and hospitality to toast the other side first and get it over with. The tactic could work well where you earn your battle field stripe and earn the respect from the host. Make sure you have a reliable member on your team to take you back to the hotel.

Mixing Liquors

There is common saying that the more you drink the deeper the relationship. But there is also a common saying "drink until you drop." If you drink in the following ways, you will definitely drop in no time!

In the western drinking culture, people mix different alcohols to make cocktails. In China, people mix liquors to get drunk faster. Sometimes towards the end of the dinner or banquet and you are still sober, someone may propose a "Triple Mix" — mixing Bai Jiu, red wine, and beer together! Of course as mentioned before, all mixed in a full glass finish in one go. You must have incredible tolerance to stay sober after that. If "Triple Mix" is not crazy enough for you, then there is also "Quintuple Mix" — adding Yellow Wine and western hard liquor like whiskey on top of the Triple Mix! If someone asks you to drink the "Quintuple Mix" at dinner, either you are asking the person to do a big favor or you have offended the person and this is his revenge. Sometimes, Chinese can be quite adventurous in mixing alcoholic drinks. Recently a few government officials were reported in the news having drunk to their death!

Rules of Giving Toasts

At a business dinner, you need to pay attention to so many rules, such as seating arrangement and the sequence of how dishes are served. Now we add to the sequence of giving toasts. If you randomly propose toasts, say people next to you, you may make your boss lose face in front of the guests.

If it is an internal company dinner without outsiders, the first toast should be given by the second highest ranking person among the group to the highest ranking one at the table. It is to be followed by the third highest ranking person to give the toast to his boss and so on. The most junior person should be the last one to propose a toast. If a junior person jumps the gun and toast to the boss before the hierarchy of the senior staff, he is viewed as disrespectful to everyone at the table. Remember that respecting ranks and order is an important part of the Chinese business culture.

If there are outside guests at the dinner, then toast should be proposed in the following order:

1. Head of Host (most senior person from host side) propose a toast to the Guest of Honor

2. Members from the host side propose toast to the Guest of Honor, in the order of seniority, and if there are too many people, then it is ok to propose toast as one group

3. Guest of Honor propose a toast to Head of Host and other members from the host side as reciprocation

4. Members from the host side and guest side can start proposing toast to each other where the heavy drinking starts.

Be Proactive or Not

As a guest, you should not be too proactive in proposing toast because you will make the host feels like you are taking control of the dinner. That will be seen as being rude and make your host lose face. On the flip side, if you are the host, then you should take initiative to be proactive. Your guests will not feel comfortable pouring liquor for themselves even if they want to drink. If you are the junior person within the group, you should also restrain yourself from proposing toast randomly. Unless everyone has become tipsy after a few drinks and loosen up, then you can go with the flow.

At some point after your team and the host team get close, you will find out at dinner table that the host team has a drinking commander "Ju Siling 酒司令 " who deploys his best drinkers to toast your senior staff with the single goal to get your entire team drunk. Now it becomes a chess game.

Reciprocate

If someone gives you a toast, it is important that you reciprocate by giving a toast back. Again, reciprocation is a big part of the Chinese culture. Since I am giving you a toast, you should give a toast in return. If you do not reciprocate, others will find you not polished or not social. Of course, if you are the big boss, then you are exempted from all these rules.

Clinking Glasses

When you are clinking glasses, make sure you hold your glass with both hands and your glass is lower than your counterpart's according to social hierarchy and to show respect. By holding your glass low, that means you are of lower ranking than the other person. On the other hand, if you are the most senior person within the group, then do not put your glass too low. Otherwise, how do others hold their glasses while they are trying to clink glass with you!

Gallery 3.5 Clinking Glass to Show Respect

Ten Rules at the Drinking Table

Here is a summary of the drinking rules for your reference:

1. Only after the bosses from the host and guest sides have given toasts, then you can give toast.

2. A group of people can give toast to one person, but the reverse is not appropriate: one person cannot give toast to a group of people, unless you are Lingdao, the big boss.

3. When you give a toast, if you do not clink the glass, you do not need to finish the glass. The amount you drink depends on how much the other party drinks, but you should not drink less than the other party. You can say "Sui Yi (随意)" before you drink, meaning, at your own will or pace.

4. If you clink the glass when you give a toast, then you should finish the whole glass while telling the other party to drink at his or her wish (say "Sui Yi"). That also shows you have good drinking etiquette!

5. Use your right hand to hold the top of the glass and your left hand to hold the bottom of the glass. Make sure you hold your glass lower than the other party when you clink.

6. If it is an informal dinner with no special guest, then you should give toast to each person at the dinner table in a clockwise direction.

7. Do not talk about business while you are drinking. Just enjoy drinking in each other's company. This is a time to build personal relationships, and business will be done in due course. Remember from previous section that for the Chinese, personal relationship comes before business relationship. After all the wine and dine, business is pretty much settled implicitly.

8. Be mindful of your manner after you drink. Do not get drunk and start talking nonsense. Do not pass gas at the dinner table. Always have someone sober on your team to be the wing man and make sure your team does not make a scene.

9. If the big boss give you a toast, that means he is really giving you face and likes you. So no matter how much the boss drink,

you need to finish your glass to show respect. Again, hold your glass with both hands and keep your glass low! Say something complimentary afterwards, such as thank you for all the kindness and attention over the years, and what a great leader he is, etc.

10. If you have a low tolerance for alcohol, yet you know that your guests love to drink, what should you do? Find someone on your team who can drink and assign the person as the designated drinker for the night. The designated drinker should take initiative to give toast to the guests and save everyone else from over-drinking.

KTV

KTV, which stands for Karaoke TV, is highly popular in China and many Asian countries as entertainment after dinner. Other than allowing you to showcase your singing in front of other people, KTV in China is an important venue for business. Many KTVs in China also offer "hostess service," or young female hostesses to accompany guests in a private setting. KTV is a sensitive topic and is often kept quiet in the business world, but because of the importance it plays in conducting business, it would be unfair for you to not know the background and find out in an awkward way. First of all, why do business people and officials in China like to have "meetings" in KTV?

This is what my Chinese-American friend, Tom, told me. He worked at a consulting firm that advised clients on Chinese government policies. Since Tom's work involved understanding government policies and their directions, building relationships with the officials became an important part of his job. Tom would invite key government officials to dinner followed by KTV. Since Tom did not speak Chinese well, he hired a young lady to be his personal assistant and interpreter. At business dinner, she would help translate back and forth. When they went to KTV after dinner, she would leave quietly as she was not comfortable with the environment. So I asked Tom: how did you communicate with your guests at the KTV without the interpreter? Tom told me that at business dinner, everyone needed to pay attention to the proper etiquettes. But once they moved into the KTV room, all the hierarchy and ranking became less important. Everyone drank and sang without worrying about ranking too much. Of course the officials get to pick the songs they are familiar with first. It did not matter even if Tom did not speak Chinese, as long as he could drink and give toast! In the KTV room, guards are down, and that is how relationships are built.

For us ladies, going to KTV with men could be embarrassing. If you don't want to go, just tell your boss before dinner, since usually it is an optional part of the evening program. It is worse if you force yourself to attend but feel uncomfortable for the entire evening. On the other hand, if your boss really needs your presence, or you are the one who needs to build a relationship with the client, then you have no choice. How do you avoid drinking too much? A female friend of mine, Sally, taught me a good tactic. Sally worked for a PR agency, so her job required her to take clients to KTV often. Yet, she was not particularly good at drinking. After Sally took her clients to the KTV, she would request for a KTV hostess who could drink to accompany her for the entire time. She would give the hostess a big tip, and in return the hostess would do the drinking for her when she was giving a toast. The hostess also had the job of getting all her guests drunk! In that case, she did not need to force herself to drink, yet everyone would have a good time at the KTV.

As mentioned earlier, fake liquor is prevalent in China. Bars and KTV are certainly one of the hardest hit locations. Most places would ask you to mix hard liquor with green tea or soda, so you cannot tell if the liquor is authentic. Moreover, KTV rooms are usually very dark. You will not be able to read the labels well to tell if the bottle and label is authentic. I have also heard that some KTVs will serve you real liquor at the beginning, say the first bottle. But as the night goes on, the waiter would bring out the fake ones. So what are the consequences of consuming counterfeit liquors? You are lucky if you only get a bad hangover the next day. Worse, it may hurt your eyesight or cause severe liver damage! If you need to take your client to a KTV, then look for a KTV that serves government officials in particular, or a place where your friends knows the owner well. It is less likely for places that serve government officials to sell fake liquor. If a government official gets sick after drinking liquor from a KTV, that KTV will probably go out of business the next day! Where do you locate these KTVs? You should ask around since places that serve officials are usually located in discreet locations.

Here is another tip to help you drink less at KTV. Other than liquor, KTV serves snacks and fruit plates. Sometimes the fruit plate comes with the room charge. Put one or two pieces of fruits like grape or cherry tomato in your glass before you start drinking. In that case, you can reduce the amount of drinking and be able to tell your glass from others: subtle yet effective.

Banquet Rundown

In case you are invited to a formal business banquet in China, here's a simple rundown so that you know what to expect. First, as a guest you should not arrive before your host. If you do arrive early, go find a café and have coffee until the time has arrived. Before you step into the banquet hall, look for a check-in desk for a seating chart and find your name. When you are seated, you will find a wine glass already filled with some red wine. Do not gulp it down immediately – it is saved for the opening toast given by the head of host later. If you are thirsty, ask the waiter for some water. But be prepared that they may not serve drinks until the banquet has officially started. When the banquet has officially commenced, the head of host will first go up to the stage and give his opening speech. After the speech, he will give a toast to everyone. Now is the time to take the glass of wine and toast with everyone at your table. The banquet is then officially kicked off, with food and drinks served. If you are hungry, try to get something to eat now as very soon people will walk over to give you toast. Then you must return the toasts at their table as reciprocation. You will be quite occupied with drinking, walking and chatting that you will not have much time to eat.

Lingdao (Boss) Attending Banquet – Big Deal

Paying attention to all the dining and drinking etiquettes is important when having dinner with your Lingdao (big boss). If you have to invite your Lingdao or an important guest to attend a banquet, like the annual party, then there are a lot more things you need to pay attention to. My friend, John, who worked at an SOE described to me all the preparation work involved when organizing an important banquet for Lingdao. It gives you a sense of all the formalities and bureaucracies involved with SOEs and government organizations.

Before the banquet started, as the person in charge of the event, John needed to find out where Lingdao would be before dinner. He needed to coordinate with Lingdao's driver on how to get to the venue location and knew exactly when Lingdao arrived. Then John needed to have the team lined up at the entrance and along the path leading to the banquet hall to welcome Lingdao when he walked in, much like welcoming a head of state. John also needed to have some contingency plans in place. What if Lingdao wanted to rest a bit before entering the banquet hall? So there must be a private room prepared for Lingdao to rest and freshen up. What if Lingdao needed to use the restroom? Which restroom should he use? Who should accompany Lingdao to the restroom? The restroom must also be equipped with all the toiletries and supplies. It is not acceptable if Lingdao went to the bathroom and it was out of toilet paper. What if Lingdao decided to not take rest and go straight to the banquet? Then the organizer needed to ensure all employees and guests had been seated. The organizer also needed to have the opening speech written and printed on a red piece of paper for Lingdao. Lingdao might not use your version, but it is important that you had one ready. Group photo taking was another complicated task. How should people line up? Seating and line up must reflect ranking of the organization. For instance, Lingdao would take the middle seat on the front row, other senior executives would take seat based on their ranking in the front row, other employees would go to the back rows, and female employees would kneel down in front without blocking Lingdao's face. All these required numerous rehearsals. What if Lingdao wanted to leave in the middle of the banquet while performance was still under way? The organizer needed to end the performance in a seamless way, and gave Lingdao a proper farewell.

Even a simple banquet required a lot of detailed planning and many rehearsals. If anything was not done properly, the entire event was considered to be a disaster! That would give Lingdao an impression that you are a careless and incompetent person, which might jeopardize your future promotions!

3 . 6

Lessons Learned at Work

Lesson 1: Stock and Worker Shortage after Chinese New Year

Whenever a foreign friend asks me what it is like during Chinese New Year (aka Spring Festival), my answer is usually "the entire country shuts down." The shutdown does not just occur during the official weeklong holidays, but five to six days before the Lunar New Year, lasting all the way until one month after the holiday. During this period, the productivity of the country is reduced significantly. Chinese New Year is viewed as the most important festival of the year, and most of the 270 million migrant workers only have this one chance to go home to reunite with the family. It is an important Chinese tradition to have the family reunion dinner the night before the Spring Festival. To ensure arriving home for the special dinner, many migrant workers head home five to six days ahead of time. My live-in maid, for instance, has already told me months ahead that she needed to go home five days before the holidays begin. Even courier service is significantly reduced due to the lack of delivery personnel during CNY period. Deliveries that usually takes one to three days will take five to six days, and if you do not get it before the New Year holidays, you will have to wait a couple weeks after the New Year to receive your package. This is why many Taobao shops will close early, since there are no courier services anyways. E-commerce sites will be impacted and need to plan ahead. When you think things should get back to normal after the Chinese New Year holidays, you are wrong. Many migrant workers and Ayi may decide not to return to work, or they may switch jobs. This result in a massive labor shortage after the Chinese New Year. A friend who owns a small café in Shanghai told me that staff turnover is worst before and after the Chinese New Year. It is safe to assume a portion of the staff would not return after the holidays. So after the New Year holidays, she and her family would need to help out at the café until replacements could be hired.

Many corporates also suffer because of the Chinese New Year "shut down." A few years ago, my company's manufacturing plant experienced shortage of workers before Chinese New Year as workers left work early for home. The remaining capacity was only half of the usual level. Products were selling well before the Chinese New Year, so inventory level was low. Since there was not enough capacity to meet customer demands, I had to cancel sales promotion activities that were originally scheduled for after the Chinese New Year. Even after the Chinese New Year capacity remained low because many workers were not back to work yet. Many stores were out of stock despite the lack of promotion activities. I was not able to meet my sales target that month due to out of stock. To make things worse, the company received punitive fines from the large retailer chains because of out of stock issues. After what I have experienced that year, I learned my lesson. To prepare for Chinese New Year, I asked supply chain to build up inventory beforehand. Also, I avoided arranging promotion activities right after Chinese New Year. So even the manufacturing plant experienced shortage of workers after the Chinese New Year holidays, I will have enough supply in the warehouse and do not need to worry about running out of stock again.

Lesson 2: Buffer for Time and Budget

If you plan to start a company in mainland China, you'd better set aside additional budget to pay for unexpected expenses like government fees, fines, agency fees, gifts, etc. For example, a famous Hong Kong restaurant chain entered the Shanghai market two years ago. It took them eight months just to get the operating license from the government for one of its restaurant locations. Meanwhile they still needed to pay rent and utilities without any income. Similar situations happened to many of my friends who started businesses in China. Besides paying for operating costs while waiting for the business to open, you may also receive ridiculous charges from real estate developers! Fred, a friend from Hong Kong rented an office space for his business in Shanghai. At the beginning, he was quite happy with the reasonable rental cost. But when he was about to start the renovation work, the developer suddenly notified him that his company must use the designated supplier for the fire protection system. Otherwise, the developer would not issue the approval letter for his company to start operation. Without that letter, his company would not be able to obtain the operating license from the government. What's outrageous was that the designated supplier quoted RMB 2 million (US$320,000) for the small project, which was eight times the market price! That was completely beyond his budget! Finally he negotiated with the supplier and reduced the price down to RMB 600,000 (US$97,000), but it was still twice the market price! My friend told me that there was a US-based multinational company who rented four floors of office space in the same building, and the supplier charged this company RMB 20 million (US$3.2 million) for the fire protection system! So if you plan to spend US$200,000 to start a company in China, my advice is to prepare at least an additional 50% budget to meet with all the unexpected expenses.

In China the laws and regulations are very detailed but oftentimes hard to follow to the exact word. It takes strong relationship with different government agencies to navigate and get things done, i.e., getting the approval chop. Inefficiencies in the system created business opportunities for middle-men. These agencies usually have good connection with the government officials, sometimes opened by family and friends of the officials, and are able to get things done faster and simpler for a fee. There is pretty much an agency out there that can help with any matter related to the government. If you choose to follow the law to every last word and do it all by yourself, you will need to build up a high tolerance for pain along with a thick wallet.

Lesson 3: Do Not Underestimate 3.15

March 15th is the World Consumer Rights Day. It is also a day that gets to the nerves of many companies in China. On that day, China Central Television (CCTV) brings to light consumer's complaints regarding certain companies, investigates and criticizes the offenders in a live show called "315 Gala." As CCTV is watched by the majority of the Chinese population, any exposure during this event can be a deadly blow. For many corporations, this is a day demands a lot of attentions from the senior management, as news can go viral on social media. In the "315 Gala" hosted by CCTV in 2013, the station namely criticized Apple's after-sales services in China. Two weeks later, CEO Tim Cook had to issue a public apology to the Chinese consumers as media sentiment continues to turn negative. Eventually Apple issued 2 year warranties to laptops sold in China versus 1 year for the rest of the world, a dramatic increase in cost. Given its importance, some companies pay extra attention when dealing with customers' complaints in March, fearing that ill-handled ones get escalated to the show on CCTV.

Personally I learned a great deal from my previous job managing 3.15. Two months before 3.15, the company organized workshop with senior managers to discuss potential issues that might arise in the 3.15 Gala. The team also conducted exercise to simulate the situation in case the company was featured on the show, and immediate steps to take. In addition, the public affairs and regulatory team formed task force and prepare plans for different scenarios in advance. And on the evening of 3.15, the leadership team and the task force team members were required to stay in the office to watch the entire 3.15 Gala program to ensure quick response in case something happens. As you read from the McDonald's incident in Chapter 2.3, prompt response to the public is critical in preventing more negative public opinions emerged. If a company statement is not issued within the first two hours, you may find waves of negative opinions from the Internet and it would become very hard to rescue the damaged brand image. If only everyone could prepare for natural disasters or fire with such precision, many more lives would have been saved.

Lesson 4: Watch Out for Professional Scavengers

It is almost impossible for a company to comply with all China rules and regulation 100% even with the world's best legal team, quality assurance program and regulatory assurance team. This is because a lot of the rules and regulations in China are subjectively and poorly defined, often contradicting with one another. Each province and even each city also have its own interpretation of certain regulations. For instance, in Shenzhen, no QS license can be issued to pre-packaged salad, because there is no such standard. As a result, law-abiding retailers are not allowed to sell pre-packaged salads in their stores. Just cross the city border in the rest of Guangdong province, including Guangzhou, you are allowed because the other cities' food health regulations do allow.

If you feel that your quality standard is so high and practiced globally without any incident, and the local regulation is silent in this area, therefore you can try to be a pioneer. Right? Wrong! Since the government know it is prohibitively expensive to monitor all companies, especially little mom-and-pop shops to ensure compliance, it actually outsources this task to the public. When someone reports a company or a brand violating a regulation to the government, and if the accusation is deemed true and the company is fined by the government, the person reporting the case will get a percentage of the fine as reward. This incentive system gives birth to a new occupation in China called "professional scavengers" who make a living by reporting companies to the government. These professional scavengers study regulations for a particularly industry. Their job is to study the every product labels, price tags, advertisements etc., and try to find mistakes companies make. If these professionals find one missing information in your label or a typo, they either blackmail the company and ask for compensation, last resort they report to the government directly to get their money reward.

For example, in China there is strict requirements on what type of information is needed on a price tag: product name, price showing to two decimal points, list of ingredients, name and address of manufacturer, date of manufacturing, telephone number of local price bureau, name of the price supervisor, QS logo etc. This is just one example on how complex it is to follow local regulations. For instance, if your "New York Cheese Cake" is not directly imported from New York, you must call it "New York Style Cheese Cake" for your product name. The term "Almond Croissant" is illegal because the Chinese translation of the nut almond refers to a Chinese medicine and not allowed as food ingredient. You must use a more generic term like nuts. When I was in the retail business, I needed a team to work on the price tags. Once a small typo was made in one price tag. As soon as we found out, we had to stop selling the product immediately. We only resumed selling the product after we had replaced the price tag in all our stores in the country. If a professional scavenger had found out about the mistake before us and reported to the regulatory bodies, we could be fined by every local government where our stores are located. That could be hundred of thousands of dollars!

Even though these professional scavengers like to target large corporations because of their deep pockets, but that does not mean they won't target small businesses. Particularly if they find out the business is owned by a foreigner. Pay extra attention to the customer facing contents you created for your business so that you won't be the target for the professional scavengers. While having the public supervise on product safety and quality is a reasonable business cost, going overboard to follow all regulations is prohibitively expensive for smaller firms.

Lesson 5: Reference Checks

One of the biggest challenges both large and small business in China face is hiring talents. On my last job, I spent three years and still could not fill up all the vacancies on my team. The moment I hired a person, another person from the team would resign to join another company. Turnover rate is high, as there are many opportunities in the market for a faster way to get promotion and raise. In the US, it is not uncommon to find employees who have been with a company for 10+ years. In China, staying at the same company for 3 years is already considered a long term employee.

When hiring is a challenge with large companies, it is even more so for small businesses. I have a few friends who run their own businesses in China, and they always complain about not able to hire people for management positions. While large companies have good brands to attract talents, it is extremely difficult for small companies to compete on pay and career path. My friend Lin started a retail business three years ago. Yet until today she is still struggling with finding a marketing manager and operation manager. Lin had no choice but to do everything by herself. Just a month ago, she told me she hired a headhunter agency to help her with recruiting. The headhunter did find her two candidates and they were supposed to meet her for interviews. Both did not show up on the day of the interview, with no notification at all. The headhunter apologized to Lin but still was not able to find Lin any good candidates. If you plan to start your own business in China, be prepared to spend a lot of your time on recruiting and getting the right people.

The lesson in this section is not just about hiring, but on the consequences of hiring the wrong person. Annie, who is the owner of a trading company in Shanghai, hired an HR manager, let's call her Ms. X. However, Ms. X did not perform during probation period, a 3 months trial period allowed by the China labor law. By the end of the probation period, Annie decided not to renew Ms. X's contract into a full time employee. The drama started the moment this conversation occurred. First, Ms. X went hysterical and refused to leave. She claimed that the company had no right to terminate her employment right away despite the fact it was still within probation period, which was surprisingly accurate according to labor law but too subtle for many to understand the technicalities. Then she started throwing things around and even smashed one of Annie's company laptops! Seeing Ms. X's behavior got aggressive, Annie called the police and hoping the police was able to put an end to this drama. But the police refused to arrest her because the damages was less than RMB 5,000 (US$ 770). Annie later half-jokingly said she wished X crashed more things, the police may be forced to take her away. The drama did not end here. As a revenge, Ms. X reported Annie's company to various government agencies for breaking regulations. Since the very first day Ms. X started, she had been collecting information about the company. It is almost impossible for a company to comply with all the rules and regulations, so it was not difficult for her to gather a few pieces of evidence. If these accusations are accurate, the informant can collect a reward, an incentive that turns people against each other in the society. Given Ms. X was able to precisely pinpoint most of the loopholes in Annie's company, she clearly came prepared. She reported Annie's company 8-9 times to various departments, such the tax bureau, labor department, social security bureau etc. She filed 4 complaints to the tax bureau alone. Even though all the violations were minor, dealing with all the audit and investigation was painful. As I was discussing with Annie, Ms. X could be a professional scavenger, which Annie should be able to find out before hiring her. Annie admitted that her company did not do a reference check. The lesson here is always conduct reference check on the candidate, including both references offered by the candidate and cold calls on her previous employers. When I was hiring before, I always use my personal contacts to verify. For a specific function and within the multinational companies, the circle is surprisingly small. For candidate from smaller firms, in addition to doing reference check with the candidate's ex-employer, you should conduct a search on the candidate on the web. Even the ex-employers' references and diplomas could be fake. Annie's case was not a standalone case. There are con artists who faked top MBA degrees from the US, transcripts from Chinese universities with cooperation from the schools themselves, and even creating an entirely fake bank branch to provide bank statement for investment references. Just because you need someone urgently does not mean you should skip the reference check. It may cost you a great deal if you hire the wrong person.

Lesson 6: It's All About Your Attitude

Attitude? You may wonder how that plays an important role in the workplace. Again it comes to the show of respect especially when dealing with government officials, even when you are right. An American friend owns a bar in Shanghai. He smartly hired a competent agent to help him apply for all the licensing in Shanghai. In a few months he was able to open the bar and business was doing great. Not having to deal with the government agencies before, he got carried away one day when the fire inspector came for a routine check. The inspector had pointed out a few areas that did not meet the standards and was planning to issue a fine. My friend found the accusations quite random and not strictly correct. He sensed that the inspector was deliberately giving him a hard time. It was the end of a long day, he couldn't help and started an argument with an attitude. Unbeknownst to him, the fire inspector was doing his routine round and typically do find a few issues with everyone. After the inspector wrote a ticket and left, my friend was naïve enough to think that he had won the battle and truth won. The next day he found a team of fire inspectors at his bar inspecting every detail like CSI. In the end, they issued a dozen tickets totaling hundreds of thousands of dollars! At that moment, my friend knew he had made a huge mistake. So he immediately apologized to the inspector and his supervisor. However, the inspector simply ignored him and left. Later on, he had to find someone who knew the head of inspector to amend the situation.

In this case, relationship - guanxi becomes important. Through that person, he met with the inspectors, apologized and gave them gifts. Finally they accepted his apology and only asked him to pay RMB 10,000 (US$1,600) in fines. After this incident, my friend became the most friendly person every time when there are government officials inspecting his bar. He would never dare to put up an attitude anymore.

Lesson 7: Don't sign anything blindly

Mary, a Chinese-returnee "Hai Gui 海归" had earned an MBA degree overseas and obtained a US passport. She returned to China for a CFO job at a large local enterprise (LLE). Later I found out she quit after only three months on the job. She told me that the company's financial reporting was a huge mess. I was curious why didn't she fix it as it could be the top reason they hired her. Mary then explained that was not the case. The company was about to go public in the US. They hired someone with a great resume to show illusion of financial compliance, and someone from the US is more likely to win the trust of US investors. She quickly found out that internal control was non-existent. Senior executives always asked her to sign off suspicious payments and reimbursements. One day, the founder CEO even asked her for US$48,000 (RMB 300,000) in cash for his personal use, and asked her to find ways to cover the trails. She knew that if she continued to stay, she would probably be arrested for accounting fraud and banned for practicing in the US by the SEC! She became so worried that she decided to quit even before her probation period ended.

While Mary was smart enough to leave before trouble found her, another former colleague John was not so lucky. John also held an MBA degree from a top university in the US. After graduation, he joined a US-based multinational company as Chief Financial Officer. Then a LLE approached him with an attractive package to join the company as CFO, preparing the company to go public. He worked there for two years and during which he accomplished the IPO. But somehow he felt he could never fit in with the rest of the management, and that strange feeling in his gut made him quit. A year later, the LLE was investigated for faking IPO documents. The prosecutor found out that all the problem documents were signed by the former CFO, which was John. In the end, he was charged and sentenced to five years in a Chinese prison. He was released from prison not too long ago.

Always remember, never sign important documents handed to you if you do not truly understand the contents. Once your signature is on the documents, you are legally responsible for the content. If you are charged, a foreign passport will not be able to protect you from jail time!

If you encounter any trouble in China and detained by the police, remember rule number one: be friendly and do not try to be tough or show an attitude. You may not be able to get a lawyer and they can indefinitely detain you without outside contacts. Arguing and showing anger is the last thing that can help. Even though you know you did not commit any crime, be humble if you want to be treated nicely. Do not be obnoxious because you hold a foreign passport, unless your father is the President of the United States! Among the people I know, there is a US citizen who was detained by the local police for tax evasion. I heard that because he was not cooperative with the prosecutor, even the US Consulate could not help to keep him out of jail. In case you really get into trouble with the police, first maintain a good attitude, don't admit to any wrong doings, and try to find a lawyer. Calling the emergency number of your country's consulate should also help.

Professional Life with a China Twist

No Privacy During Job Search

In many developed western countries, companies by virtue of non-discrimination laws would not accept personal curriculum vitae (CV) that discloses an applicant's personal information like age, gender, political affiliation, marital status to avoid violating the Prevention of Discrimination Ordinance. In the recruitment process, the interviewer is not allowed to ask the candidate such personal information either. Otherwise the interviewer, and even the company, can be accused of discrimination, which is a serious legal issue. But in China, if you do not disclose your personal information, you may not even get the chance to be interviewed. This applies to local companies as well as MNCs. CVs I received before not only have personal information like gender, date of birth, marital status, home address, but also a photo! When I worked for an American company in Hong Kong many years ago, the company's HR policy states that if there is a photo attached, the CV must be discarded right away. Disclosing personal information applies to positions at all levels in China. Not too long ago there was a headhunter calling me regarding a senior marketing position at a MNC. We had a nice chat on the phone about the role. Towards the end of our conversation, the headhunter asked me about my age. Not remembering I was actually in China, I got upset because of her question. So I replied her "Why do I have to tell you how old I am? In the US that is considered discrimination! (The headhunter was probably thinking: you are in China right now, Ms. Ching!) I think you should look at my experience and my capability, not my age! Moreover, if you want to know how old I am, do the math yourself!" The headhunter then apologized to me unwillingly. Later that day, after I had calmed down, I realized it was totally unnecessary for me to get mad at the headhunter. This is the norm in China, and there is nothing I can do about it. And of course that headhunter never called me back again. So next time when a headhunter asked about my age, I would reply the headhunter with an approximate range in a polite tone. If you are thinking of finding a job in mainland China, be prepared to answer all kinds of personal questions that recruiters would not ask in Western countries. You may also want to invest in a nice passport photo that can be attached to your CV.

Online Search of Your Colleagues

Similar to people in the US who like to look up a new colleague's photos on Facebook, people here search about their colleagues. So don't be surprised to find out that everyone in the company seems to know a lot about you on your first day of work! They will use Baidu (Bing and Google are for the more sophisticated with VPN) to search for your history and photos. Especially if you are the manager of a team, your subordinates will be curious about their boss, especially hobbies and gossips. If there is anything that you do not want your subordinates to know, find a way to remove information if it is on the internet! Chinese search engines and websites can do that for a fee through trusted intermediaries.

Horoscope Specialists

Young Chinese professionals are fascinated by the western horoscope in addition to the traditional Chinese zodiac signs. When you first join a company, your horoscope is one of the first questions people may ask you, especially among the female staff, along that line would be your blood type. Based on these information, your colleagues will be able to give you an analysis of your personalities, whether certain people can work well with you based on their zodiac signs. In extreme case, I have heard that some managers use zodiac signs as an important screening criteria when recruiting. On the other hand, if you happen to be an expert in zodiac signs, you can also exchange expertise with your Chinese colleagues. This is definitely a great way to break ice and start an interesting conversation.

"Blue Blood" Interns

When working in Mainland China, you have to be prepared for receiving the "blue blood" interns to work on your team. In local Chinese teams they are called the "Government Officials' Second Generation" or "Rich Families' Second Generation." They come from rich and powerful families who know the heads of a lot of companies. These eager parents want their only child to be able to piece together an impressive resume that includes job experience from large multinational companies, financial institutions or consulting firms. That will help the child to go study overseas or find a high profile job in the future. Therefore, they will leverage their connections with the senior executives from large companies, and ask them to arrange an internship for their child.

My friend Peter who run a private equity fund in Shanghai received a request from a government official, asking him to take his son for a short internship. This wasn't a big deal, so Peter agreed. But the funny thing was that he didn't know it was a "buy one get one free" deal. Peter not only needed to take the official's son, but also the son's girlfriend! They "worked" or showed up for one week. Then they requested the company to issue an employment letter as well as a strong recommendation letter for US College applications, which of course had already been written! So I asked Peter what type of work he assigned to these "Blue Blood" interns? He replied with a wink and told me that you could not really assign them any real work because one, they probably were not capable enough and two, unwilling to spend any time to work hard. Yet you needed to make them feel they were valued beyond getting coffee for the staff or just sitting and surfing the internet. So usually he would ask them to conduct simple online search, like looking up China's GDP information, then asked them to put all the data together in a simple excel file.

Another friend Jenny who worked at a fashion magazine in Beijing also shared a similar story with me. Her company recently hired a rich second-generation as intern. The young intern became the talk of the office very quickly! Her work outfits were all from luxury brands from head to toe, and the handbag she carried to work cost the same as Jenny's monthly paycheck, if not more. She also drove a Porsche to work, which made everyone felt awkward. The editor of the magazine of course would not assign her any work. What's worse the editor asked Jenny to look after the intern. Unlike other interns who would get the coffee and make the photocopies, this one needed additional babysitting. In fact Jenny was the one who poured her tea during the first few days of work. What really drove Jenny crazy was that she also needed to think about what types of simple task to assign to the intern everyday, such that to keep her occupied, but not too busy.

If you are a manager in China, be ready to receive these "Blue Blood Interns" when your boss asks you to. You also need to know how to take good care of them. Otherwise if they complain to mommy and daddy that they are not having a good time at the company, both you and your boss may get into trouble!

CHAPTER 4

Survival Guide

Whenever I have friends who are about to move to China or will be coming for the first time, they often ask me for things to look out for. This section is devoted to my personal, or friends and families' experiences to give you a better idea of the little things that may make a difference.

4 . 1

Key Chinese Phrases You Should Know

Most Often Used Mandarin Phrases

While many other tour books will teach you common phrases, I am limiting this section to the top six Chinese vocabularies which I believe are most often used to help you ease into your first journey in China:

1) Nǐ Hǎo (你好) – meaning "hi" or "hello." Even Hollywood stars need to learn this phrase when they visit China to meet with their fans! Greeting your host or guest with this phrase will definitely give your Chinese counterparts a warm impression.

2) Xiè Xiè (谢 谢) – meaning "thank you." In any language, the phrase "thank you" is probably one of the most popular and useful. Next time when your Chinese friend gives you tea or liquor, make sure you reply with "Xie Xie" to show your appreciation.

3) Bù Yào(不要) – meaning "no" or "I don't want it." This term is important particularly under the following circumstances: (1) when pushy street vendors try to sell you things you don't want; (2) when

the taxi driver is trying to give you recommendations on restaurants or hotels; (3) when you are having dinner with your Chinese friends and they try to offer you some weird dishes. In this situation, make sure you add the phrase "Xie Xie" after you said "Bu Yao" so that you do not sound rude.

4) Fú Wù Yuán (服 务 员) – meaning "waiter/waitress" or "flight attendant." In China, instead of saying "excuse me" to get the attention of the local restaurant staff, you should use"Fu Wu Yuan" instead, and in a loud tone to be heard far away. Anything other than "Fu Wu Yuan" (like "Hi", "Excuse Me", or "Sir/Madam") does not work in these bustling local joints. At first, you may not feel comfortable yelling out loud in public places. In fact, quite a few of my foreigner friends have difficulty calling out the words "Fu Wu Yuan" despite having lived in China for years. As a result, they always have a hard time getting the attention of the service staff in restaurants. Likewise, don't be surprised if you see your Chinese colleagues screaming loudly to get the waiter's attention. They are not being rude, they are just doing what is needed.

5) Má Fán (麻烦) – meaning troublesome. One cannot take things for granted in China. Sometimes you may need to go through a lot of troubles to get a simple task done. Next time to express how annoyed you feel, you can use the phrase "Ma Fan." Just don't express it to the government official or you will receive unwelcoming treatments, which will add to your "Ma Fan."

6) Directions – if you need to ask for directions, remembering the four directions in Mandarin will be quite helpful.

East: pronounced as "Dōng (东)"

South: pronounced as "Nán (南)," same "Nan" as in "Nanjing"

West: pronounced as "Xī (西)," same "Xi" as in "Xi'an"

North: pronounced as "Běi (北)," same "Bei" as in "Beijing"

Hand Gesture for Counting 1-10

Although there are many different dialects within mainland China, it is the same when it comes to hand gestures for counting, though slightly different in Hong Kong and Taiwan. Since a picture is worth a thousand words, Gallery 4.1 shows the hand gesture that the local Chinese use for counting from one to ten.

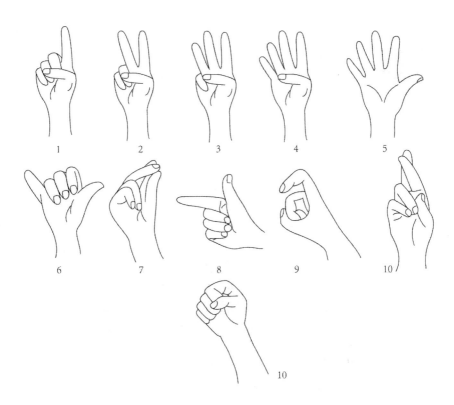

Gallery 4.1 Hand Gesture for Counting 1-10

4 . 2

Safety

Beijing & Shanghai

A lot of people wonder if it is safe to be outside at night in Beijing or Shanghai, and in my opinion it is fairly safe inside the cities. In Beijing, since it is the nation's capital, security is understandably tight. As for Shanghai, since it is an international metropolis, the city government also puts in a lot of effort to ensure that the city is safe. Therefore, there tends to be little serious crimes in these cities; the most common crime is probably pickpocketing, especially before Chinese New Year when most people need money to return to their hometown. I have a few friends who had their new phones and wallets stolen right before Chinese New Year. In general, it is relatively safe if you are inside the city perimeter, but the situation can be very different once you go outside of the city. Therefore, if you have to leave the city perimeters for business purpose, it would be much safer if you are accompanied by others.

Other Cities

The level of safety differs with different cities, so as a general rule of thumb, it is not advised to go out alone at night, or you should avoid going to secluded places.

Children's Safety

There have been instances where kidnappers abduct children in supermarkets, on busy streets, or around kindergartens. It is advised that parents keep a close watch on their children in public places. This is the reason why a lot of children, even as they enter middle school, are accompanied to and from school by their parents or grandparents as there have been cases of kidnapping. Don't be surprised next time when you pass by a neighborhood in mid afternoon and see long lines of people waiting outside of a school. Those are parents or grandparents who waited to pick up their child from school.

4 . 3

Pollution

Air Pollution

When I asked my foreigner friends what they don't like about living in China, pollution definitely comes first among all answers 99% of the time. Among the four key cities, Beijing has the worst air quality as it is surrounded by cities with heavy industries in Hebei province. Air quality in Beijing is at 'unhealthy level' or worse in almost half of the time out of a year, if not more. Many company executives with family refuse to be relocated to Beijing because of the poor air quality there. As a result, many MNCs are facing challenges in recruiting professional managers for their Beijing operation. I also have friends who were relocated to Beijing before but then requested the company to move them back to Shanghai as the family members couldn't stand the air pollution. Shanghai's air quality is slightly better than that of Beijing, but still quite bad especially during winter times.

Regarding air pollution, there are three things you should pay attention to. First, you should download the 'Air Matters' APP onto your smartphone before you arrive in China (I have heard from friends telling me they had problems downloading the APP when they are in China). It allows you to get real time air quality information from the local official government source and from local US embassy measurement (if there is one in that city). Even when you travel around China, it will show you the air quality index of the city you are at. Every morning when I wake up, that is the first APP I used to check whether the air quality is good or not. If the air quality index is high (and I usually refer to the US embassy measurement), I will wear a mask when going out.

So why are there two measurements? That is related to the second point. The Chinese government uses a different standard to interpret air quality than the US embassy. The most obvious difference is on the interpretation of PM2.5 articles level in the air. For example, the measurement of PM2.5 articles (which is the vital particle that causes all kinds of cardiovascular diseases) are often times different between the Chinese government and the US Embassy reading. Even if the measurement are the same, the interpretation is different. If PM2.5 level is at 100, then the US Embassy would classify the air quality as 'unhealthy' (WHO advises that PM2.5 level above 35µg/m3 is considered unhealthy) and would advise people to stay indoor; while according to the Chinese government standard, the air quality is only considered as 'Lightly Polluted'. Local schools follow the Chinese government standards while international schools usually follow the US Embassy reading.

By now you have downloaded the APP, and understood how to interpret the air quality index from different sources. Lastly, you need to get protection to combat the poor air quality. During the days of heavy pollution, it is advised that you stay indoors. Even so it does not mean the air quality inside your home is of acceptable quality. To improve the air quality in your household, you could purchase air purifiers, and make sure they are the types that can filter PM2.5 particles. However, those high quality air purifiers do come with a pretty high price tag. Each unit costs around US$1100-1600, and you will need one unit for each room. Just to equip each room with a unit will easily cost you US$3000-4000 in total! This is definitely the additional cost one needs to pay living in China.

Air Quality Index, China Standards vs. US Standards

China Standards	US Standards
0-50: Excellent	0-50: Good
51-100: Good	51-100: Moderate
101-150: Lightly Polluted	101-150: Unhealthy for Sensitive Groups
151-200: Moderately Polluted	151-200: Unhealthy
201-300: Heavily Polluted	201-300: Very Unhealthy
301-500: Severely Polluted	301-500: Hazardous

Illustration 4.1 Air Quality Index, China Standards vs. US Standards

Gallery 4.2 Example of different air quality index reading

When you have to go outdoors, it is advised that you wear a N95 grade mask which filters out the PM2.5 particles. It is useless if you wear only a surgical mask as it does not block PM2.5 particles. Also be wary of all the masks sold online, in supermarkets or pharmacies that claim to be N95 grade. There are only a few number of international brands like 3M that produce N95 grade air masks. If you have little ones at home, make sure you get a child size mask as the adult ones would be too big for their little faces. I usually buy mine directly from the 3M flagship store on TMall online so that I know for sure I am getting the authentic ones.

Air pollution usually gets worse during winter time as many families living in the rural area burn coal to warm their homes, emitting high level of sulfur dioxide (SO2) and soot - which is the PM2.5 particles. I still remember during the winter of 2013, air pollution was really bad in both Beijing and Shanghai as families in the rural area were burning coal at home for heating. The air quality index was over 300 in Beijing and over 200 in Shanghai for weeks! All the local and foreigner families rushed to buy air purifiers and air masks online or in stores. The entire China went out of stock overnight! My colleagues and I would be discussing where we could get masks and air purifiers for our home as we were really concerned about air quality! It was after that terrifying air pollution period where people started to pay attention to air quality in China.

Gallery 4.3 Heavily Polluted Days during Winter time

Water Pollution

With concern over the quality of tap water heightened by news story such as the hordes of dead pigs found in a major river in Shanghai in March of 2013, a lot of people choose to install water filters and order bottled water for home consumption. When you order bottled water, there are a few things to keep in mind: first, you should order from established brands. I have witnessed some roadside shops filling bottles with tap water. Since you are paying for it, you might as well get clean and safe drinking water in return. Some bigger brands are Nestle, Watsons, Ice Dew from Coca Cola etc., and their ordering hotline can be found online from their official websites. Secondly, you should always place the order during office hours, otherwise you might be scammed. Marco, my Taiwanese colleague, had a bad experience with ordering bottled water and ended up losing money. Marco just moved to Shanghai from Taipei and was looking for bottled water home delivery service. He found a number on the internet and called to purchase water vouchers that night. A man who did not sound like any customer service personnel answered his call. Without feeling suspicious at all, Marco placed order of 50 vouchers of bottled water. The next day, a delivery man arrived with the vouchers and he paid the delivery man US$240 (RMB 1,500) in cash for the 50 vouchers. But later when Marco tried to order bottled waters with the vouchers, he found out that they were fakes. And of course, the scammer and his RMB 1,500 were nowhere to be found. So remember, only order from reputable brands and call their official customer hotline number during office hours.

4 . 4

Wine & Dine & Shop

Eating is an integral part of Chinese culture, and a lot of "weird things" can go onto the table. For instance, the consumption of dog meat, though technically illegal, is fairly common in restaurants in the western and northern parts of China. As it is considered to be a delicacy, be prepared to be brought to these restaurants by local clients if you happen to go to business trips in these areas.

Recent Food Scandals

Many food safety issues have been brought to light in China. Below are some of the bigger issues that were reported:

"Refusal oil" or "Di Gou You (地沟油)" in Mandarin – this is the pinnacle of unsafe Chinese food. You may understand it as "recycled oil" made by unethical merchants refining kitchen waste into cooking oil. Large amounts of chemicals are used in the refining process, and basically a lot of cancer-inducing chemicals are produced, and one could only imagine what would happen after eating it. News reports have shown that not only do small eateries and restaurants purchase this kind of oil for its cheap price, but some higher-end restaurants purchase it as well. So how do you avoid it if it is potentially everywhere? Your best bet is to stay away from the very cheap and small restaurants, and keep in mind that if the food is too cheap, it is probably not safe.

Fake alcohol – due to the high demand for alcohol, the production of fake alcohol came into operation. It is likely that there are all sorts of fake alcohol in the market, but the most common ones are red wines, white wines, and hard liquors. For instance, the recipe for fake wine is simple: just mix alcohol (which is likely to be ethanol for industrial use), food coloring and grape juice or flavoring together! The cost of making fake wine is probably a few RMB, but the fake wine can be sold for RMB 100+! The profit margin is huge. In recent years, many small wine shops have opened in the mega cities; since they source from questionable suppliers, a lot of these small shops may be selling fake wines without knowing. You may think that the content would be okay if the wine bottle is authentic, but people are willing to pay good money for empty liquor bottles online; the bottles of the famous "Moutai" can sell for up to US$160 (RMB 1,000) for the vintage ones. Since there could be fake wine inside of real bottles, it is advised that liquor be purchased from reputable sources, such as large supermarkets or online retailers. My practice is to bring back a bottle every time I travel abroad, since the price is cheaper abroad anyway. The Chinese customs allows for foreign passport holders to bring in two bottles of liquor per visit, whereas Hong Kong, Macau, and Taiwanese residents may bring in one bottle.

Gallery 4.4 Suspicious wine shop located at a busy street in Shanghai

Other illegal food additives – there are many recent news reports about illegal food additives, such as chemical flavorings in hotpots, antibiotics used in seafood and poultry, chemicals that are used to alter the texture and outlook of any meat into seeming like beef or pork, fake eggs, tainted baby formulas, methanol-laced vegetables and herbal medicines, etc. As a consumer it is often difficult to distinguish the fake goods from the authentic ones, therefore it is safer to purchase goods from large and reputable retailers, or one could produce items from scratch. As a result of the seemingly endless list of problematic food items, many retailers in large cities such as Shanghai and Beijing have taken the opportunity to offer organic meat and vegetable at a higher price.

Fake cigarette – there are usually fake cigarettes where fake liquor is being sold. It is the same as buying liquor; it is advised to purchase cigarettes at reputable stores. Of course, since smoking is bad for your health, it is advised that one does not smoke altogether.

Imported Food

If you are concerned about the safety of local food in China, you may consider purchasing imported food items. With a growing number of foreigners moving to the mega cities, many high end and online grocers like www.yhd.com have started to cater to their needs by offering a greater selection of imported goods. However, as the import duty and shipping cost of these items are also factored into their prices, they will be expensive. The usual markup is two to four times the price at the good's place of origin. For example, a box of Morton's salt costs US$0.99 (RMB 6.2) in the United States, but it sells for over US$3 (RMB 20) at high end supermarkets in Shanghai. A bottle of Wesson cooking oil sells for US$3.2 (RMB 21) a bottle, but sells for US$7.7-9.2 (RMB 50-60) in China! For foreigners to maintain the same quality of living in China as is in their home country, one actually needs to pay extra on many daily necessity items. Living cost definitely is not cheap anymore in China.

A lot of my expatriate friends actually would stock up on packaged food and household products when they go back to their home country for holidays and bring back to China. Note that fresh food, like fruits and meat are not allowed to be brought into China though. Javier, my Spanish friend, was trying to bring in some Iberia Jamon since Jamon sells at very high price in China. Unfortunately he was stopped at the China customs and all his Jamon was confiscated! Javier told me that he was asking the custom officer whether he could just eat all the Jamon on the spot! Of course the custom officer refused and said that he should feel thankful because they did not fine him for bringing in meat without declaring to the custom! When Javier saw the custom officer 'threw' away the Iberia Jamon, he felt his heart stopped beating!

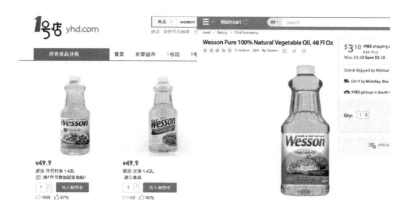

Gallery 4.5 Price comparison of Wesson Cooking Oil, China vs. US

Cloth Shopping

Since it is relatively inexpensive, many foreigners like to get their clothes tailor-made in China. So what is there to look out for when you are buying clothes in China?

Tailor-made Clothing

The centers for tailor-made clothing are the markets of Dongjiadu (董家渡) in Shanghai and Silk Street (秀水街) in Beijing. The shops can tailor make articles of clothing such as suits and traditional wear for men and qipao (long Chinese gown) for ladies. Usually men's dress shirts and pants can be readied in a day's time, and some can cost as little as US$16 (RMB 100) if you pick cheap fabrics. For a qipao, it costs around US$40 and up, depending on the fabric and style. If you don't have time to go pick up the tailored-made clothing, you can also ask the shop to send to the hotel you are staying at. For whole suits, it may take 2-3 days to be made, while ladies' qipao can take 5-7 days.

International Brands

Many international clothing brands have established shops in China, but due to the implementation of various taxes by the Chinese government, the prices of these goods can easily be 20-30% more expensive than in other countries. For luxury brands, the mark up could be up to 50%. This is mainly the reason why many Chinese go on shopping sprees when they travel abroad since it really is much cheaper than buying them in China.

So-called "International Brands"

While strolling through Chinese malls, you may notice many foreign-sounding brand names, but in reality they are all local brands. Many local brands try their utmost to appear "internationalized", so that they can target higher-spending consumers by appearing to be more prestigious. The funniest thing is that oftentimes these brand names are just a jumble of letters that no one can pronounce, so if you come across weird brand names, keep in mind that they are most likely local brands.

Useful Websites:

Online Grocer	www.yhd.com
Online Shopping	www.taobao.com; www.jd.com
Travel (Flights, Hotels, Trains)	www.ctrip.com; www.qunar.com; www.taobao.com
Train Tickets Reservation	www.12306.cn
Books	www.dangdang.com
Amazon China	www.z.cn
Restaurants listing	www.dianping.com
Online Cake Shop	www.lecake.com
Courier Service	www.sf-express.com
Food Delivery Service	www.ele.me; www.waimai.meituan.com

4 . 5

Public Holiday Schedule

The holiday calendar in China is simple yet complicated at the same time. The simple part is that there are only seven public holidays for a total of eleven days, which is outlined in Illustration 4.2.

The complicated part is how the holidays are arranged. In order to extend holidays to encourage consumer spending, the government tends to turn one-day holiday into holidays that last a couple of days. But since there is no free lunch in the world, those extra holiday days have to be compensated by the employees working on weekends. Below is an example:

If Qing Ming Festival falls on a Tuesday, the government would turn the Monday before into a holiday but would require employees to work on the previous Saturday. In that sense, you would have to work for six days the week before and get three continuous days off the next week (Sunday, Monday and Tuesday), and you would resume work on Wednesday. Some people may take some annual leaves to make for an extended break. Therefore, you may find that some Chinese companies are still in operation on weekends but are gone for the whole week after.

Public Holiday Schedule in China

HOLIDAY	DATE	NO. OF DAYS IN HOLIDAY
New Year	January 1st	1
Chinese New Year / Spring Festival	Lunar calendar January 1st – 3rd	3 (7 when combined with weekend and substitute work days)
International Working Women's Day	March 8th	Most companies offer female employees half day off
Qing Ming Festival (Tomb Sweeping Day)	April 4th	1
International Labor Day	May 1st	1
Dragon Boat Festival	Lunar calendar May 5th	1
Mid-Autumn Festival	Lunar calendar August 15th	1
National Day	October 1st – 3rd	3 (7 when combined with weekend and substitute work days)

Illustration 4.2 Public Holiday Schedule in China

For longer holidays like the Spring Festival and National Day, the arrangement becomes even more complicated. Usually you are required to work on the weekends before and after the holiday, and it is not uncommon to be working seven days straight. That happened to me before, and by the seventh day I was close to having a mental breakdown.

Many websites have holiday arrangements posted, but do not hold them to be absolutely accurate. Every year the State Council will publish the next year's holiday and working arrangement, so it is best to check its website for the most up-to-date information. However, they tend to publish the information very late, usually in early to mid December, which makes Chinese New Year holiday planning a bit tricky.

Another important tip is that book your travel early for Chinese New Year and the National Week Holidays. As many Chinese choose to travel overseas during these long holiday break, air ticket price tends to go up significantly as the holiday approaches. Unless you do not mind paying an astronomical price for flights. A few years ago, I was too busy at work and did not have time to plan a trip for CNY. Two months before CNY and I finally searched for flights, however it was already too late. Tickets of the date I wanted were all sold out, or became prohibitively expensive! For example, a round trip economy class ticket from Shanghai to Tokyo would cost US$1600! I just could not convince myself to pay US$4000 on air tickets for the whole family only to travel to another city within Asia, while I would only need to pay one third of that price if I booked earlier. So in the end, we were stuck in Shanghai for CNY. It was cold and many places were closed for the holidays. We got really bored as there was nothing to do. Since then, I would book my flights at least four to six months before the holiday.

2017 Public Holiday Schedule

January

	S	M	T	W	T	F	S
New Year	1	2	3	4	5	6	7
	8	9	10	11	12	13	14
	15	16	17	18	19	20	21
	22	23	24	25	26	27	28
	29	30	31	Chinese New Year			

February

	S	M	T	W	T	F	S
Chinese New Year				1	2	3	4
	5	6	7	8	9	10	11
	12	13	14	15	16	17	18
	19	20	21	22	23	24	25
	26	27	28				

April

	S	M	T	W	T	F	S
Tomb Sweeping Holiday							1
	2	3	4	5	6	7	8
	9	10	11	12	13	14	15
	16	17	18	19	20	21	22
	23	24	25	26	27	28	29
	30						

May

	S	M	T	W	T	F	S
Labor Day	1	2	3	4	5	6	
	7	8	9	10	11	12	13
	14	15	16	17	18	19	20
	21	22	23	24	25	26	27
	28	29	30	31			

Dragon Boat Festival

September

S	M	T	W	T	F	S
					1	2
3	4	5	6	7	8	9
10	11	12	13	14	15	16
17	18	19	20	21	22	23
24	25	26	27	28	29	30

October

National Week Holiday + Mid-Autumn Festival

S	M	T	W	T	F	S
1	2	3	4	5	6	7
8	9	10	11	12	13	14
15	16	17	18	19	20	21
22	23	24	25	26	27	28
29	30	31				

Holiday	Substitute Work Day

Gallery 4.6 2007 Public Holidays Schedule

4 . 6

Getting Around in China

Traffic Safety

When the pedestrian light turns green, we all know that cars will stop and it is supposed to be safe for pedestrians to cross the road. However, do not take that for granted in China. When you are in China, you need to pay extra attention to all sorts of traffic as there are many crazy and clueless drivers. You may often see inexperienced drivers who back up on highways, exit the highway by cutting across several lanes at once, drive on the shoulder of the road, drive in the wrong direction, change lanes without signaling or even looking, stop on the road to run errands without turning on the emergency lights, throw litter out the car window, drive 20km/h on the passing lane while chatting on their mobile phones, etc. Drivers in China basically drive like they were riding bicycles, ignoring all rules and regulations. You need to pay attention to the following three rules. First of all, cars usually do not yield to bicycles and pedestrians, so as a pedestrian, you must be careful when crossing the road, even when it is green light for pedestrians. Second, watch out for the electric or gas scooters. These bikes look similar to motorcycles, except that they are powered by batteries or natural gas and do not required licenses, thus they are relatively cheap. However, in terms of speed, they can still reach 60 km/h. These scooters are the most reckless; they could be driven on the sidewalk, overtaken cars on the roads, or driven in all sorts of direction. Since these scooters often do not have licenses and are usually driven by parcel delivery men or young people, it could get very problematic if you have a run-in with them. If the situation occurs, you should yell to make sure that the other people around you would help you stop the perpetrator and call 110 to report to the police. Thirdly, the traffic laws in China dictate that if an automobile is involved in an accident with a cyclist or pedestrian, the burden of the law is on the automobile driver. When the police arrive, they will determine a ratio of responsibility for each party involved. In other words, the automobile driver is responsible for the costs incurred by sending the injured to the hospital, and he would be reimbursed accordingly after the police determine how much responsibility each party is to hold in the incident. Of course, it is very difficult to claim the money back. Given the nature of this law, some ill-intentioned individuals may even create these incidents in order to extort or blackmail. Therefore, the best thing to do if you are driving in China is to avoid the pedestrians and cyclists in order to avoid any trouble.

Bicycles

Bicycles are a good alternative as the traffic becomes increasingly congested and taxis are harder and harder to find in big cities. One thing to keep in mind is to not purchase a bicycle that is too expensive, since it would be an easy target for thieves; another thing is to buy a good lock. The last thing to note is to observe the road signs as some busy roads prohibit the use of bicycles. Started recently in Shanghai, police would fine cyclists who ride their bicycles or motor scooters on pedestrian walk or on roads where bikes are not allowed. If you live in Shanghai or Beijing, and do not wish to buy a bike worrying about the bike being stolen, you may check out this bike sharing app called mobike.

Electric Scooters

Electric scooters are a good means of transportation to travel to farther places that bicycles cannot reach. They are powered by batteries, so when they run out you can simply recharge them at home, and you do not need a driver's license to drive one. However, these scooters, especially their batteries, tend to get stolen a lot as well, so you may want to invest in a good lock or take the battery with you after you parked the vehicle. If you are in Guangzhou, then riding electric scooters and motorcycles is not an option as the local law prohibits it.

Getting a Driver's License

If you want to drive in China, you will need a local driver's license. Should you already have a license from Hong Kong or Taiwan, then all you need to do is to pass a written test and there is no need for a driving test. However, do not underestimate the written test; it is not as easy as it sounds, and in most cases you will need at least a 90% for a passing score. If your license is from other countries and there is no Chinese translation of your license, then you will first need to have it translated to Chinese by an agency recognized by the local government, followed by the written test which is available in English.

Of course, if you have no license at all, then you will need to take a written test, followed by a driving test, just like what the locals do. In case you find the whole process being too complicated, you can always find an agency to help you with the application at a charge (in China, whatever license you are trying to apply, there is always an agency out there who can help you get the license in a more effective manner).

Public Transport Card

It is essentially a pre-paid smart card that deducts the fare every time you ride on certain public transportations. It can be purchased at the local subway train stations, but they can usually be used only on the local subway trains and public buses. In Shanghai, some taxis have also installed the system for fare payment by the public transport card.

Buying Plane Tickets

In China, most people purchase plane tickets online, and some of the more popular websites include Ctrip (www.ctrip.com) and the travel section on Taobao (www.taobao.com). If you have registered for alipay or e-banking, you can directly pay for your purchases online. If not, some online agents also allow for payment on ticket delivery.

Buying Railway Train Tickets

If you want to buy railway train tickets, you will still need to go to the train station or designated selling counters around the city, with your ID. You can also reserve a ticket online via the official train ticket site www.12306.cn (registration required in Chinese language) or via Ctrip, but you will still need to pick up the ticket at the train station in person. It is advised that you go pick up the ticket in advance instead of the day of travel, unless you are willing to arrive at the train station at least two hours before the train departs and you can bear with the chaos at the train station. In case you cannot make the trip yourself, you can ask the local delivery services or LinQu 邻趣 (more on LinQu in Chapter 2.3) to pick up or buy for you. They usually charge RMB10-20 as service charge. However, keep in mind that valid identification document is required for the purchase of railway tickets, so even if someone else is to make the purchase for you, you will need to provide a photocopy of your ID.

CHAOS AT THE TRAIN STATION

Train stations in any size-able city are typically packed by massive crowds. These stations may have been constructed within the last decade which they are not ready to meet the demands of today. As people's wealth level improves, they tend to travel more. Train service meets the basic needs of the low to middle income population. Unfortunately some of the riders lack the basic etiquettes in public. Since the railway system was run by the state, the service level is always dismal. These two factors tend to make the train station experience less than pleasant.

Starting from the moment you arrive at the station, you may need to get a ticket or pick up one if you booked online (which is preferred). The ticketing hall, which is sometimes a block away from the main station, could be the beginning of your unforgettable journey. Despite there being dozens of ticketing counters, each line is still usually 20-30 people long and sometimes chaotic. You need to be careful to line up for the right window: Today's tickets only, Pickup only, Dual language or Regular window. Also check their lunch break time, because when the clock strikes, the window will be shut and if you are the unlucky one right behind the last one served, you will have to wait for an hour or run like the rest of the line for a new queue all over again.

Also be aware that some people just don't like to line up for their turn. As time goes on, you will observe certain people trying to cut in, which results in fat lines (i.e., several people trying to jostle for the same forward position). I have even seen an old man cutting right into the front of line, and when stopped by others, he claimed his senior citizen status to mute complaints. But it turned out that he was a professional ticket buyer paid to buy tickets for others! Even when you got to the front of the line, there could be people trying to extend their hands into the counter out of their turn.

It could be frustrating and even daunting for foreigners to buy tickets under such circumstances. The key is to defend your position and stop people from taking advantage. These people typically back off if you ask them directly to line up.

For foreigners, you need to show your passport before you can pick up your ticket, which means the automatic machines that recognizes national IDs won't work for you. Once your passport is checked at the station for the first time, you can get the tickets from designated travel agencies without the hassle. So budget two hours minimum just for the tickets if it is your first time to the train station. Also, always watch out for your possessions in crowded places.

Traffic Restriction

Traffic Restriction

One of the most troublesome aspects of Chinese traffic, especially in Beijing, is the so called "traffic restriction", a.k.a. "Jiao Tong Guan Zhi (交通管制)" in Chinese. Essentially, it is the police blocking off traffic to make way for the cars of government officials, who shall not be stuck in traffic like the rest of us. Traffic restrictions are not pre-announced, so if you find yourself in one you can only blame your bad luck. This kind of restriction happens more frequently in Beijing than other cities simply because it has the largest number of government officials based in the city. This also explains why the traffic in Beijing is bad despite having some of the widest roads in the country. Therefore, it is advised to factor in more commute time if you are to travel around in Beijing, or learn to take the subway.

Air Traffic Restriction

There is traffic restriction on roads, and there is also air traffic restriction. Flight delays are commonplace in China, and most of the time it is due to "air traffic restriction". No one further explains what "air traffic restriction" really is, but one explanation is that commercial airliners have to give way to government officials traveling by planes. Another plausible explanation is that the military is conducting drills or missions, and so the air space is completely sealed off. Regardless of the reason behind, when "air traffic restriction" occurs everyone will just have to sit on the plane and wait. Also, it is advised to take trains rather than plane to the South during typhoon or monsoon season, which starts from May and last until August/September. During the monsoon season, flights could be delay by 6 hours or longer or be simply cancelled. If you really have to travel by plane, take the earliest flight out as the morning flights are less likely to be delayed or cancelled.

Watch Out while Traveling in China

Do Not Touch Things that are Lying Around

Many families like to visit the countryside or farms that are located on the outskirts of cities for a family day out, but beware about touching things when you are on farms or in villages. One time I was traveling with some friends from abroad, and we were driving from Beijing to Hebei province when we stopped by a scenic village on the way. One of my friends saw that the fruits on a nearby tree were ripe, so he picked one off. Suddenly a man came out of nowhere and claimed that by picking the fruit off, my friend had destroyed the effectiveness of his "fengshui tree" and asked for RMB5,000 (US$800) in compensation, otherwise we would not be able to leave the village. It was essentially extortion, but the problem was my friend did pick off the fruit. My friend was quite upset about being extorted and suggested to call the police, but we told him that it was fruitless to do so, since there was no police in small villages, and it would take a while before they came from the nearest town. Moreover, the police would most likely be on the side of the villagers when they came. After some haggling between us and the villager, we finally paid RMB200 (US$30) for the "feng shui fruit" and settled the issue. The moral of the story is: don't touch things mindlessly when you are in small towns and villages!

Renting a Car

A Beijing friend was driving his wife and daughter to the countryside for some fun in the sun, and when he arrived, he saw that everyone parked on the side of the road, so he did the same thing with his own car. However, they went back to the car after lunch and realized that all the tires were punctured. With nowhere to complain to, he could only drive the car very slowly back to Beijing for repair. When he told us the story, we tried to figure out why his car became the target. We believed it was either because my friend was driving a nice car (it was a BMW 3 series) or parked in the wrong place. It is not uncommon for nice cars to be the target of malicious pranks in China. If you don't want to risk your own car, you can consider renting one for traveling. The names of some car rental agencies are China Auto Rental (神州租车), eHi Car Services (一嗨租车), and Topone (至尊租车); however, you must have a Chinese driving license for car rental.

4 . 7

Taxi

Taxi Calling App

It has become increasingly difficult to get a taxi during rush hours or when it is raining in large cities in China. This is why taxi calling App has become very popular these days. Seeing the success of Uber in the US, the big Chinese internet players quickly copied the model and launched similar apps in China in early 2014. The most popular ones are Didi-Dadi and Kuaidi-Dache ("Dadi 打的 or Dache 打车 " in Mandarin means getting a taxi). Uber also entered China in late 2014. You can reserve a taxi or private car in advance using these apps, or you can call a taxi for immediate use, given there is one nearby. Bear in mind though that you cannot settle the taxi fare by cash. You need to either tie a local credit card to your account, or pay via one of the online payment platforms like Alipay or WeChat payment. All these taxi apps also offer limousine cars if you don't want to have a taxi and willing to pay a higher price for a private car.

In order to grab market share, every taxi calling app is now subsidizing both taxi drivers and passengers. It is actually cheaper to get a taxi using the app than finding a taxi on the street. For instance, last week I took a taxi from home to the Bund in Shanghai. It was a 20-minute ride and cost me US$5.5 (RMB 35). On my way back home,

I called an Uber and it only cost me US$4 (RMB 25)! Besides subsidy, these taxi calling apps always run promotions. There was once I took a Didi-dadi limousine to the airport and it only cost me US$16 (RMB 99). A normal taxi ride would have cost me US$26 (RMB 160)! So try to look for these promotions next time when you are calling a taxi using an app.

Note that ever since the acquisition of Uber China by Didi-dadi, your Uber account overseas would no longer work in China if it is linked to an international credit card. You will need to download Uber China from the China store separately. Also, Uber China only accepts local credit card for payment and no longer offers English interface as it used to be.

Do Not Ask for Restaurant Suggestions from Taxi Drivers

It seems reasonable to ask taxi drivers for local restaurant suggestions when you arrive at a new place and don't know where to go, but in fact it could be a scam. The following are two real life stories involving scams by taxi drivers.

The first story is of my colleague Liz, with whom I went to Sanya (popular tourist destination in China) for the shooting of the TV commercial. It was the first day she arrived, and she was with two crew members deciding where to go for dinner. Three of them hopped on a taxi when they had not decided where to go. They asked the taxi driver for any local restaurant recommendations. The driver quickly suggested a place that served local delicacies and seafood. After driving for about thirty minutes, they arrived at a so-called "seafood restaurant" in the countryside. The driver said, "You can eat here, and I will drive you back to the city after I finish dinner here as well." Liz felt that something was fishy and asked if the driver could take them to another place. The driver insisted, somewhat eerily, that they ate here and that the food was "very authentic." Since they were out in the middle of nowhere, they had no choice but to comply. The restaurant's menu had no prices, and they did not dare asking, so they ordered several dishes and a steamed fish. After all, how much could a small fish and some normal stir fry dishes cost? The final bill came out to be US$500 (RMB 3,000), so it was roughly US$160 (RMB 1,000) per person! You could definitely go to some very, very nice restaurants at that price. Liz complained to the manager and found out that the tiny fish had cost US$160 (RMB 1,000), while each dish cost US$50-60. In addition, each person was charged US$30 for tea and other amenities. They had no choice but to pay the bill, and fortunately the taxi driver did drive them back to the city afterward. When I arrived the next day, no one dared to venture out to find restaurants, so we all opted for the safe option of ordering room service in the hotel.

The second story is told to me by a Taiwanese friend Sue who was a consultant. She and a colleague from Beijing were in Guangdong for business trip once, and they had also asked the taxi driver to recommend some restaurants. The driver enthusiastically drove them to a remote place with a few shacks and said that they served the most authentic local food there. Despite the driver's good intentions, Sue got a good scare when she saw the inside of the shacks. It was almost like a zoo, as there were cats, dogs, peacocks, raccoons, field mice, owls, etc. locked up in cages. The worst part was that all the animals looked depressed. Sue wanted to leave, but since they were again in the middle of nowhere she couldn't find a cab to leave on, so she reluctantly stayed and ate some rice with peanuts, while her Beijing colleague feasted on the wild game. Fortunately this restaurant did not rip them off, and the driver drove them back to the hotel after the meal. So if you are to ask locals for food recommendations, be sure to find out what exactly the local delicacy is.

Both of the above stories happened when the visitors are accompanied by local Chinese, so the scams or unpleasant surprises do not only happen to foreigners. The main reason why taxi drivers take unsuspecting visitors to these restaurants is because they get a "commission" from the restaurant, so your best bet for finding a good restaurant is to ask local friends and colleagues. If you are visiting a city and really have no idea where to go for restaurants, you can search on Dianping; it is similar to Yelp and provides restaurant reviews. It is available on the app store free of charge, and it has a function that displays restaurants that are closest to your geographical location and has a map function that can guide you to the restaurant you want to try. However, Dianping is only available in Chinese.

Taxi-phobia

An American friend of mine has been to China a good number of times for business trips, but he says he still gets uneasy riding in a taxi here. On some occasions the driver had my friend get off the cab before reaching the destination, which may have to do with miscommunication due to language barriers. To avoid confusions, if you have to travel to any of the Big 4 cities, for instance, you may consider using the app "That's". Besides restaurant and entertainment recommendations, it has a taxi printout function that shows the address and location of where you want to go. That way, you can simply show it to the driver to prevent any misunderstandings. Currently this app is only applicable to Shanghai, Beijing, Guangzhou, and Shenzhen; for other cities, it would be very helpful to write down the address of your destination and also the phone number and street intersection of where it is at.

The Smell

During the winter time, a taxi ride in Northern China could be a smelly one. This is mainly because a lot of taxi drivers, in order to seize as many business opportunities as possible, tend to stay in the car for days. Since they eat and sleep in the car, obviously they would not have a place to take showers. Often times you will be faced with the dilemma of being suffocated by the stink in the car or being frozen by the outside cold should you choose to open the windows. Also, since traffic jams are commonplace in China, you will also have to deal with inhaling car exhausts if you have the window opened. My personal tip is to roll down the window a little bit and sit close to it, much like how a dog would breathe while riding in a car. Another option is to wear a face mask to filter the smell, or get a limo from Didi.

Getting Fapiao (Receipt) For Your Taxi Ride

In most cities in China, the taxis are metered, so remember to ask the driver to print out a copy of the fapiao (receipt) before you leave the cab. Also, make sure the words printed on the fapiao are clear; information such as time, price, and the car license number should be present. If you suspect the driver have taken a longer route, you can report it to the complaint hotline. In Shanghai, if the incident is verified by checking the car's GPS, a refund will be made to the customer in the amount of double the paid fare, and the driver will be fined by the company as well. An important reason of getting the fapiao is to retrieve items that you have left on the car, which happened to my friend a couple of times when he left his unlocked iPhone on the cabs in Beijing, Shanghai and Shenyang. He had to pay the driver his gas money and a one or two hundred RMB reward, but he was able to get his phone back every time.

4 . 8

Staying at Hotel

Smoking / Non-smoking Rooms

If you are staying at an international hotel chain, the premises are usually all non-smoking, so there should not be any issues. However, in smaller cities and towns, there may only be local hotel chains, and it is very important to state your preference for smoking or non-smoking room when you make the reservation. Especially if you opt for non-smoking rooms, since there are usually only a few non-smoking floors in local hotels, they may be unavailable if you do not book in advance. If you stay in a smoking room, the hotel staff may offer to perform a "de-smoke process" to rid the room of the smell, but in actuality they will just spray some air freshener around. Other than the rooms, you should be prepared that there will be people smoking in the hotel lobby, restaurant, etc. during any time of the day. Do not be surprised if you find yourself surrounded by middle-aged men smoking and lighting cigarettes for one another during your breakfast buffet.

Massage Services

Another thing to look out for, especially in local hotels, is the massage services. Oftentimes, these are "massage services" with other services included. Francis, a friend of mine from Hong Kong, once went on business trip to a second-tier city and had stayed at a local four-star hotel. He ordered the in-house massage service, and after twenty minutes, a lady in her early twenties showed up, dressed in a low-cut shirt and hot pants. Francis was starting to get the idea that something was wrong but still let her in. The so-called 'masseur' started the massage service, but after a while, the lady started to probe Francis to see if he wanted "other services". Francis rejected her offer, and she left after the thirty-minute massage session. After hearing this story, I asked Francis how come he was not tempted. Francis' first answer was that he was not that type of guy (of course). Even if he wanted to, it was just too much risk. What if that 'masseur' was with a local gangster group? He has heard many cases of foreigner got blackmailed by prostitute or detained by local gangster for money. In fact, after that incident, Francis said he would never order massage services in local hotels in China again.

Being Approached by Young Women/Men Outside of Hotels

This happens to many men regardless of ethnicity and nationality. My friend Raj, an Indian guy, was staying at a five-star hotel in downtown Beijing on his first visit to China. He was walking around the hotel looking for an ATM, and during that short fifteen minutes walk, he was approached by four young women! One asked if he wanted to go for coffee, another said she could take him sightseeing, and he did not even understand what the last two ladies said to him. My friend joked that he never thought he would be so popular with the ladies. Another friend of mine, who is from Hong Kong, was even directly approached by a man who asked if he wanted women in front of the hotel. As shocking as it sounds, please keep in mind that prostitution is illegal in China if you come across this kind of situation. If you are approached by any stranger, offering to take you to a bar or coffee, it is safer to say no and walk away.

4.9

Finding an Apartment

Find a House that Faces the South

This is especially applicable in Northern China; since the winters there are long and harsh, people from that region tend to care a lot about whether the house is facing the south. This is mainly due to the fact that more sunlight would reach houses facing the south, making the house brighter and warmer, and thus would require less heat. If the house or apartment that you are looking at is not facing the south, you may be able to bargain for a lower price with the owner! But in return, be prepared for a cold and depressing winter!

Houses with Balconies

Many houses do not have a designated laundry area, and it is not common to use laundry dryers in China. If there is a balcony you could put out clothes or sheets to dry. For Shanghai in particular, the rainy season starts in May/ June every year, thus it is customary for the locals to put out their sheets to dry beforehand so they wouldn't become moldy. An apartment with a balcony would ask for higher rent than one without.

Check for Odor in the Bathroom

In the numerous apartments that I rented before, the bathroom's drainage pipe had constantly emitted an unpleasant odor. This is because in many buildings in China, the drainage pipe connects the sewage pipe to the flushing water, as a cost saving measure. (While in many countries, it is separated into two pipes: one for the toilet and the other one for drainage.) This one-pipe design, however, also allows the smell of the sewage water to be emitted from the drains. The smell is very difficult to get rid of, as I have tried many different ways but still not successful. So I would highly recommend that you check for odors in the bathroom prior to renting or purchasing.

Be Prepared for Very Cold Winters in East China

As mentioned before, apartments/ houses in South region (south of the Yangtze River) usually are not equipped with central heating, so it becomes very cold indoors in winter. Further south the winters are comparatively milder, but in areas like Shanghai and the cities in the Yangtze River Delta, winters are cold and last longer as well. Usually the temperature starts dropping in November, and it does not become warm again until April. The Shanghai winters may be tolerable for those who are used to living in Europe or the United States, but for those of us who are from places much closer to the equator (myself included), the first winter was quite harsh. If you don't like cold weathers, what can you do? One option is to find a house with floor heating system; however, these houses are limited in number and are generally more expensive in terms of rent and your gas bill. Another option is to buy an electric heater (see Gallery 4.7). Note that it uses electricity instead of oil and is much warmer than the fan heaters or infrared heaters found in the market. Of course, using this heater will up your electricity bill as well, though not as much as using the floor heating system. If you are unsure of where to buy it, you can order it online and have it delivered to your door. My advice is to get it at the beginning of the winter season when the new models are out and stocks are available. I remembered last year's winter temperature suddenly dropped and I wanted to buy one for my live-in maid, but all the models went out of stock! I had to wait for two weeks before inventory arrived.

Gallery 4.7 Electric Heater for the Winter

Prepare at least Five Months' Worth of Rent

For renting apartment or houses in China, it is common for the landlord to request for three months' rent at a time, in addition to the two months' rent as safety deposit. So that is five months' worth of rent which could be a lot of money! In some cases, the landlord may even ask for six months' rent or twelve months' rent at a time to secure his cash flow. Of course, if you are willing to pay for six months or twelve months' rent at once; you may be able to bargain with the landlord for a lower rental price. Thus it is important to make sure you have enough cash when renting a house. Most MNCs offer cash advance to expatriates who just moved to China and do not have enough local currency to pay for moving expenses. So do check with your company for cash advance option in case your landlord asks for five months' worth of rent when you sign the lease.

Rental Tax and Tax Receipt 'Fapiao'

Fapiao is basically an official receipt, and Chinese tax laws allow foreigners (including residents from Hong Kong and Taiwan) to use it to offset their income tax. You can request the landlord for fapiao, which is the receipt the landlord gets after paying taxes for their rental income. Some landlords may ask you to pay additional for the taxes (typically 6% of the rental fee). So when you negotiate rent with your landlord, make sure the rent includes tax as well.

Temporary Household Registration for Foreigners

When you move into a new accommodation, including serviced apartments, by law you have to register yourself at the local police station within 24 hours. Some properties' management office would take care of that for you, but if you need to complete the registration yourself, remember to bring your passport, the original and a photocopy of the rental agreement to register at the local police station. Upon completing the registration, you will receive a "temporary household registration for foreigners", which is needed for opening a bank account, applying for work visa, the one-year visa-free resident permit, driver's license etc.

If the Rented Accommodation is Sold, the Tenant Gets Evicted

In China, the laws protecting the rights of the tenants are not very comprehensive; therefore the tenants usually get the worse end of the bargain when situations arise. For instance, if a property is sold and the new owner is unwilling to extend a new rental contract, the tenant will be evicted. Thus there is risk in paying too many months' rent in advance. It has happened to my friend before when the safety deposit was also lost when the property was sold. Therefore, it is advised that if you are not going to renew the rental agreement, you should properly communicate with the landlord beforehand. If a problem arises, you can contact the local consumer council for intervention. A friend of mine once paid the rent a week late since he was on business trip, and when his rental agreement ended he found that the property agent had deducted ten percent from his safety deposit as penalty as was stated in the agreement. He sought help from the consumer council, found out that the law prohibits landlords from fining tenants and instead could only charge a very low interest rate, and ultimately the agent withdrew the fine.

4.10

Domestic Helper "Ayi (阿姨)"

Ayi (the Domestic Housemaid)

In China, "Ayi (阿姨)" is the general term for referring to domestic helpers (the term literally means "aunt" and is a common way to address a middle-aged woman). It is very common to hire domestic housemaid to help with house chores or child caring in China. It started out because of the cheap labor cost. In Guangzhou and Shenzhen, the average salary for live-in maids are around US$480-$560 (RMB 3,000-3,500) in 2016, while in Beijing and Shanghai, their salaries are from US$800 -$1000 (RMB 5,000-6,500). The level of salary demanded by domestic helper in China is still much cheaper compared to childcare in western countries.

While domestic workers are categorized by either being full-time or hourly-paid workers in most western countries, there are many types of Ayi in China. The common ones are full-time live-in maid, nanny, confinement lady (one that takes care of the newborn baby and the mother after she has given birth), hourly-paid Ayi, cleaning maids, etc. What gave rise to such specific division of labor? In my opinion it is mainly due to the demands of the rich in the mega cities, who demand that the various domestic helpers they hire be professional in the specific skill set that they possess. In other words, since many of the Ayi are hired to help with childrearing tasks, the parents want nothing but the best for their only child. In turn, this spoiled many of the Ayi working in big cities, since now they are paid just to do a fraction of the work.

So figuring out what type of Ayi you want to hire already seems complicated. The harder part is how to keep your Ayi happy and 'motivated'. Let me share my personal experience here: The first Ayi I hired was back in 2011, right after I gave birth to my daughter. Her name is Xiao Cui and apparently she is very good at negotiation. During the two years she worked for me, Xiao Cui had threatened to quit three times, and every time I offered to raise her salary as a result. Her monthly salary started off at RMB 3,000 and, after four times of increase, was last at RMB 4,500, which was 50% increase over the two-year period! In fact, that rate of salary increase was better than most jobs on the market!

In addition to the 'expected' annual salary increase, don't forget that you are expected to give your Ayi red pocket "hong bao (红包)" during Chinese New Year ("hong bao" are little red packets with money inside that Chinese give out during Chinese New Year). How much should you give? A few hundred or a few thousand dollars? The expected amount in Shanghai/ Beijing is roughly equivalent to a month's salary. Recently during my interview with an Ayi, she had already requested that she wanted two-months' worth of salary as "hong bao" for Chinese New Year (and of course she did not make it through my interview). Another point to note about Chinese New Year is that a lot of Ayi quit, with or without notice, after the holidays. So now you have to struggle whether you should give the Ayi "hong bao" before or after the holidays? If you give it before, what if the Ayi doesn't come back to work after CNY? If you give it after the holidays, maybe she will be upset and quit right after she collected the "hong bao". A friend of mine once gave her Ayi a generous "hong bao" to wish her a happy holiday and hopefully worked harder when she came back after the Chinese New Year. After the holidays, her Ayi did not return. She didn't even call my friend to say that she was quitting. My poor friend had to scramble to find someone to take care of her two toddlers while she and her husband returned to work!

4 . 1 1

Mobile Phone and Data Card

Due to the expensive mobile phone roaming fees, one of the first things people do as they arrive in China is to register for a Chinese mobile number. Which carrier is better? Where do you buy network data cards? We will briefly discuss the above in the following section.

Pre-paid Phone Cards

If you will not stay in China for long, you can use pre-paid phone cards instead of signing up with a mobile phone carrier. ID registration is required to purchase a SIM card, because the Chinese government needs to be able to trace every mobile communication. It is advised that you bring your passport to the official sales offices of the different carriers to purchase a pre-paid phone card. You can also purchase pre-paid cards from small street vendors or online, but you still need to take your ID to the mobile carrier's sales office to register first before the card can be activated.

When your pre-paid card is running out of money, there are a few ways to top-up the card: 1) Purchase top-up cards online at sites such as Taobao; 2) purchase top-up cards at convenience stores or newspaper stands; 3) add value at the carrier's sales offices. There are also monthly plans for adding value to your card, which could save you some money.

Monthly Plans

You can opt for monthly plans if you don't want to add value to your phone card every month and if you need other services, such as roaming. You will have to bring your passport to the carrier's sales office if you want to sign up for these phone plans. Credit card or bank card will also be required. If you don't have them you can pay a deposit, which ranges from RMB3,000-5,000. Your monthly plan fee can be deductible from the deposit. When you first sign up for a mobile plan, additional services such as international calling and roaming are usually not yet available. They will become available once your credit is established after a couple of months. Oftentimes there are additional benefits if you sign up for plans; for instance, China Unicom offers plans that give you a free phone when you sign up.

Comparison between China Mobile, China Unicom and China Telecom

CARRIER	ADVANTAGE	DISADVANTAGE
China Mobile	• Reception is best out of the three in remote areas • Has more sales offices • 4G is available if your phone is 4G enabled	• Foreign 3G mobile phones cannot use China Mobile's 3G network; can only go online with GPRS and speed is slower
China Unicom/ China Telecom	• 3G and 4G network are available	• May not have reception in remote areas • Does not have as many sales offices as China Mobile

Illustration 4.3 Comparison between China Mobile, China Unicom and China Telecom

Phone / Message Fraud

Frauds involving mobile phones in China come in many forms, below are some of the more common ones to look out for:

You may receive a short message asking you to check your bank account for money that has been transferred into it and to contact the sender if you haven't received it. Of course, money does not fall from the sky, and you should ignore these messages altogether.

Around holiday times, frauds may take advantage of the fact that many people travel abroad. Sometimes the messages may seem to come from people that you know, and the following is an example of what I received one New Year's Eve, "Hi, this is the landlord. I'm traveling right now, so please deposit your rent to my wife's bank account: 1234-5678, (Name of wife). Please let me know once you have made the deposit." And of course, this is a total scam.

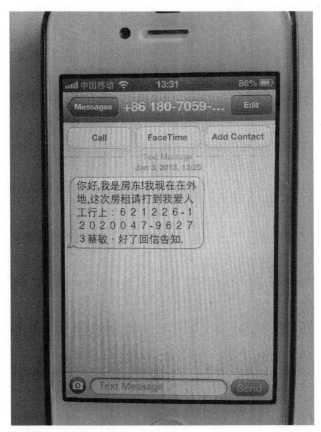

Gallery 4.8 SMS Fraud

Another common kind of fraud is that the perpetrator would call your phone and hang up after one ring, and the point of this is to lure you to call back. The most annoying thing is that they like to call in the middle of the night so you may think that it is an important call. Sometimes these are pay calls, and you would be charged if you call back, and other times the perpetrator may try to gather your personal information if you return the call. So if you find any suspicious missed calls on your phone, do not call back.

It is best to be cautious when you are handling weird phone calls or messages. Even if the person calling you can speak very good English, that does not mean he or she can't be a swindler.

4 . 1 2

Visiting the Doctor

It is quite a hassle if you become sick in China. The following are real stories to align your expectations with reality, so if you do need to visit the doctor, you will know what to expect.

Buying Medical Insurance

Unless you don't mind visiting the crowded inpatient unit or emergency room of public hospitals along with the rest of the Chinese populace, you may opt to visit foreign-run clinics or hospitals to shorten your waiting time. However, each visit to foreign-run clinics could cost at least US$100-120 (RMB 600-700), and it would cost at least US$250 (RMB 1,500) if you visit the emergency room of foreign-run hospitals. Therefore, you should have an estimate of how much will come out of your pocket if you don't have medical insurance coverage. You can consider buying insurance that has worldwide coverage; the only inconvenience is that Chinese hospitals usually do not bill the insurer directly, so you will have to file for reimbursement on your own. If you would like to purchase insurance locally, you can look into BUPA or China Pacific Insurance. Their coverage is similar, and they allow for direct billing by hospitals. For your reference, medical insurance that covers both inpatient and outpatient for a family of three would cost around US$17,500 (RMB 110,000) per annum.

Being Accompanied to Public Hospitals

If you do go to a public hospital in China, bring someone who can speak Chinese with you. The main reason is that everything, such as registering, getting an injection, being put on the drip and getting your medicines, requires you to pay first. It is after you pay and are able to present a receipt then you will receive your service or treatment, and it will be chaotic if you attempt to do everything by yourself. One time I accompanied a colleague to the hospital emergency room as she was experiencing gastric pain. First we had to register at the reception. We then had to pay the registration fee at the cashier, which was located in another building. After we come back with the receipt, we were then put into the queue to see the doctor. After an hour of waiting, we saw the doctor and asked for a painkiller injection, for which the doctor issued an invoice. I returned to the cashier with the invoice to pay, got my receipt, picked up the injection, and helped my poor colleague to the injection area. After the injection, the doctor issued a prescription, and of course we had to pay first, and then we went to the pharmacy to pick up the medicines. I probably walked back and forth from the cashier to the various departments and offices for ten times before the ordeal was finished. If I were not accompanying my colleague, how would a patient in pain manage on his own?

Speaking Mandarin

If you don't speak Mandarin, you must find a Mandarin speaker to accompany you to local hospitals, since no one can communicate to you in English at the hospital. A Korean friend of mine visited a public hospital once for eye discomfort, and no one could understand what problem she had. She ended up going on a tour around the hospital and saw the dermatologist, otolaryngologist, and finally the ophthalmologist, which my friend had no idea what was being said. At the end, she opted to return to Seoul to seek treatment.

Being Put On Drip

It is common practice for Chinese doctors to put their patients on drip, no matter you are suffering from fever, cold or toothache. Official data once shown that the average Chinese person goes through 8 bags of IV fluid in one year! Sometimes, the doctors even put antibiotics into the drip for their patients. In case you have to go to a local hospital, and you find your doctor suggesting that you be put on drip, make sure to ask for the reason why and also for the content of the drip. It may feel very strange to be put on the drip so easily, since foreign doctors tend to issue the drip after issuing medications and injections, but in China it is the other way around.

Information on Foreign-run Clinics and Hospitals (you can check on Bing for the most updated contact information)

City	Name of Clinic / Hospital
Shanghai	• Shanghai United Family Hospital and Clinics 上海和睦家医院 (has emergency unit) • Parkway Health • World Link Medical Centers • Raffles Medical Center • Huashan Worldwide Medical Center 华山医院外宾部
Beijing	• Beijing United Family Hospital and Clinics北京和睦家医院 (has emergency unit) • China – Japan Friendship Hospital 北京中日友好医院 • Peking Union Medical College Hospital – International Medical Services 北京协和医院 - 国际医疗部 • Vista Clinic
Guangzhou	• Guangzhou First People's Hospital 广州市第一人民医院 • Guangdong General Hospital – Concord Medical Center 广东省人民医院 – 协和高级医疗中心 • Guangzhou Can Am International Medical • Eur Am International Medical
Shenzhen	It is very close to Hong Kong, you may consider traveling to Hong Kong for treatment

Illustration 4.4 Information on Foreign-run Clinics and Hospitals (you can check on Bing for the most updated contact information)

4 . 1 3

Bank Affairs

Opening a Bank Account

You can open up a bank account with your identification document and temporary residence permit at any bank branch, and if you would like, you can also set up electronic banking there. If you have enough cash deposited, you can upgrade your account to a VIP account and enjoy banking services at special counters, amongst other benefits. There are many banks in China, and below are a few of the more popular ones with foreigners:

- Industrial and Commercial Bank of China (ICBC): Probably the bank with the most number of branches, but also the longest queues, especially around lunch time. Many companies also choose ICBC as the payroll bank as it is one of the largest banks in China.

- China Merchants Bank (CMB): The bank with the best service by popular opinion; its credit card also offers many benefits.

- Hong Kong and Shanghai Banking Corporation Limited (HSBC): This is a good choice if you will need to make money transfers from China to overseas, since it waives the handling fee for these transactions for its Premier customer. HSBC also introduced global banking online which allows you to wire foreign currency out with only a click. (However, one is not allowed to wire RMB out of the country without converting it to foreign currency first. See section below on how to convert RMB to foreign currency.)

Applying for Credit Card

Local banks are reluctant to issue credit cards to foreigners as there were many cases of foreigners leaving China without paying off their credit card bills in the past. Recently I tried to apply for a credit card from ICBC that convert points to airline mileage. Even though my payroll was with ICBC, and I also had term deposit with the bank, my application still got rejected! The only way for foreigners to get approval on credit card issued by local banks is through company corporate card. So if your company offers you a corporate card, take it! With a local credit card, you can sign up for Alipay and Wechat payment and allow you to make online purchases easily.

If your company does not offer corporate card, there are two ways you can try to get a local credit card. Option 1: If the company you work for is one of the world top 500 companies (note, it has to be world top 500. Fortune 500 or US top 500 doesn't count), and you have payroll slip, large local banks like ICBC, Bank of China, China Merchant Bank may approve your credit card application. Option 2: You may check with Citibank as it offers a Premier Miles credit card to foreigners with proof of income in China. My friend from Canada told me that she couldn't get any credit card from local banks even though she holds a senior position at Starbucks China. Citibank is the only bank who is willing to issue her a credit card. With this card, one can convert points to airline miles too!

Financial Services and Products

Majority of the financial products in China are only available to mainland Chinese citizens, not even citizens from Hong Kong, Macau, or Taiwan. Fixed deposit probably is the only and safest option to foreigners, which is also not a bad option given the decent interest rate level in China these days. (as of September 2016, the standard interest rate for one-year fixed term deposit is 1.75%)

Online/ Mobile Payment

It is similar to Paypal and is a popular online payment method in China. You can open an account at www.alipay.com or download Alipay from the China app store, and link it to your bank account and/ or local credit card. It is accepted by most online shopping sites, for electricity, gas or water bills, and for topping up your mobile phone or data cards. WeChat also launched its mobile payment site in 2013. As WeChat is becoming increasingly popular, many ecommerce sites also accept WeChat payment as well.

Foreign Currency Exchange / Money Transfer Out of China

China has currency control measures, so it is difficult to exchange foreign currencies or to transfer money out of China. Firstly, RMB cannot be transferred out of the country. If you need to make a transfer you will first need to change the RMB to a foreign currency. You will need the following documents for foreign currency exchange:

1. Identification document;

2. Work permit;

3. Labor contract;

4. Monthly payroll slip;

5. Proof of tax payment

You must submit the original copies of these documents to the bank. Photocopies are not accepted. All the documents should refer to the same time period. These are used to assess how much salary you have earned in China, and consequently how much foreign currency you can exchange. Every time you want to exchange foreign currency, all of the above documents must be submitted again.

You may also choose to bring RMB out of the country personally if you do not want to exchange into foreign currency. Each person can bring up to RMB20,000 OR US$5,000 in cash out of China each time. A friend of mine actually crossed the Shenzhen-Hong Kong border ten times in one day in order to bring RMB1 million out of China!

Tax Matters

The personal income tax in China is progressive, with the tax rate in the highest income bracket reaching 45%, which is much higher than many Asian countries. Your income tax is automatically deducted from the monthly salary, so the amount on your pay slip is the after-tax income. Below are some tips regarding tax issues in China:

Tax Receipts "Fapiao (发票)":

Companies in China require official tax receipts, or "fapiao (发票)", for reimbursement of business-related expenditures. Bear in mind that the Chinese tax authorities only recognize fapiao and not the printed or handwritten receipts by merchants. Usually the merchants would not offer to give you a fapiao, as issuing one would make the transaction "official" and thus taxable, so you must request for one. There are also a few kinds of fapiao; in smaller cities they are usually like checkbooks, and the merchant would write the information on it and tear it out for you. Another kind has a header, and the merchant would ask if you want a personal fapiao or company fapiao. If you are using it for company reimbursement, the header should be the company's registered name in China. You should also check if the fapiao has the official stamp on it, since without the stamp it is invalid. The last kind is where the customer needs to go online to print your own fapiao, which is offered by limited merchants, such as Starbucks in Shanghai.

Tax equalization:

If the Chinese tax rate is higher than that of your native country, you may consider asking your Chinese employer for tax equalization. That way, you will only be accountable for the tax rate of your country, and your Chinese employer will bear any excess tax amount. However, not many employers are willing to offer tax equalization these days due to high cost.

Tax-exempt expenditure:

As a non-Chinese citizen, if you do not get tax equalization from your company, you can opt for a portion of your expenditure to be tax exempted, which would ultimately decrease your taxable income. According to tax ordinances, the following items can be exempted from taxation:

- House rent
- Meal (but excluding foodstuff you buy from supermarkets)
- Chinese language training

- Transportation expense for home leave

- Children's education cost

- Laundry

Please note that it should be clearly stated in your labor contract which items and what amounts are covered by the company in the form of reimbursement. Since these items will be reimbursed to you, your before-tax income will subsequently be lowered. As much as 50% of the salary can be allocated as the tax-exempt expenditure, but the exact amount is to be worked out on individual cases with your employer. These reimbursable items must be supported by official receipt fapiao.

Tax break:

According to Chinese law, if a foreign citizen resides in China for over 5 years and has not left China for a period of 30 days continuously, he becomes a permanent China tax payer and is liable for worldwide taxation by the Chinese government. Thus, many foreigners would leave China for 30 days when they have lived in China for almost 5 years to evade this law, and this is referred to as the "tax break." And if a foreigner did not take a tax break after living in China for 5 years, he or she will need to take annual tax break by leaving the country for 30 days every year. So it is very important not to forget about the five year tax break. Otherwise, it is more troublesome to take it every year.

Tax liability for frequent visitor:

Even if you do not reside in China but you stay in China for more than 180 days within a 12-months period, you are still liable to pay China taxes. It does not matter even if your salary is not paid in China or if you only visit periodically for business trips. Pay attention that the period involved is the past 12-months period and not the past calendar year, and the days that you pass through customs, regardless of time, are counted in the 180 days as well. I actually have a friend from Hong Kong who created an excel program to log all his trips to China to ensure he did not pass the 180 days line, as China tax rate is significantly higher than that of Hong Kong!

Eight things to prepare before your first visit to China

1. Install a VPN on your phone and laptop if you still want to stay connected with your friend via FB and gmail

2. If you use gmail, set up another email address from hotmail, yahoo, qq, msn for local use

3. Download these useful APPs for your China trip:
   - Instant Messaging: WeChat (make sure you get it from the China store to get the Wallet function)
   - Subway: Metro Shanghai, Metro Beijing, Metro Guangzhou
   - Dining: Dianping
   - Map: Tencent Map
   - Translation: Pleco or Google Translate (only works if you have VPN)
   - Air Quality: Air Matters

4. Make sure your health insurance could cover your medical bills in China

5. Bring your own medicine, e.g. Zyrtec, Imodium, Pepto bismo etc.

6. Bring a N95 grade mask and keep it in your bag wherever you go. If you are moving to China, buy air purifiers and ship them over.

7. If you are moving to China, you and your family will not be able to travel anywhere for the first 2-3 weeks (not even within China) as you will need to submit your passport for work permit application. So be prepared to be stuck at home at the beginning

8. If you have kids, pack as much kids stuff as possible (e.g. children's books, apparels, shoes, toiletries). They are really expensive in China and the quality may not even be as good as what you can get in the US/ Europe

Epilogue: Key Apps For Your First China Trip

CHRISTINE CHING

Christine Ching (Chinese name 程姬絲) is a native Hong Kong Chinese who have lived and worked in Asia and North America. She was finalist in the Miss Hong Kong Beauty Pageant 1999. She holds a Master of Engineering degree from University of Toronto, and an MBA degree from Stanford University.

Christine wrote Grasp China based on her experience working in China since 2002. In her early years working in China, Christine consulted for many large multi-national companies on their China market strategy. Later she held position of Head of Strategy at Kimberly Clark China (2009-2012), and Marketing Director at Starbucks China (2013-2016). She understood the most common types of problems a foreigner would encounter when working in China as she had already lived through those issues herself.

As a Hong Kong Chinese who grew up abroad, Christine possesses both Chinese and Western mindsets. As a foreigner to mainland China, Christine is exposed to all the cultural differences or sometime even shocks. As an ethnic Chinese, Christine is able to understand the nuances in the Chinese culture where a westerner would otherwise easily miss. This rare combination allows Christine to provide a

unique perspective resonant to the western audiences. To write the book Grasp China, Christine interviewed hundreds of locals and expats across the spectrum: from business professionals, real estate agents, to taxi drivers. The tightly weaved stories add color and authenticity to the content.

Christine currently lives in Shanghai, China. She is the author of "Grasp China 搞定中国" (in Chinese) published in Hong Kong and Taiwan in 2013.

Christine can be reached through email at graspchina@yahoo.com or through the Grasp China Facebook page.

REFERENCES

[1] http://www.chinadaily.com.cn/china/2015-02/02/content_19466412.htm

[2] China Statistical Yearbook 2015, Figure 25-1 http://www.stats.gov.cn/tjsj/ndsj/2016/indexch.htm

[3] http://www.yum.com/company/our-brands/china/

[4] China Statistical Yearbook 2015, Figure 6-1, 6-6, 6-2 http://www.stats.gov.cn/tjsj/ndsj/2016/indexch.htm; Beijing, Shanghai, Guangzhou, Shenzhen Statistical Annual Reports 2015 http://www.sei.gov.cn/ShowArticle.asp?ArticleID=261378; http://www.shanghai.gov.cn/nw2/nw2314/nw2318/nw26434/u21aw1109178.html

http://www.gzstats.gov.cn/tjgb/qstjgb/; http://www.sztj.gov.cn/xxgk/tjsj/tjgb/201604/t20160426_3606261.htm

[5] https://www.ft.com/content/3c521faa-baa6-11e5-a7cc-280dfe875e28

[6] http://gs.offcn.com/html/2015/10/35460.html

[7] http://finance.people.com.cn/n/2013/0302/c70846-20654337.html

[8] https://www.theguardian.com/business/2015/oct/29/global-luxury-goods-market-exceeds-1tn-euro

[9] http://www.masterkong.com.cn/activition/product.shtml

[10] China Internet Network Information Center (Jan 2017) http://www.cnnic.net.cn/hlwfzyj/hlwxzbg/hlwtjbg/201701/ t20170122_66437.htm

[11] http://www.iimedia.cn/41787.html

[12] Numbeo www.numbeo.com

[13] https://club.1688.com/threadview/33938764.html

[14] http://www.gsk.com/en-gb/media/press-releases/2014/gsk-china-investigation-outcome/

[15] http://finance.ifeng.com/leadership/jdrw/20090420/559813. shtml

Made in the USA
Middletown, DE
05 June 2017